# DOGMA ➤ *Volume 3: God and His Christ*

A PROJECT OF JOHN XXIII INSTITUTE
Saint Xavier College, Chicago

# Dogma

**Michael Schmaus**

*Volume three*
God and his Christ

Christian Classics
Westminster, Maryland
1984

# Contents

# I

## The Christ Event

# ◄ 1

## *The Jesus Who Preached and the Christ Who Was Preached*

Christianity is not primarily a collection of truths and commandments; rather, it is the living Jesus Christ. All its declarations of truth are to be understood as statements either of Jesus himself or about him. All its moral commandments are to be interpreted as directions for the living of the Christian faith, that is, for the imitation of Jesus Christ.

The key point for the understanding of Jesus presented to us in Scripture is that his life did not end with his recorded death, as if all that remained were his influence on posterity. On the contrary, the New Testament writings give direct testimony to the glorified Lord, living and present in his universal, total, and indeed revolutionary act of salvation. Everything which took place up to the time of his death is portrayed in Scripture as an introduction to his post-historical life and activity. The risen and glorified Lord is the central content of the Christian proclamation and the primitive Christian faith: the early Church awaited the second coming of the Lord and his final revelation of salvation with longing. The resurrection event itself is at the heart of the primitive Church's faith, insofar as it was through his resurrection that Jesus attained to his life as the glorified Lord (cf. Phil. 2:8–11).[1] Although the Acts, the New Testament Epistles and the Book of Revelation testify in a special way to faith in the reality and efficacy of the

3

salvation brought by the glorified Lord, the accounts contained in the four gospels are likewise concerned with his resurrection and his risen life. This emphasis on the bodily transfiguration of Jesus Christ does not lead to any diminution of the reality of his historical life. Even though the narratives concerning it are oriented towards faith in the resurrected Lord, the existence of Christ in history is nevertheless presented as sober fact. The life and death of Jesus Christ are recounted in order to vouch for the reality of the resurrection. The glorified Christ is not a myth, not an invention: on the contrary, he is identical with the historical Jesus. Moreover, the New Testament witnesses to Christ attain through this view of the earthly life of the Lord a deepened understanding of the Resurrected One himself. Who this One is, what he desired, what he attained, can be gathered from his earthly life.

There is another aspect to this. As the identity between the historical Jesus and the risen Lord ensures the reality of the latter, so inversely, this identity guarantees the genuine physical character of Jesus' suffering. For the discussion with the Jews—that is, for effective proclamation about Jesus—the scandal which the execution on the cross implied had to be surmounted. For the Jews it was absolutely unimaginable that one who was executed should be the God-sent Messiah (cf. Mt. 27:39–44). In the resurrection of Jesus, however, God gave his confirmation precisely to the Crucified One. The resurrection was the divine ratification that Jesus was truly the Messiah promised by God—the Christ.

The intention to proclaim the Resurrected One as the Crucified One and the Crucified One as the Resurrected One becomes clearly evident in the speeches of Peter and Paul in the Acts of the Apostles (see Acts 2:22–24, 3:13–15, 10:36–43, 13:27–34). The same conviction is expressed in the letter of Paul to the Philippians (2:8–11), just as in the demand which Peter makes after the death of Judas for the restoration of the full complement of apostles. The one to be newly chosen, he said, must have been with the original apostles during the entire time when the Lord Jesus went in and out among them, beginning with the baptism of John until the day on which Jesus was taken up from them, in order that this man too could be a witness to Jesus' resurrection (Acts 1:21f.; cf. 1 Cor. 9:1; Acts 2:22–40, 4:8–12, 8:30–35,

10:41, 13:23–41). The witness of the earthly life of Jesus was thus capable of testifying to his resurrection as well. He who had experienced the reality of the risen Lord would also have the power to testify to the earthly life of Jesus, and in fact as a witness who saw and heard.

The pre-eminence which the risen Lord received in the primitive Church's testimony to Christ thus led to this: that the earthly life of Jesus was viewed in the light of the glorified Messiah. The New Testament speaks of the historical Jesus only out of a faith deepened by the experience of Easter and the working of the Spirit. This does not indeed mean that the historical figure of Jesus was invented; but it was interpreted from the standpoint of the Easter faith. Accordingly, the gospels do not present a historical account in the usual sense of the word, but the account of a faith. This account is characterized by several factors, namely, selection, interpretation, and actualization. Jesus' apostles did not relate all that they knew of him; they selected only deeds and words of Jesus which they considered significant for men's salvation. They arranged these in what they considered to be an appropriate form. They had to make the understanding of Jesus, his words and his deeds, accessible to their listeners; accordingly they had to convey the words and deeds of Jesus in a language that suited the comprehension of the listeners. The character of this translation was affected by the insight and individuality of the translators, the apostles and writers of the New Testament, as well as by the individuality and the needs of the listeners. It made a difference whether it was a question of catechizing, or of a mission sermon, whether the listeners were Jews or Greeks.

Moreover, in their explanation and proclamation of Christ it was necessary for the Apostles to be alert to the difficulties and questions arising in the congregations, which had to be answered on the basis of their own experience of Christ. This again occasioned a specific interpretation of Jesus Christ, the historical figure as well as the risen Lord. In a negative respect, this procedure on the part of the apostles had the result that in their proclamation of Christ they did not present the historical course of Jesus' life, they did not offer the original context of his words and action; rather, they pieced together, in a manner which seemed appropriate to them, what they had experienced and learned as seeing and hearing witnesses. Thus, one can proffer neither a biography nor a chronology of Jesus on the basis of the New Testament witness to Christ. The constantly recurring link-words "then" and "in those days" are purely redactional comments, not essential particulars.

For the New Testament writings, the gospels in particular, their character as faith-accounts is of fundamental importance. With regard to the gospels, their origin must be discussed in greater detail. The gospels came into being in three broad stages. The first stage was the words and deeds of Jesus which the disciples had experienced and heard. The second stage was the passing on to the congregations of that which had been experienced concerning Jesus and heard from his lips. In this all the factors became operative that have been described above. At the same time, small units of text naturally developed in which certain utterances and saving acts of Jesus were placed together for purposes of proclamation. Moreover, a larger, more closely knit unit of this kind is formed by the story of the passion, whose course is described, on the whole, with great similarity by all the evangelists. The more Christians who had neither seen nor heard Christ were placed in the service of proclamation, the greater seemed the need to offer the preachers aid. Thus it came about that things were put down in writing to assist proclamation. What Jesus had said was indeed to be retained, yet not in such a way that it would be made known to posterity by a simple report, as with any other historical event; rather, the account was designed to serve as the foundation for the faith and the preaching of the Christian community. The collection of such textual units into larger works constitutes the third stage. The oldest collective work of this kind lies before us in Mark's Gospel. Mark came from Jerusalem. He was not a disciple of Jesus but was perhaps over a long period of time a companion of the apostle Peter. According to the oldest tradition, Mark, after the death of the apostle Peter, wrote down what the Lord had said and done as well as he remembered it from the teaching discourses of Peter. Mark thus became the creator of a new type of writing, which is the gospel.

Taking this collective work as a basis, two additional larger collections of the Jesus tradition, the Gospels of Matthew and Luke, were soon afterwards produced independently of one another. These are indebted for their greater quantity of material both to written sources and to the wider-flowing stream of oral transmission. They have the same literary character as the Gospel of Mark. They do not provide us with a historical report, but with a theological interpretation of the words and deeds of Jesus, and of his personality. Each has his own distinctive interpretation, so that it is possible to speak of the theology of each of the synoptics. It may not be out of place to give a couple of examples. It is clear that both Matthew and Luke have made use of a collection of the sayings of Jesus (a document frequently called "Q"), and in this document the proclamation of the reign of God is very much in the foreground. In the case of Mark, by contrast, it is the crucifixion and resurrection of Jesus which form the center of interest and the rest of the gospel is built around these events. He wants to show how it came about that Jesus was crucified, so that it is possible to call the gospel "a passion narrative with a lengthy introduction" (M. Kähler). On the other hand he also wants to show that Jesus is the promised Messiah and the Son of God.[2] Matthew tries to show that Jesus is the Messiah who was foretold in the Old Testament but received from the beginning with skepticism and ever more strongly rejected. Luke, whose theology can only be understood in connection with Acts, is characterized by a careful distinction of the periods of salvation history. The time of Israel (the Old Testament) is followed by the time of Jesus (the gospel), and this is followed by the time of the Church. Jesus is the center of time (H. Conzelmann). For Luke, Jesus' life is a journey towards Jerusalem, and he knows what awaits him there. Theological interpretation of the historical Jesus has gone furthest in John's Gospel.

In virtue of their peculiar character, these four accounts were named by the Church in the middle of the second century not simply the "Life of Jesus" but rather the "Gospel"—that is, they were characterized by a word which until that time (and this continued to be true throughout the second century) had referred to the oral message of salvation regarding Jesus, the God-sent Messiah.

In accordance with the development of the gospels a threefold

method of exegesis has been developed, namely, tradition criticism
(*Traditionsgeschichte*), form criticism (*Formgeschichte*) and redaction criticism (*Redaktionsgeschichte*). The last endeavors to
discover the redactional interest of the evangelist. The second endeavors to disclose the textual units, the gospel before the gospel,
which underlie the collecting activity of the evangelist. The first
endeavors to sift out and crystallize the words of Jesus themselves, the *verba ipsissima.*

Given these circumstances of exegetical investigation, the question cannot be avoided whether the gospels' accounts of the
earthly life of Jesus are authentic or whether the figure of Jesus
has been so colored and modified by the Easter faith that we are
no longer able to discern the historical reality.

The problem frequently presents itself in theology under the
head of the relationship of the Jesus who preached to the Christ
who was preached. The liberal theology of the last century was of
the opinion that the image of the historical Jesus had been utterly
distorted by the New Testament writers, features completely foreign to his historical personality having been attributed to him.
From a different point of departure the demythologizing theology
put forward by Rudolf Bultmann and, with various nuances, by
his adherents, reaches a similar conclusion. It is in essence this:
that by his proclamation of the Reign of God, Jesus had no intention of announcing special events, whether of the near or distant
future; he in no sense claimed for himself the identity of Son of
God or Son of Man; on the contrary, he was concerned with emphasizing, in a mythological mode of expression which belonged
to his time, the character of decision which the present moment
bears. In other words, he conceived of himself neither as a bringer
of salvation nor as one sent from Heaven on a divine mission.
Jesus' disciples, however, saw in his death an example of the conquest of those forces, egoistical and materialistic, that are inimical
to life (*dasein*). The death of Jesus thus became significant for
the understanding and realization of a truly human life, and in this
way became a historic event. Henceforth it is of concern to every
man. The disciples brought this faith to expression in terms of a
thought form which was natural to their milieu—namely, the concept of a "resurrection" of Jesus—and thus proclaimed the "risen
Christ."

For a discussion of the extent to which this view is supported by the *a priori* belief that a divine intervention in the course of history is impossible, and how far it is determined by a consideration of what Christian elements can still be meaningful to contemporary man, the reader is referred to the first volume of this work, on the foundations of theology. Insofar as this approach lays claim to interpret Scripture according to its true sense, one must object that the witnesses to Christ most certainly knew how to distinguish myth from reality, and that they considered the Risen One as a reality, as can be clearly seen from the fifteenth chapter of the first letter to the Corinthians. So far as they were concerned, the risen Lord has meaning for salvation for only one reason: because he actually existed. Nevertheless note should be taken of an important element in this program of demythologization, which is its concern with the fact that Jesus becomes meaningful for men's salvation only through proclamation and faith. Jesus' life, suffering and death and being raised from the dead are aimed at men: they are not events which rest in themselves, self-enclosed. They receive their meaning only when they reach the individual man in order to draw him into the life of God. Nor, equally, may it be overlooked that the gospels are constituted of testimonies of faith which had their origin in the Easter experience of Jesus' disciples and the working upon them of the Spirit. This means that the gospels witness only indirectly to the Jesus of history.

Nevertheless the figure of Jesus in its historical reality can be discerned through the biblical testimonies. In this inquiry a twofold danger must be avoided: uncritical carelessness, on the one hand, and excessively critical skepticism on the other (A. Vögtle). In view of the present state of research we must say that, however much Jesus is, for the New Testament kerygma, the risen and present Lord whose return is ardently desired, the fact remains nonetheless that the responsible bearers and interpreters of the Jesus tradition knew themselves to be bound to Jesus; and furthermore, whatever their divergences as to approach and terminology, the theological inquiries lead essentially to the same assertions concerning Jesus. We should do greater violence to reality by minimalizing our knowledge concerning the historical Jesus than by holding too confident an estimate of the historical value of the gospels (A. Vögtle; see the section on the resurrection of Jesus).

According to the present state of scholarship we must say that although Jesus is, for the New Testament message, primarily the risen and glorified Lord, whose return is longed for, still according to the gospels, there is a completely certain historical basis for the message about Jesus, namely his violent death. And this in its turn is only understandable if there was some reason for his execution. The reason given is a special claim made by Jesus, his claim to be the Messiah. This explains the hostility of the authorities towards Jesus (see Mark 14:61 and parallels). Further, Jesus is described by both the synoptics and John as a figure with marked characteristics, his own very individual attitudes, reactions, and manner of speaking, which cannot be explained simply in terms of his milieu. On the other hand, his words and deeds are intelligible only when viewed within the world of late Judaism. This is especially true of his controversy with the Pharisees. Then again there is his style of speaking, which consists for the most part of short, pregnant statements related to some particular episode.

An interpretation was necessary. During Jesus' life his disciples experienced his claim to be the Messiah, but Jesus' idea of messiahship had little in common with that of late Judaism. Subsequently the disciples had to preach Jesus to their contemporaries as the Messiah despite this difference of understanding. But the interpretation that they adopted was not the only one that would have been possible, as we can see by comparing the New Testament with the apocryphal gospels. These were almost certainly written as a form of protest against the recognized gospels. For the apocryphal gospels, the historical Jesus is the Messiah also, but his life story is told in a framework of myth and legend, to satisfy curiosity. It was very important for the early Church that the Lord whom they were announcing should be identical with the Jesus of Nazareth known to their contemporaries. The reason for this is as follows: Jesus' resurrection could not be announced without preaching his death as a salvific death. But it was precisely Jesus' death on the cross which was a scandal to both Jews and Gentiles, and much more of a hindrance to faith than an invitation to it. The idea that Jesus' death could be the death of the Messiah stood in irreconcilable contradiction to the messianic hopes of the Jewish people at that time. An explanation had to be given of how it came about that Jesus was executed.

Further, the disciples were concerned to show that they were not mythologizing in preaching Christ as the Messiah, but that this announcement corresponded to the mind of the historical Jesus, to his words and deeds. Jesus spoke and acted in such a way that he could be and had to be proclaimed to the world as the Messiah, the Son of Man. Mark, especially, has Jesus announce emphatically that the time is fulfilled and the reign of God is at hand (Mk. 1:15). That this announcement is not an empty one, Mark shows by describing how·Jesus enters battle against the powers of destruction, sickness, death, and sin. Jesus' claim to be the Messiah is expressed with extreme force in the statement which is certainly authentic: "If anyone comes to me and does not hate his father and mother, wife and children, brothers and sisters, even his own life, he cannot be a disciple of mine" (Lk. 14:26 and parallels). Rudolf Bultmann has maintained that Jesus' messianic claim was an invention of the early Christian community, but in this case the question must be asked how such a conviction could arise in the community, and further, how it could come to such irreconcilable hostility between Jesus and his opponents. The proclamation of Jesus as the Messiah is inexplicable if it does not have its basis in Jesus himself, in his words and deeds. The conception of the reign of God and of the Messiah which Jesus puts forward in the synoptics is very different from that which was common at the time and it was precisely this difference which aroused the hostility against him.

Especially remarkable is the interest which John's gospel, combining emphasis both on eyewitness testimony and meditative interpretation, has in the historical Jesus, the incarnation of the divine redeemer. If John bears witness to Jesus in the form of a gospel again, some two or three decades after the first three gospels were composed, the only available explanation for this is that he wanted to emphasize again as strongly as possible the identity of the heavenly Christ with the historical Jesus against docetic or gnostic conceptions. Reduction of the earthly Jesus to a purely heavenly figure is branded by John as the characteristic act of the Anti-Christ (1 Jn. 4:3; Jn. 1:14). The entire gospel of John was written in order to support the belief that the historical Jesus of Nazareth was the Christ the Son of God (20:31).

In the light of this interest of the New Testament in the historical facts it is understandable that, despite much difference in matters of detail, the authors all come to essentially the same statements about the historical Jesus. It would be just as much of a mistake to minimalize our knowledge of the historical Jesus as to trust too readily the historical value of the gospels. Extra-biblical witnesses for the historicity of Jesus are not totally lacking, but play only a small role. The Roman author Suetonius gives an indication in his biography of the emperor Claudius (2,4). The Roman governor Pliny writes to the emperor Trajan that the Christians sing hymns in alternating choirs to Christ as God (Letter 10,96). The Jewish author Flavius Josephus likewise makes some indicative remarks (Antiquitates 20,9,1). Tacitus reports of Christ, whom the procurator Pontius Pilate sentenced to death, in his Annals (1,54).

From the gospels it may be calculated that Jesus appeared publicly in the land and to the people of Israel around the year 28–29 and taught publicly for somewhat more than two years. He is portrayed as a man of the Jewish people. His birthplace is Bethlehem. His home, however, is in Nazareth, a small town in despised, half-heathen Galilee. Jesus comes from a religious family. He speaks Galilean Aramaic, which differs from that spoken in Jerusalem. In Nazareth nothing extraordinary had been observed of him before his public appearance, apart from the event of the twelve-year-old in the temple. For this reason his acquaintances are taken unawares by his work, and attempt to bring him home (Mt. 12:47; Mk. 3:32; Lk. 8:20). After this he found no approval among them (Mt. 13:53–58; Mk. 6:1–6; Lk. 4:16–30). The burdens of the day make him so tired that he falls asleep. He gets hungry and thirsty. He weeps over his dead friend. He is seized by sorrow and agony in the face of death. He enjoys a meal in a hospitable house, and rebuking observers call him a glutton and a drunkard. There are men who are especially close to him.

There are many words in the gospels which may be immediately recognized as his own original formulation, although they occur in a context shaped by the apostles. The "Amen" which introduces his sayings in the gospels is a word belonging so exclusively to him that we do not find it at all in the remainder of the New Testament, nor is it used this way in any extra-biblical literature. In the word "Abba"—Father—the intimate term of address for

God, a completely new use of language emerges in which is reflected a new relationship with God opening up depths of unutterable profundity. As J. Jeremias has remarked, these two words
by themselves contain the essence of Jesus' message of salvation
and his consciousness of sovereignty. When we are seeking to
evaluate the historical character of the gospels, it would be perilous
to leave out of account the fact that in the ancient world religious
and other traditions were very often faithfully preserved over a long
period of time without anything being written down. Examples of
this are the maxims of the rabbis. Such a procedure seems very
probable with respect to the words of Jesus, for the message which
he brought was certain to have a startling impact on his hearers,
owing to its newness: it would readily impress itself on their
memories in its content as well as its form. The call to salvation
represented by the Beatitudes, the threats of divine retribution, the
I-formulas, the maxim-like wisdom sayings, the similes, the parables and the illustrative stories—all these would live vividly in the
minds of hearers. The reliability and substantial fidelity of the
gospels are not, on these grounds, to be doubted, even though they
were first written down several decades after Jesus' death (Mark
between 64 or 67 and 70; Matthew and Luke after 70).

The authenticity of the figure of Jesus delineated by the evangelists also comes to light when we situate it in relation to the religious currents of its time. Many of his teachings can be understood more easily against the background of contemporary religious
movements; but on the other hand, Jesus stands in such contrast
with the currents of his time that he and his teaching could not
have been invented. It may be said that the reality of the Jesus
witnessed to by the evangelists shows itself through his continuity
with his milieu as well as through his simultaneous discontinuity,
through his *Sitz im Leben* in the period, and at the same time
through his infringement of and his opposition to the religious
thought and life of his time. A brief look at the religious groups
at the time of Jesus can bring this out more clearly.

All, whether members of the liberal lay and priestly aristocracy,
the Sadducees, or of the Pharisees or the Essenes, were at one in
this: that God's will was to be done so that he might bring in the
era of salvation. The group of Pharisees, the "separated ones,"

held that God had revealed himself not only in the books of the Old Testament but also in the tradition of the ancients—that is, in the additional oral development of the patriarchs' teaching. Their aim was to bring into being a holy people to whom God might send the promised Messiah. Most of the scribes belonged to this party. They tended to look down on the popular masses, believing that the people could not fulfill the law because their grasp of it was inadequate. The Essenes formed the most extreme group of those endeavoring to bring the true Israel into being on the basis of a particular form of legalistic piety; the community of Qumran, organized by the priestly Teacher of Righteousness, is unique in its form of life in the late-Jewish penitence movement. The Essenes were distinguished from the Pharisees by the fact that they secluded themselves in special settlements. For them the written Law alone was authoritative and this was to be carried out completely. The Pharisees were frequently branded as hypocrites by the Essenes, because they required the direct fulfillment of the Law, yet made many small exceptions. The Essenes understood themselves as the community of the new covenant, as the sons of light, the chosen ones. According to the rule of their order, the sons of light must have love for one another but at the same time hate all sons of darkness. Jesus had to come to terms principally with the piety of the Pharisees, for they governed public life.

Naturally there were many who belonged to none of these groups, but in the simplicity of their hearts prayed and waited for the salvation of Israel (Lk. 2:58). The question for all was this: How is the will of God to be understood and how is it to be fulfilled? But precisely to this question there was no answer to be obtained from the leading circles. Jesus saw the people as a flock without a shepherd. He knew himself to be sent to the lost sheep of the house of Israel (Mt. 15:24, 10:5; Mk. 6:34; Mt. 9:46).

John the Baptist played a special role. His preaching of repentance fell approximately within the years 27–28. That Jesus had connections with him is certain; however, it is very difficult to define the relationship more exactly. In any case, the salvation preaching of Jesus differs essentially from John the Baptist's preaching of the Law.

To all these considerations it must be added that those passages in the gospels which cannot be made intelligible if taken from the point of view of the disciples after Easter are for this very reason marked as primitive, pre-theological components of the Jesus tradition. All things considered, it may be said that Jesus' words and actions, even though not transmitted with literal accuracy, are nevertheless reported by the evangelists with substantial correctness, though they are often placed in different contexts and undergo specific interpretations.

Although the original substance of the words and actions of Jesus can thus be attained through the apostolic formulations, it is faith alone that opens up the understanding of Christ. If the New Testament witness to Christ consists in accounts that are not so much historical as kerygmatic, and hence witnesses of faith, then the appropriate response to them is our own faith in return. This likewise follows from the content itself which is proclaimed, since it is nothing other than the risen Christ, living and present. But Christ cannot be affirmed as an object: he always remains subject. Hence proclamation can aim only at personal encounter with Jesus Christ. This takes place in faith; faith is the surrender of the believing I to the Thou of Jesus Christ. If even ordinary encounter between persons requires faith as a preliminary, this is true of the encounter with the glorified Lord in a special and unique way. For in the resurrection he has entered into the mystery of God, and so, in being proclaimed, he speaks out of the mystery of God. The one who hears through this proclamation is called into the mystery of God. The way of rational knowledge does not lead to this encounter, but only the way of decision, in which man submits himself to the divine mystery. Because the historical words and actions of Jesus are most intimately related to the life of the Risen One, their true sense can be grasped only in faith; indeed they are in their totality nothing other than forms of expression of the one Jesus Christ. Faith, in the form of a personal encounter, naturally includes the acceptance of Jesus' words and teachings (assent to revealed truth); this, however, is only one element within the total event of faith.

In the last analysis, man is capable of decision for Jesus only when he is empowered to make it by Jesus himself. In the call, of

which man becomes aware through the gospel proclamation, Christ
so acts upon the genuine hearer that his hearing of the call
through the words of men becomes at the same time a following of it; that is, faith is at once both grace and a human decision.[3]

*Notes*

[1] Except where otherwise indicated all Old Testament quotations in this
book are from the *Revised Standard Version and the Apocrypha*, copy-
righted 1957 by the Division of Christian Education, National Council of
the Churches of Christ in the U.S.A., and used by permission. New Testament quotations are from the *New English Bible, New Testament*, © The
Delegates of the Oxford University Press and The Syndics of Cambridge
University Press, 1961, 1970. Reprinted by permission.

[2] Cf. F. Müssner, *Praesentia salutis* (Düsseldorf, 1967), pp. 84–98;
W. Marxsen, *Der Evangelist Markus* (Göttingen, 1959).

[3] See the article "Jesus Christus," by A. Vögtle, in *Lexikon für Theologie v. Kirche* V (1960), pp. 922–932.

# ◄ 2

# *The Reign of God*

The resurrection of Jesus Christ is portrayed in Scripture as that event which releases the radical movement of history towards the ultimate future salvation of man, which will consist in an eternal, blessed dialogue of creatures with God, offering himself to them unveiled. God's gift of himself to men, the encounter of men with God which it has made possible, and the dialogue of salvation which it has brought into being are designated in Scripture by the expression "the Reign of God." The connection between the resurrection of Jesus and the Reign of God is so close (cf. 1 Cor. 15) that the resurrection of Jesus can be understood in its saving sense only when it is interpreted in the light of the idea of the Reign of God. In order that this relationship may be seen more clearly, we will sketch the New Testament message of the Reign of God before we analyze the New Testament's proclamation of the risen Lord. The proclamation of the Reign of God belongs to the oldest passages of the preaching of Jesus. According to the Synoptic Gospels, Jesus summarizes the meaning of his coming with the phrase "Reign of God."

In the Gospel of John, the expression itself recedes; it is found only twice (John, 3:3,5). In fact, however, the Gospel of John is in accord with the Synoptics, inasmuch as it speaks of the condition which they term "Reign of God" in terms of the expression "new life."

The phrase "Reign (Kingdom) of God" means in the first place

not a political or a geographical reality, but the saving historical
action of God; the Reign of God is thus to be understood dynamically. When the phrase "kingdom of heaven" is employed in
place of the expression "kingdom of God" in the Gospel of
Matthew, this can be traced to the fact that in the Old Testament
the name of God was not pronounced, out of reverence. Obviously
the author was thinking of Jewish Christians, who came from this
Old Testament tradition. It may be assumed that Christ himself
also made use of the expression "reign of heaven." At the beginning of their history men brought on themselves a catastrophic
situation in that they attempted to withdraw from the Lordship of
God. They were to attain salvation in the reign of God which
Jesus proclaimed and re-established. In Christ himself the sovereign saving action of God has burst forth, inasmuch as the
Father has bestowed on him a glorified and transformed existence,
as the completion of his divine-human being. The risen Lord so
operates in the history of men, indeed in the whole of creation, that
his own glorified existence will ultimately prevail in men and creation. Consequently, the final state of the universe will be a transformation of creation according to the archetype of the risen Lord.
In this sense creation is seen as the location where the sovereign
action of God takes place. Thus, beyond the dynamic meaning, the
concept of the Reign of God attains at the same time a spatial
meaning.

Jesus' proclamation of the Reign of God can be understood both
in its historical origins and in its radical novelty only against the
background of the Old Testament and the ancient Jewish teaching
and hope concerning God's reign. In the Old Testament, what
Israel expected of the future was summarized in the concept of
the kingship of God. Perhaps the Sinai covenant was already understood as a covenant of kingship (M. Buber). In any case, the
conception of the kingship of God originated not later than the
period after the taking of Canaan, and thus before the introduction
of the Israelite kingship (Ex. 15:18, 19:6; Num. 23:21; cf. Dt.
33:5). It was considered to have its foundation in the fact of creation (Jer. 10:6–22; Ps. 113; Mal. 1:14). By analogy with the
religious conceptions prevalent on all sides, Yahweh is praised in
the psalms as the great king of the entire world, and specifically for

this reason, that he is its Creator and at the same time its Judge (Pss. 2; 23; 47; 49; 93; 95:3-6; 96; 97; 99; 103:19; 113; 145; 147).

The Lordship of God, which extends over the whole of creation, concentrates more and more in the saving acts of God for his people, who have been constituted and formed through the call of Abraham, Moses, and David. God is in a special way the King of Israel his people, the people of God (Ex. 33:1-5; Num. 24:8; Dt. 8:14; Judg. 8:23; I Sam. 8:7; 12:12; 2 Sam. 14:13; Is. 6:5; Jer. 2:6f.; Amos 2:10; Mic. 6:4; etc.). The people of Israel also consecrate cultic songs of royalty to him (Pss. 5; 24:7-10; 48; 68; 84). They submit to the Lordship of God (Ex. 19:4-8; 24:3-8).

God carries out his rule by means of earthly representatives. These were first of all the judges. The judges understood themselves to be the representatives of God's Lordship. The belief in the kingship of God at first occasioned hesitation concerning the introduction of an earthly kingship (Judg. 8:23; 1 Sam. 8:7; 12:12). When the people, adapting themselves to the kingdoms existing around them, nevertheless demanded a king for themselves too, God commanded Samuel to anoint a king (1 Sam. 8:15ff., Pss. 97:8; 99:2). The earthly king is the deputy of God. The earthly king was not considered, as in Egypt and Babylon, as the incarnation of God (divine kingship—apotheosis of the king). He, as well as the people, had to submit himself to the Lord God (1 Sam. 12:14; 2 Sam. 7:14, 20; 2 Kings 1:15; 1 Chr. 29:23; 17:14; 28:5; 2 Chr. 9:8; 14; 26:9; 13:8). The earthly king rules on the authority of God (1 Chr. 17:14). He sits on the throne of the Lord (1 Chr. 29:23). The kings are called the anointed of the Lord (Messiah, Christ; 1 Sam. 10:1; 16:13). They are filled with the Spirit of the Lord (1 Sam. 10:6; 16:13). God gave the kingship of David special promises: Out of his family was to issue the Anointed One of the Lord, who was to set up the ultimate reign of God and thus bring final salvation. From the lineage of David, the King of the future will come forth, who will bring full righteousness (2 Sam. 7:12-16; 1 Chr. 17:7-14). The kingship instituted in Zion is the visible form of the reign of God (1 Kgs. 8:15ff., Pss. 97:8; 99:2). The earthly king is the deputy of God.

The Lordship of God over his people points towards his Lordship over all people (Amos 9:7; Jer. 10:7–10; Ps. 22:29). At some future time it will encompass the entire earth and comprehend all peoples. As the final reign of God will be universal, because it is cosmic in scope as a result of the fact of creation (1 Chr. 29:11f.; Pss. 29:10; 74:12f.; 103:19; 145:10–13; Dan. 4:31–34), so the goal in the future is also universal, over and above God's election of the people of Israel (Mic. 4; Oba. 15; Amos 9:7; Zech. 14:9; Jer. 10:7–10; 15:20; 30:20–22; 36:25–27; Is. 11: 44–55; 65:17–26; Pss. 2; 22:29; 29:4f.; 47; 93:1f.; 96). It was Deutero-Isaiah who connected the idea of the Kingship of God with eschatological thinking (see the small Isaiah "Apocalypse," Is. 24–27; also Is. 41:21–22; 44:6; 52:7–10). The Kingship of God aims at the bringing about of a new aeon, in which all peoples will be obedient to one world king. God will prevail as universal King. He will reveal himself as God and King in Israel and in the whole of humanity (Hos. 2:21ff.; Is. 14:1; Jer. 31:31ff.; Ez. 34:24; Zech. 14:9; 10:9, 16f.; Oba. 21; Mal. 1:14). God will hold judgment, which will be effected in terrible catastrophes (Is. 24:21f.; 41:14; 59:15f.; 63:1; Joel 30ff.; Pss. 46:6; 48:4; 96:8; 97:1ff.; 99:1). But the judgment of God will at the same time bring salvation for Israel and all other peoples (Lev. 26:3–13; Dt. 30). Peace and righteousness will reign on the earth forever (Is. 11:1; 61:1f.; Jer. 31:31f.). A new world will begin (Is. 65:17; 66:22f.; Zech. 14:9ff.; Zeph. 3:15f.; Ez. 38:22ff.). In consequence of the faithlessness of Israel *vis-à-vis* the divine covenant partner, a radical new beginning is required, in order that salvation come (Jer. 31:31f.; Is. 6; 33:22; 24:23; 44:21f.; 43: 16f.; 48:6). This comprises an inner renewal (Hos. 14; Ezek. 36:25f.; 11:19; Jer. 31:33f.), as well as the external restoration of the people itself (Is. 25:8; 30:27ff.; 32:1; 33:17; 52:7–10; 62:2; 60:1ff.; Dan. 11:32–35). Then the earth will overflow in blessings (Jer. 23:6; Hos. 2:20; 11:6; 65:20ff.), and all peoples will do homage to God (Is. 18:7; 60:4ff.), not only Israel but all nations (Is. 2:22f.; 19:25; 45:22; 51:4ff.; 55:5; 66:9; Zech. 8:23; Zeph. 2:11; 3:9), and indeed the whole of creation (Hag. 2:6f.; 32:15ff.; 65:17). Relying on the promises of God, whose perpetually new coming determined the history of Israel, the prophets take careful note of historical movements and changes. No quiet or delay is allotted to them, no building up of a fixed historical position; they must reach out for the unknown but nevertheless assuredly Coming One.[1]

God will appoint an earthly bearer of power who is filled with his Spirit. He will go forth from the house of David, which has been plunged into deep degradation, and will bring about a state of prosperity which lies beyond all experience and so can be depicted only in similes (Is. 9; 11:1-9; Mic. 5:1ff.; Jer. 23:5ff.; Ez. 17: 22ff.; 34:23f.; 37:24f.). The bearer of this divine commission will have a difficult way to travel. He will appear as the servant of God who fulfills his mission in affliction and suffering, in distress and death (Is. 42:1ff.). But precisely through his death he will bring the reign of God to its final, indestructible form (Is. 53:1–12). He will bring about its universality (Is. 2:2f.; 49:6; 56:7).

The Spirit of God will be the life-power of this coming Reign (Is. 32:15; 44:3f.; 11:1-6; Ez. 37:1ff.; Zech. 4:6; Hag. 2:5; Joel 2:28).

However, if salvation also embraces all peoples and the whole of creation, it nevertheless does have a boundary: death. Only in the last books of the Old Testament, in those of the Hellenistic period, does the hope of an overcoming of death through a further life in peace gradually emerge (Wis. 3:7f.; 5:15f.; 6:19f.; Dan. 12:2f.). Thus, transcendent and immanent expectations begin to push against each other.

In later Judaism these hopes were further developed. They took on the most manifold forms, world-immanent and world-transcendent, particular and universal, individual and collective. The character of the reign of God as something still in the future is affirmed repeatedly. This does not hinder, however, the affirmation of the Lordship of God already in the present. The existence of Judaism itself can, according to this conception, be considered as clear evidence for the Lordship of God. For the observance of the Law or the praying of the first commandment (Dt. 6:4f.), which forms the beginning of the prayer which every adult Jewish male must recite daily at morning and evening, meant, according to the teaching of the rabbis, the same as taking the yoke of God's reign upon oneself. Since, however, such submission to God's Lordship takes place in the inner man, the reign of God is not yet manifest, but hidden. The concealment is intensified by the fact that a great segment of mankind does not recognize the Kingship of God. Three times daily each Jew prays that God's reign will come soon. In the "Eighteenth Prayer" (11th Benediction) it reads, "Hasten to be King over us." In the kaddish spoken at the worship in the synagogue, it is said, "And may God bring His Kingship to prevail in your life and in your days and in the life of the entire house of Israel and in the days close at hand."[2]

As far as the form of God's reign is concerned, the hope for it in late Judaism was influenced by the political oppression of the people. Broad circles understood it as release from the yoke of the Romans, as material wealth, as earthly security, as the restoration of the Davidic kingship and the creation of this into a world dominion. A small group advocated the expulsion of the Romans by force. The majority counted upon a direct intervention by God. God could not for long leave his people to humiliation by a godless and lawless world power. Of course the Kingship of God was seen to be active also wherever God's will was fulfilled. But the hopes of the people were directed towards a transformation of the total state of affairs.

The Old Testament is the history of the reign of God. It describes how God's reign progresses, how God establishes it step by step, how he makes it prevail against the opposition of man. Since God's reign does not take away human freedom, there comes a momentous struggle between the reign of God and human self-assertion. The attempt at rebellion against the reign of God is all the greater, in that the alluring gods in the vicinity of the chosen people show themselves to be powerful, indeed at times appear to be stronger than the God of Israel. They lead the people who trust in them to victory. Here the question arises: What is our God? Is he truly the Lord over all lords? Many texts in the Psalms and the Prophets read like an answer to this question: Our God is still more powerful than all gods, even though at times it appears to be otherwise. In many texts one can perceive that they are meant as aids to overcome doubt. With the experience of the might of the gods is combined the temptation to desert to the sensually pleasing cults of the surrounding paganism. Thus the acknowledgment of the Lordship of the One God is again and again mixed with worship of the heathen gods who were recognized in the vicinity of the chosen people. Again and again God afflicts the apostates in order that they may turn back to him in repentance and remorse. Because the history of Israel was a constant exchange between man and God, a final and unconditional seriousness was inherent in it. In all decisions it was a matter of the question God's glory or man's self-glorying, God's honor or man's honor, the Lordship of God or the lordship of the gods? It always turned out that when the people chose its own honor and the lordship of the gods, its own honor and dignity were lost; when it decided for God's honor, honor and glory came to the people itself. When it chose God's kingship, it decided at the same time for its own salvation, for God is a King of grace. He is terror for their enemies. Thus the people can praise the victory of God as its own victory and its own victory as the victory of God:

I will sing to the Lord, for he has triumphed gloriously;
    the horse and his rider he has thrown into the sea.
The Lord is my strength and my song,
    and he has become my salvation;
This is my God, and I will praise him,
    my father's God, and I will exalt him.
The Lord is a man of war;
    the Lord is his name.
Pharaoh's chariots and his host he cast into the sea;
    and his picked officers are sunk in the Red Sea.
The floods cover them;
    they went down into the depths like a stone.
Thy right hand, O Lord, glorious in power,
    thy right hand, O Lord, shatters the enemy.
In the greatness of thy majesty thou overthrowest thy adversaries;
    thou sendest forth thy fury, it consumes them like stubble.
At the blast of thy nostrils the waters piled up,
    the floods stood up in a heap;
    the deeps congealed in the heart of the sea.
The enemy said, "I will pursue, I will overtake,
    I will divide the spoil, my desire shall have its fill of them.
    I will draw my sword, my hand shall destroy them."
Thou didst blow with thy wind, the sea covered them;
    they sank as lead in the mighty waters.

Who is like thee, O Lord, among the gods?
  Who is like thee, majestic in holiness,
    terrible in glorious deeds, doing wonders?
Thou didst stretch out thy right hand,
    the earth swallowed them.
Thou hast led in thy steadfast love the people whom thou hast redeemed,
    thou hast guided them by the strength of thy holy abode.
The peoples have heard, they tremble;
    pangs have seized on the inhabitants of Philistia.
Now are the chiefs of Edom dismayed;
    the leaders of Moab, trembling seizes them;
    all the inhabitants of Canaan have melted away.
Terror and dread fall upon them;
    because of the greatness of thy arm, they are as still as a stone,
till thy people, O Lord, pass by;
    till the people pass by whom thou hast purchased.
Thou wilt bring them in, and plant them on thy own mountain,
    thy place, O Lord, which thou hast made for thy abode,
    the sanctuary, O Lord, which thy hands have established.
The Lord will reign for ever and ever.

(Ex. 15:1–18)

At the end of the line of prophets stands John. He lives at the turning point in the history of salvation. He sees the hour of judgment and grace standing before the door. He sees God's bearer of power, who rises above all preceding bearers of power and sets up God's reign with the greatest intensity possible for the duration of the present world-forms, approaching. Here the reign of God will obtain a might which it has not possessed till then, which it was the purpose of all previous forms to prepare for, which itself is, not yet the end to be sure, but the anticipation of the final shape of God's reign to be established beyond human history (Mt. 3:2–12). The reign of God will come as a judgment upon human self-glorification. Only those will escape its terror who devote themselves to the Lord in repentance and conversion. Consanguinity with Abraham is not sufficient for membership in the impending reign of God. It is not established upon blood, but upon the Holy Spirit (Lk. 3:16f.). The one who will found it stands already among the people, but is as yet unknown (Jn. 1:26).

Jesus took up the people's expectations and hopes for the reign of God, but transformed them in a radical way. He freed them from political-nationalistic elements, and gave them a universal validity. Precisely the fact that Jesus had a conception of the kingdom other than that of the ruling powers of his time led to his execution. After the initial high hopes with which his proclamation of God's reign was greeted, his supporters grew fewer and fewer, until the nation's leaders changed over to open enmity and determined on his death, in the conviction that it would be in the interest of the people if Jesus died, in order that the nationalistic expectations of the kingdom should not be destroyed. In a dramatic scene Jesus had characterized himself as King (Jn. 18:33–38), but at the same time added of what sort this kingship was. He is the king of truth. Thus the promise of the angel, which according to Luke 1:32 was bound up with the announcement of his coming, was given its proper meaning. Love unites with the truth proclaimed by Jesus and exhibited through him. Truth is nothing other than the unveiled mystery of God. The Lordship of God is accordingly a Lordship of truth and love; that is, it serves human salvation. In that Christ took away sin and closed the breach between man and God, in that he summoned sinners to conversion (Mt. 9:13; Mk. 2:17), he established the reign of God. For men this meant liberation for true freedom, for that freedom in which man is no longer a slave to his egoism and pride. Christ raised up the Lordship of God in that he sought and saved what was lost (Lk. 19:10).

It is not first a question of shaking off the yoke of Rome, but of casting off the yoke of sin. Accordingly, neither is the Kingdom of God confined to the people of Israel. It is to embrace the whole of humanity, the entire world (Mt. 8:11f.; 11:21–24; 12:41; Lk. 10:13; 11:31; 13:28f.). The Kingdom of God will not bring judgment but salvation (Lk. 5:32ff.; 15:1ff.; Mt. 15:24; 20:1ff.). It will be the highest fulfillment of everything that God effects with men and of what they may expect in confident hope. The proclamation of this coming world-period is the message of salvation. To enter into God's Kingdom (Mk. 9:47) means to enter into life (Mk. 9:43–45), to be saved (Mk. 10:24ff.), to enter into the joy of the Lord (Mt. 25:21–23). It is the opposite of being cast out into darkness (Mt. 25:30). Whoever does not enter into the

Kingdom of God enters into hell (Mk. 8:36f.; 9:47).

The Reign of God is a gift of God. Only God himself can set it up. Man cannot compel it to come about. It is grace. It is a gift and act of God. Man, however, is summoned to open himself to God's action. The summons is to conversion, turning around, the changing of the entire direction of life. John the Baptist demanded conversion. However, with him this call was connected chiefly with the threat of judgment. John shows himself as an Old Testament believer when he allows God's grace no great scope. According to the words of Jesus, God's reign is pure grace, which is not forced upon man, but which man must grasp hold of in freedom if it is to take effect on him in a saving way.

God establishes his reign through his Son Jesus. The close attachment of the reign of God to Jesus is a problem both of its present and its future. Jesus himself proclaims the eschatological character of the Lordship of God. But at the same time he proclaims its nearness, indeed its presence. The question is how the present and the future of God's reign are related to each other and whether the future meant is near or distant. Insofar as the Reign of God is visible and audible in Jesus, in his actions and words (Lk. 11:20; 13:18f.), it manifests its presence; in particular in the forgiveness of sins, in the conquest of Satan (Mt. 12:28), and in Jesus' acts of power—the healing of the sick, the raising of the dead, the multiplication of the loaves, the walking on the water and the stilling of the storm. It is likewise made tangible through Jesus' entry into Jerusalem (Mk. 11:1–10), the cleansing of the Temple (Mk. 11:15–17), the Last Supper and the commission of the Twelve as the core of the new community of salvation. But at the same time the Reign of God is depicted as a reality of the future when references are made to its nearness, its coming, the day of God, the judgment, the final entrance into God's reign and the inheritance of life (Mk. 1:15; 9:1; 13:29f.; 13:32; 14:25; Lk. 10:9; 22:18; Mt. 10:15; 12:41f.; 13:30; 25:31ff.). These and similar texts lead to the supposition that Jesus expected the final coming of God's Reign in his own lifetime, in his generation (see Mk. 9:1; 13:9–13; Lk. 21:20–29; Mt. 10:23). Such texts were utilized and interpreted in the sense of what is called a "consistent eschatology" (A. Schweitzer, M. Werner). But it cannot be overlooked that they stand in contrast to others which reckon with a great lapse of time before the return of Christ (Mt. 24:3–14; 24:36; Mk. 13:10). Jesus holds himself aloof from any discussion of dates. The appointed day is unknown even to the Son (Mk. 13:32). The Kingdom of God does not come according to calculation (Lk. 17:20; cf. 1 Thess. 5:1ff.).

The representatives of an extreme eschatology attempt to explain the development of the Church and Christian theology from the fact of the delay. The statements of Jesus concerning the present and the future of God's Kingdom contain, in fact, a tension which cannot in the full sense be resolved. In any case one cannot mechanically place side by side the statements referring to the present and future and simply count them up. Rather, they are entwined in the entirety of Jesus' proclamation. It is evident that Jesus places no weight on the dating. What concerns him is the promise of divine salvation and the summons to conversion. Present and future statements in his preaching belong so closely together that the already present beginning of God's Lordship can never be spoken of in any other way than that the present discloses the future as salvation and judgment, and, on the other side, that the future can never be spoken of in any way other than that it opens up and illuminates the present and thus enables the present day to be seen as the day of decision.[3] The Reign of God is truly present dynamically, but will be consummated only in the future (R. Schnackenburg).

This tension between the present and future is also reflected in the early Church, according to whose faith and preaching it has its *Sitz im Leben* in the activity of Jesus himself. Even when the phrase "Reign of God" recedes, yet in all the New Testament writings, the salvation proclaimed is that salvation which Jesus procured for men. In this sense the New Testament witnesses to Christ locate the reign of God in Jesus himself. The Lordship of God is thus realized in the Lordship of the Son. He it is who, during his earthly life, on behalf of God forgave sins, broke the lordship of Satan, and now grants salvation as the risen Lord, in the Holy Spirit. Thus Jesus, the risen Lord himself, exercises the kingship until the day on which he will subject everything to the Father (1 Cor. 15:28). In this proclamation the stress is sometimes laid more on the present, sometimes more on the future. At the same time, the past is not overlooked. For the salvation brought about by Christ is always bound to the saving acts of the historical Jesus.

The full form of the Lordship of God established in Jesus was first achieved only through death. The death of Jesus is represented in Scripture neither as a tyrannous act of the heavenly Lord nor as a historical misfortune nor a historical accident, but rather as the realization of the eternal, divine plan of salvation. "For God so loved the world that he gave his only Son, that whoever believes in him should not perish but have eternal life. For God sent the Son into the world, not to condemn the world, but that the world might be saved through him" (Jn. 3:16-17).

The cause of Jesus' death lay in God's free will. It lay at the same time in the free will of Jesus. For he had taken the Father's decree unconditionally into his own free decision (Mk. 14:21,41; Lk. 18:31). Jesus died into the will of the Father, so to speak. The reason that death first of all was the medium for the full establishment of God's Lordship lies in the fact that in the complete surrender of Jesus, as the representative of the whole of humanity, to the will of the Father, the rebellion against God at the beginning of human history was in principle overcome, so that God could again exercise to the fullest extent his saving reign of love, and man in the deliverance from sin could enter anew into a dialogue with God. The dialogue with God had often been broken off, had again and again been resumed anew by God, but it never became a lasting reality. Through the death of Jesus a permanent dialogue between God and creation was inaugurated, in that it was begun between God and Jesus Christ, and, specifically, it was begun in a manner appropriate to sinful man. The full breakthrough of the Lordship of God in Jesus Christ took place in his resurrection from the dead, and indeed in such a way that Jesus himself thus became the Lord. The creative power of his death is attested to in the Gospel of John, chapter 12, verses 23-32. Jesus is the firstborn from the dead. According to the Letter to the Hebrews (2:10-12), it was fitting for him, for whose sake and through whom everything is, in order to bring many children to glory, to perfect the founder of salvation through suffering. Indeed the sanctifier and the sanctified all originate from One. For this reason he is not ashamed to call them brothers, since he says, "I will proclaim your name to my brothers. In the midst of the congregation I will praise you."

The apostle Paul brings the coming Lordship of God most clearly into relation with the risen Lord. In the risen Lord the Lordship of God had prevailed at one point in creation, and that the decisive one, insofar as Christ is the center of creation and the total movement of the world is oriented towards him. The glorified Lord so acts through the Holy Spirit on the world, especially on men, that what has become a reality in his case will become a reality for all. With the resurrection of Jesus the final future has been inaugurated: Jesus, at the right hand of the Father, continues to work for the formation of that future until the hour of his return. In the risen Jesus the future into which all are called has already begun. In this future the transcendent reality which always penetrates the world—or rather, the transcendent God—will come into the visible world with such power that a blessed dialogue will ensue between God, who will reveal himself unveiled, and the creature, and this will endure for eternity. Hence the fullness of God's Lordship mediated through Christ will consist in the saving encounter with God the Father directly, through Jesus Christ in the Holy Spirit (1 Cor. 15:20–28). In his hope for the Reign of God all the Christian's expectations of the future are radically transformed.[4] (Further consideration will be given to these relationships in the volume on the Last Things.)

## Notes

[1] P. Hoffman, "Reich Gottes," in H. Fries, *Handbuch Theologischer* II, pp. 414–428; R. Schnackenburg, "Basileia," in *Lexikon für Theologie* II, pp. 25–31.

[2] Strack-Billerbeck, *Kommentar zum Neuen Testament aus Talmud und Midrasch* (1922), p. 418f.

[3] G. Bornkamm, *Jesus von Nazareth* (Stuttgart, 1956), pp. 84ff. (New York: Harper & Row, 1960).

[4] Cf. J. Moltmann, *Theologie der Hoffnung*, 1966³; G. Saufer, *Zukunft und Verheissung*, 1965; E. Bloch, *Das Prinzip Hoffnung*.

# ‹ 3

## *The Salvific Activity of Jesus*

### THE RESURRECTION FROM THE DEAD

The resurrection of Jesus is the foundation and the main content of the preaching and the faith of the primitive Church. Paul in particular explains the resurrection of Jesus together with his death on the cross—the two inseparably forming a single mystery of salvation—as the center of his message of salvation (1 Cor. 15:1–21). When, in place of Judas, who was eliminated from the circle of apostles, another was to be chosen to make up the full Twelve, Peter, as we have noted, stipulates that the man should be one who has been with them throughout the entire time from the baptism of John to the day on which Jesus was taken up from among them. In other words, he demands that the one chosen should have been a witness of the resurrection (Acts 1:21f.; cf. 1 Cor. 9:1; Acts 2:22–40; 10:41; 4:3; 13:23–41; 4:8–12; 8:30–35).

First the scriptural witness and the teaching of the Church concerning the resurrection of the Lord will be discussed, then the sense in which it can be said to have taken place, and finally its meaning for salvation.

### THE TESTIMONY OF SCRIPTURE

#### *Some General Observations*

It must be pointed out in the first place that Scripture offers us no direct account of the event of the resurrection itself, nor a

30

report of any continuous presence of the risen Lord among his disciples.

The resurrection of Jesus Christ is a mystery of faith in the strictest sense of the word. Of course the empty tomb, and most especially the appearances of Jesus, offer grounds for faith in the risen one: but they cannot compel this faith and cannot serve to make the manner of the resurrection intelligible in the positive sense. The resurrection is not an event within history, which can be established by means of historical research. Since it cannot in the strict sense be "proved," neither can it furnish the "proof" for Christianity. As it becomes credible through the Easter appearances, it is a motive—but not a proof—for belief in Christ. But its knowledge-function does not go beyond this.

The mystery therefore concerns not only the That but also the How. The mystery character of the resurrection is founded basically not in the fact that it is a happening beyond experience, but in the fact that the resurrection lies within the realm of the mystery of the incarnation, insofar as it represents the final consequence of it. In the resurrection there is revealed the perfect form of the incarnate God.

According to the rationalist theology of the last century and the rationalist-based demythologizing- and existence-theology of the present (cf. R. Bultmann and his disciples and followers, especially W. Marxsen; also the non-Bultmannian Swiss theologian R. Buri), the historical reality or the actual event is only the Easter faith of the disciples, not the resurrection of Jesus. According to these scholars the Easter faith does not arise out of the experience of the really living and present Jesus, awakened from the dead, but in another way, either through a visionary experience (D. F. Strauss), or through the experiencing of the crucifixion of Jesus as the end of a purely inner-worldly and isolated existence (Bultmann), or through the interpretation of certain occurrences (Marxsen).

Because of their great influence, the attempted explanations of Bultmann and Marxsen should be sketched out here. Both pursue the intention to make the biblical resurrection faith accessible and understandable to modern man. Bultmann proceeds from the anthropological, philosophical, theological *a priori* that modern man, with today's self-understanding, is not able to admit the intervention of supernatural forces in history, but understands all expressions of this type as mythological. These mythological expressions must therefore be examined to see what they offer for the self-understanding of man. Another presupposition of Bultmann's is contained in the thesis that biblical revelation does not represent a communication of truths and doctrine, but rather a call to the fulfillment of existence, that the word of the Bible can be rightly heard only in a personal decision. Further, Bultmann is convinced, on the basis of tradition- and form-critical exegesis, that the "legend of the empty tomb" and "the Easter stories which report proofs of the corporeality of the Risen One" are later constructions. (In this connection he calls the Pauline text, 1 Cor. 15:3–8, unfortunate; he interprets it as a compromise of the apostle in the apologetic against Gnosticism and so minimizes it.)

On the basis of these premises Bultmann explains that only the Easter faith of the disciples is historically determinable. This faith, however, is nothing else than faith in the cross as a salvation event. But that the cross is a salvation event can be learned only through the Christian proclamation of it. Christ encounters us as the Crucified and as the Risen One only in the word of proclamation. Faith in this word is truly the Easter faith. The historical source of the proclamation is not to be questioned, because any proof would make faith illusory. The first disciples arrived at their Easter faith through reflection on their former association with Jesus. Aside from this, the question about the source of the disciples' Easter faith or about the happening behind this faith is unimportant.

One must concur with Bultmann that the resurrection is not a (historical) event, susceptible of historical research, in that it is not in the strict sense a proof for Christianity, in that the event itself cannot be proved, and finally in that the resurrection is effective for salvation only through the proclamation and in faith. However, he is in opposition to the gospel when he sets aside the testimony of the apostle Paul (1 Cor. 15) for the actuality of the resurrection event, and when he does not admit the disciples' resurrection faith was motivated by the appearances of Jesus.

While Bultmann considers the resurrection in itself unimportant, W. Marxsen formally denies the resurrection as an event. The resurrection witness of the disciples, according to him, is an "interpretation" of certain occurrences (seeing Jesus = knowing) which befell them after the death of Jesus. The content of this conviction is not the coming-to-life again of Jesus, but rather the consciousness that "the fact of Jesus goes on." They draw this conclusion out of the suggested "occurrences." Originally the disciples had interpreted these occurrences as a commission, a legitimizing of their mission. This functional meaning developed into a personal one, in accordance with which the Jesus kerygma developed. For this the disciples made use of the expression for the resurrection which was at hand in the Jewish apocalyptic.

It must be granted, in line with Marxsen, that, directly, we can go only as far as the disciples' conviction. He stands, however, even more clearly than Bultmann, in opposition to the text of 1 Cor. 15. However, Marxsen is right in his assertion that the disciples, in attesting to their experiences after the death of Jesus, made use of an expression, "he has risen," taken from Jewish apocalypticism. But while in that context it means a return to the earlier form of life, the New Testament resurrection witnesses intend to say that Jesus, who was dead, lives again and in truth, not only in his influence, but ontologically, although differently than before his death, Marxsen also wrongly assumes that the disciples had an experience that was undetermined in itself, which they decided was an experience of Christ only through reflection. In reality the New Testament describes the Easter experiences of the disciples *a priori* as encounters with the person of Jesus (cf. J. Kremer, *Das älteste Zeugnis von der Auferstehung Christi,* Stuttgart, 1966).

In general one can validly eliminate any type of purely psychological origin of the Easter faith: such a hypothesis would not sufficiently take into consideration the emotional state of mind of the disciples after the crucifixion, when they had seen all their hopes dashed. The thought of the resurrection would have contradicted completely their emotional and mental state. All the emotional prerequisites and conditions are lacking for a psychological explanation. Nor is this situation altered by the repeated promises which Jesus had given of his resurrection or by the resurrection hopes of late Judaism. These expectations were in no way realized by the disciples after the death of Jesus. The vision-theory is in contradiction to the historical extent and duration of the Easter faith of the disciples. The resurrection witnesses knew well how to distinguish between myth and reality, and, incidentally, they sharply emphasized the contrast. Again it is Paul especially who puts so decisive an emphasis on the resurrection of Jesus, that according to his conviction, the Christian proclamation, the Christian faith loses all sense, it becomes absurd, if Jesus be not risen from the dead (1 Cor. 15:1–19). The disciples were overcome by the experience of the resurrected Lord. After this experience a compulsion lay upon them which they could not escape. They could not remain silent about that which directed and drove them after the resurrection, or rather after the appearances of the resurrected Lord (Acts 3:16; 4:19ff.; 1 Cor. 9:16).

The reality of the resurrection of Jesus and of the resurrected Lord does not really mean that the resurrection can be ascertained and proved as a historical happening in the sense of other historical happenings. It is, so to speak, a real happening on the edge of history, but it is effective within history. It represents a historical-suprahistorical, an immanent-transcendent occurrence, insofar as it stands as a real happening, although of a different kind from human experience, in close connection with the data of history. In his resurrection Jesus did not return to the temporal-spatial world, as did Lazarus, whose resurrection Thomas Aquinas describes as incomplete. It is to be noted first of all that Lazarus, as well as the others whom Jesus raised from the dead, later died again. Jesus, however, after the resurrection, remained forever living, and as the Living One ontologically present in history, effecting salvation in a mysterious and hidden way. Further, it is to be noted that the Risen One belongs to another order of existence. Thus, in his appearances he was not always immediately recognized by his own. In order (to be able) to be seen, he had to interpose the order of existence into which he had gone in the resurrection into our world of experience.

This can be explained in a twofold way. Either it can be granted that the resurrected Lord, through powerful impulses, so affected the disciples that they translated the influences so received into the form of the Resurrected One. According to this interpretation, the appearances are a synthesis of objective happening and subjective striving for recognition. Such an interpretation has its parallel in the natural process of recognition. Or one could also say, with even stronger emphasis on the objective elements (in an objectivized vision, so to speak): Christ, although possessing a completely different mode of existence, took on shape and color which are proper to our range of experience, in order to be recognized by his own. But, in either case, what happened to the disciples cannot be based simply on an observation, but rather on a believing understanding.

Also, in emphasizing the reality of the resurrection happenings, one must definitely accept the concern (if not the theses) of Bultmann and Marxsen. The resurrection of Jesus remains ineffective for salvation if one understands it only as a happening by itself. Their view brings out that it is a happening *for us*. It becomes saving only through the proclamation and in faith. Only in the proclamation and in faith does the resurrection effect the salvation of man. So the resurrection is ordered towards proclamation and faith. On the other hand, however, the proclamation and faith would remain empty and senseless if the reality of the resurrection were not at work in them. Through the proclamation the resurrection is actualized and made present as a saving event for every generation. Not only the simple assertion of the resurrection, but also the theses about it would be lacking in truth, unless in the word of the proclamation and in faith. Behind Bultmann's thesis stands the dualism of nature and existence, of object and subject, so that nature, or object, as the case may be, is excluded.

The New Testament resurrection testimony concerns the present and living character of the transfigured and glorified Lord. A lesser accent falls on the event of the resurrection itself, and of course there is lacking any description whatsoever of the process. The resurrection is understood as a presupposition for the presence of Jesus and his being alive. One can say: from the experience of the appearances the disciples conclude, whether by direct logical conclusion or in a wider sense as a corollary of their faith, back to the happening of the resurrection.

*The Scriptural Texts*

Now we shall present the scriptural texts in which the Easter faith of the disciples is expressed. In these we must consider not only the historical reality but also the origin of the Easter faith. As a rule the texts speak of both elements at the same time. However, in the interests of a clear analysis, the two elements must be distinguished.

One of the earliest available resurrection texts, and at the same time the most important, occurs in the fifteenth chapter of the first letter to the Corinthians, a community in which the Greek mentality, opposed and hostile to the resurrection faith, together with an all too gross concept of the risen Christ, had provoked disagreement. In this letter Paul wants to defend and deepen the already existing resurrection faith, and at the same time to purify and clarify it. Verses 1 to 25 are as follows: "[1] And now, my brothers, I must remind you of the gospel that I preached to you; the gospel which you received, on which you have taken your stand, [2] and which is now bringing you salvation. Do you still hold fast the Gospel as I preached it to you? If not, your conversion was in vain. [3] First and foremost, I handed on to you the facts which had been imparted to me: that Christ died for our sins, in accordance with the scriptures; [4] that he was buried; that he was raised to life on the third day, according to the scriptures; [5] and that he appeared to Cephas, and afterwards to the Twelve. [6] Then he appeared to over five hundred of our brothers at once, most of whom are still alive, though some have died. [7] Then he appeared to James, and afterwards to all the apostles.

"[8] In the end he appeared even to me. . . . [11] This is what we all proclaim, and this is what you believed. [12] Now if this is what we proclaim, that Christ was raised from the dead, how can some of you say there is no resurrection of the dead? [13] If there be no resurrection, then Christ was not raised; [14] and if Christ was not raised, then our gospel is null and void, and so is your faith; [15] and we turn out to be lying witnesses for God, because we bore witness that he raised Christ to life, whereas, if the dead are not raised, he did not raise him. [16] For if the dead are not raised, it follows that Christ was not raised;

[17] and if Christ was not raised, your faith has nothing in it and you are still in your old state of sin."

This text shows that the basic concern of the apostle about the faith in Corinth is the resurrection of the dead through the coming again of Christ. The apostle speaks of the resurrection of Christ only in order to have an argument for the teaching of the resurrection of the dead at the end of time. The sense of the argument can be formulated thus: if and because Christ is raised from the dead, we also will be raised. Our hope in the resurrection would fall away, if Christ were not risen. If, however, this has not happened, then the proclamation and the faith are deception and self-delusion. For the sake of a conclusive argument Paul accents most strongly the reality of the resurrection. Underlying his argument is the governing principle of this letter: as Christ, so the Christian.

The textual basis of his argumentation is a proclamation and confessional formula stemming from tradition. It was already composed when Paul became Christian. It apparently served missionary and catechetical, perhaps liturgical purposes (cf. Lk. 24:34; Rom. 1:3ff.). Paul took over this formula either in Damascus or in Jerusalem. When he preached the gospel in Corinth (ca. 52), he had made use of it. In the first letter to the Corinthians he reminds his readers of it and repeats the formula in verses 3–7. Whether Paul had revised it slightly cannot be determined with certainty. That it essentially represents an old tradition and was not created by Paul is shown by a number of words and phrases ("for our sins," "according to the scriptures," "on the third day," "the Twelve") as well as by the rhythm of the speech with its parallelism. The formula represents a very old layer in the church's proclamation of the resurrection of Jesus in a formulated composition. It is the official ecclesiastical form of the proclamation of the resurrection. It reaches back into the ancient Palestinian community, to about the year 40 or perhaps the middle of the 30's, and it constitutes the norm for the later testimony to the resurrection of Jesus. The appearances were spoken of as the ground for the resurrection faith. The origin of the text out of the Jewish province and its use in Corinth confirm the essential unity of the resurrection faith in the Jewish- and gentile-Christian

world. Paul appends his own Christ experience to the tradition
(cf. Acts 9:1–30).

But this very addition seems rather to compromise than to en-
sure the argument, since the appearance of Christ which fell to
his lot, reported three times with some variations in the Acts of
the Apostles, poses some problems for exegesis.

The text provides the norm for the understanding of all the
other resurrection testimony, particularly for that in the Acts of
the Apostles; and these, in turn, explicate more clearly the content of the tradition.

Some texts, in which the resurrection of Jesus appears as the
content of the early apostolic kerygma, clearly have their locus
in the cult of the early church (Phil. 2:6–11; 3:14; Eph. 3:10).
One can cite here also the baptismal formulas, at first christological in form, later trinitarian (Rom. 10:9; Jn. 20:28; Mt.
28:19). In these is expressed the fullness and the power of the
primitive resurrection faith.

The speeches of Paul in Acts (13:16–41; 17:22–31; 20:18–25;
22:1–21; 24:10–21; 26:2–23; 28:25–28), which have the resurrection of Jesus as their central point, appear much more credible, despite their rather schematized form, when viewed in the
light of such creedal formulas. According to Acts 13 (26–38)
Paul, in a speech at Antioch in Pisidia, describes the suffering of
Jesus as the fulfillment of Old Testament prophecy, his burial as
a historical fact, and his resurrection again as the fulfillment of
prophetic promises, as also the appearances of the risen Christ
to the Apostles. In 1 Corinthians Paul preaches Christ as the
firstborn of those who sleep and as the type or model of the
resurrection of those who believe in him; but in the speech in
Pisidia the event of the resurrection is seen as a matter of salvation history. It is the preliminary climax of this. In this speech
the issue is not only that Jesus still lives on as the Risen One,
but that his resurrection occupies a place of outstanding importance in the course of salvation history, is in fact its culmination.
This is the reason why Paul in this speech passes over in silence
his own personal experience of the Risen One.

Finally we must mention the Gospels (Mk. 16; Mt. 28:1–20;
Lk. 24; Jn. 20:1–23) and Acts (1:3–11). The entire train of

thought of the Gospels is directed towards bearing witness to the resurrection of Jesus.

The resurrection passages of the Gospels differ from the pre-synoptic testimonies treated above by the fact that they relate the resurrection of Jesus to the overall context of his life and activity, and consider it as the climax of this. The conviction won from the experience of Easter that Jesus lives on as Lord and Messiah and is actively and salvifically present among his followers led back to reflection on his deeds of power (Mk.) and words (Mt. and Lk.). These were more deeply understood in the light of the Easter experience and at the same time they provided the basis for the "following" of Christ in daily life. It became all the more necessary to base this following on the historical Jesus, as the initial enthusiasm of Easter began to slacken in missionary activity and in the life of the community amid the demands of daily living. It is understandable then that the resurrection passages despite their importance take up a relatively small space in the Gospels in comparison with the treatment of the historical Jesus.

The testimonies of the Gospels and of Acts are uneven in this respect. This is especially true of their accounts of the appearances. As we would expect from the manner of their origin sketched above, they presume the framework of the creedal formula of 1 Cor. 15 and of the speeches in Acts. They are testimonies of faith. In the synoptic Gospels Jesus foretells his resurrection as the consummation of his passion. The resurrection itself is described in a particular schema: empty tomb—appearances—ascension. The basic intention of these descriptions is, on the one hand, to bear witness to the crucified Lord as one who still lives, and is actively and salvifically present, and on the other hand, to stress the identity of the One resurrected and glorified with the man crucified.

With all the discrepancies in the reports (number and names of the women at the tomb; different motives for going there; differing statements of time; different descriptions of the angels' appearances with regard to number, place, time, message; varied reactions of the women: amazement, silence, joy, speech; contradictions regarding the number and place of the appearances), the texts give unanimous witness to the burial, the empty tomb, its discovery by the women, the heavenly message of the resurrection of Jesus, the visible appearing of the Risen One. In contrast to the apocryphal gospel of Peter, dating from the middle of the second century, the canonical Gospels offer no description of the actual happening of the resurrection. (To make a judgment on the contradictions in the resurrection texts, note what was said above about the "truth" of the Gospels.)

The earliest report is that of Mark, free from anti-Jewish polemic or apologetic and later theological reflection. The women learn at the empty tomb, from a young man in white clothing—which means from a heavenly world—that Jesus lives, that he goes before the disciples and Peter to Galilee, and that he will show himself to them there, "as he himself has said." Mark therefore refers the meeting in Galilee back to the word of Jesus himself. According to Matthew, the resurrection of Jesus is the fulfillment of his own announcement. The angel appears as guarantor for the announcement of Jesus. According to Matthew Jesus announced his resurrection, not the meeting in Galilee. The meeting was, according to him, foretold by the angel on his own authority ("I have said to you"). This means: the disciples were called to Galilee by heavenly guidance. The angel, however, because of his authoritative way of acting, could be interpreted as a veiled mention of the Risen One himself. Then it is the Lord himself who sends the women to the disciples. The apologetic component is important. It is reported that the guards were bribed and spread abroad the rumor which persisted up until the formulation of the Gospels, that the body of Jesus had been stolen. Matthew brands this rumor as nonsense based on deceit. Perhaps the evangelist invented the story of the bribe in order to make laughable, in the form of a story, the rumor about the theft of the body.

Of greater importance is Matthew's account of the appearance of the Lord to the Eleven on a mountain in Galilee. "When they saw him, they fell prostrate before him, though some were doubtful" (Mt. 28:17). Jesus reveals himself as the Lord and commissions the Eleven to go teach all nations. At the same time he promises them that he will remain with them till the end of time. This is all the more noteworthy because at the same time he takes his leave from them. His resurrection becomes the condition and ground for a much more interior closeness. (The words of Jesus are very probably modeled upon Ex. 3:6–12; Jer. 1:4–9; Dan. 7:14.) The appearance does not force faith.

The text of Luke exhibits three differences from that of Mark and Matthew. The testimony of the women about Christ's resurrection seems to the Apostles to be mere women's idle gossip. Instead of a single angel Luke introduces, in accordance with the Jewish law of testimony, two angels as witnesses of the Easter message (cf. Dt. 17:6; 2 Cor. 13:1; 1 Tim. 5:19; Heb. 10:28). In addition he does not have any announcement of the meeting in Galilee. Instead the angel recalls the prediction of the death and resurrection by the historical Jesus himself. So the Easter message in Luke's Gospel is founded on the Jesus of the pre-Easter period.

A second story peculiar to Luke is that of the disciples on the road to Emmaus (Lk. 24:13–53). The purpose of this story is probably to point out that Jesus' fate corresponds to the image of the Messiah in the Old Testament, which is also true of the encounter of Philip with the chamberlain of the Ethiopian queen, Candace. Luke is here using popular tradition, meant to illustrate both the Easter faith and the way to it. It is noteworthy that when the two disciples returned to Jerusalem after their experience of Jesus they did not even get a chance to give an account of it, but were told by the Eleven: "The Lord has truly risen and has appeared to Simon." This statement was already a traditional formula, which Luke has scarcely altered (cf. 1 Cor. 15:5; Mk. 16:7). If Simon is mentioned specially it is to point out that among the members of the group he is the principal witness to the resurrection. It is not the disciples of Emmaus but Peter who is the guarantor of the faith of the church in Jesus' resurrection. Luke follows this account with a report of an appearance of the Risen One to the disciples gathered in Jerusalem. At first the apparition provokes shock and bewilderment. The disciples believe they have seen a "ghost." This is not a Jewish but a Hellenistic conception. Luke wishes to counter any tendency to spiritualize the experience by emphasizing the reality of the risen Christ. That is, this account represents an attack on Hellenistic spiritualism. The person they see identifies himself with Jesus of Nazareth by a three-fold demonstration: the disciples are to examine his hands and feet; they are to touch him, in order to see that he is flesh and blood; when they still cannot believe because of joy and amazement, he asks them to give him food to eat. Then he reminds them of the words he spoke to them when he was still with them. He opens up to them the sense of the Old Testament, which had already spoken of the death of the Messiah and of his resurrection, and that he would preach repentance for the forgiveness of sins. Then he makes the disciples his witnesses and promises to send them the Spirit. He goes with them towards Bethany, blesses them, and departs from them. They return to Jerusalem full of joy.

When we examine the historical reliability of this account, the question arises whether the events Luke sketches could have taken place all in one evening. It should not be forgotten that after sunset the gates of the city were shut. It is obvious that Luke is not presenting a step-by-step account of the events but puts them all together in one "picture." We must distinguish between what Luke testifies to, namely the reality of the risen Christ, and the manner in which he testifies to it. Here we see the linguistic difficulty of dealing with, on the one hand, the reality of the risen Jesus, and the new form of his being on the other. Luke presents the first with the means which lay within the conceptual horizons of his time.

We cannot separate Luke's Gospel from the Acts of the Apostles which also stems from his pen. It takes up for its beginning the concluding words of the Gospel, where Jesus says to the Apostles that they are to be his witnesses (Acts 1:8). The feast of Pentecost is for Luke the beginning of the time of the Spirit, given by the risen Lord (Acts 2:33). The signs and wonders which the Apostles and other leaders of the church work (Acts 2:43; 5:12) continue the signs and wonders of Jesus, which represented God's attestation of him (Acts 2:22).

Through his holy Spirit the risen Jesus is present in the preaching of the church and in its life of faith: "The Apostles bore witness with great power to the resurrection of the Lord Jesus" (Acts 4:33). Witness to the resurrection and to the Risen One consists in the witness of his salvific activity in the church, which shows itself in charisms and wonders and in the success of their missionary endeavors (see A. Kremer, *Die Osterbotschaft der vier Evangelien,* Stuttgart, 1967, and P. Seidensticker, *Die Auferstehung in der Botschaft der Evangelisten,* Stuttgart, 1967).

The resurrection story has a character all of its own in the Gospel of John, which was composed in Asia Minor around the end of the first century and mirrors this time and situation in its account. In the death of Jesus John sees the fulfillment of the "history of salvation" and the beginning of the "time of salvation" (Jn. 19:28; 12:32). For this reason he sees precisely in the death on the cross the Easter resurrection and glorification of Jesus (Jn. 12:23–32; 3:14ff.). The Gospel of John contains three resurrection stories, that of the empty tomb (Jn. 20:1–18), that of the appearance of Jesus to the disciples (Jn. 20: 19–23), and that of the appearance to Thomas (Jn. 20:24–29). The final chapter, added later, reports the appearance at the Sea of Tiberias (Jn. 21).

The first account is the most important. It expresses John's concern to lead his readers to faith in Jesus as the Christ so that in this faith they may have community of life with Jesus (Jn. 20:31).

John's account of the empty tomb, despite many common elements, has some characteristic differences from those of the synoptics. According to John, the empty tomb is discovered by Mary Magdalen. It does not occur to her that Jesus has risen from the dead, however, but only that his body has been taken from the tomb. No angel points out that the tomb is empty. Two angels are mentioned, but they form simply a guard of honor, as it were. On hearing Mary's story, Peter and John hasten ("run") to the empty tomb. John arrives first but stands by to allow Peter to enter first. Chapter 20, verse 8, continues: "Then the disciple who had reached the tomb first went in too, and he saw and believed." The Evangelist does not, at first, give any grounds for this faith. The empty tomb cannot be considered a proof for the resurrection. In accordance with the overall orientation of the Gospel, however, it must be interpreted as a "sign." It must be remembered that John writes out of a personally felt union with Christ and from a point of view which is basically ecclesial. His words are not a historical report, but a proclamation of faith. If this is understood, even the strange statement of 20:9 has meaning:

"Until then they had not understood the scriptures, which showed that he must rise from the dead." The point apparently is that the two disciples believed, even though they had not previously understood scripture as a prophecy of the event (Jn. 2:22). Faith in Jesus leads to a deeper understanding of the Old Testament, but this itself does not serve as the foundation of the faith. Peter and John return home: the risen Jesus does not appear to them. It seems that in this passage the Evangelist does not wish to base faith in the risen Lord on his appearances. On the other hand it is obviously his chief concern to set forth the meaning of the risen life of Jesus. This takes place in the scene which follows, where Jesus appears to Mary and states the meaning of his resurrection himself. If the Gospel presents the faith of the two disciples as the basis of the church's faith, still it is Mary Magdalen who brings the announcement which Jesus desires to give to the disciples. Jesus obviously appears to her in a form which is entirely normal and natural, "of this world" (cf. Lk. 24:15), yet she does not recognize him, but thinks he is the "gardener." When he calls her by her name she does not fall down in adoration before him like the disciples in Matthew 28:17 and she does not, like Thomas, call him "My Lord and my God" (Jn. 20:28), but simply calls him, as she always had, "Master." It would be possible to say, Mary did indeed recognize Jesus, only not as risen. However it is in this character, as risen, that Jesus reveals himself, not in order to teach Mary but in order to give her a commission for the disciples. He says to her: " 'Do not cling to me, for I have not yet ascended to the Father. But go to my brothers, and tell them that I am now ascending to my Father and your Father, my God and your God.' Mary of Magdala went to the disciples with her news: 'I have seen the Lord!' she said, and gave them his message" (Jn. 20:17f.). These words are a testimony of Jesus to himself, a message to the church he leaves behind. It is Jesus himself who makes the proclamation. The intermediary persons only hand on what he has said. As a result of the resurrection a new relation is established between Christ and his disciples. They are called his brothers, and so his Father is their Father: there is a familial community of life. The Christ who has returned to his Father is close to his brothers. A new community has arisen and only the person who belongs to it is capable of hearing and accepting Christ's witness about himself. This enduring community is established through the resurrection. Such a community cannot exist with the earthly Jesus (Jn. 20:17).

The crucifixion, resurrection, and glorification of Jesus form, according to John, one unified salvific event which can be seen from different viewpoints. In 20:17 John views the Easter-event as the return or ascent of Jesus to his Father. Jesus' path is completed in his return to the Father (cf. Jn. 13:1,3,33,36; 14:2f.; 16:5,10,17,28; 17:13). This ascent is at the same time an anticipation of their return to "my Father and your Father" (Jn. 14:1–4).

The appearances of Jesus reported from 20:19 on, to the disciples and Thomas, stem from a synoptic tradition which has been refashioned in the spirit of the Gospel of John. The appearance to the disciples is transposed to Jerusalem and described as a coming of Jesus (Jn. 20:19; cf. Lk. 24:36; Rev. 2:1; 5:6). As in Matthew 28:18, Jesus comes in power. If Jesus identifies himself to his disciples by showing them his hands and side, still the accent is on the majesty of Jesus and on his power to save. The response of the disciples, however, is not adoration, as in Matthew, but joy (Jn. 20:20; cf. 16:22). This is an expression of their awareness of familial community with Christ. He promises them peace and gives them the commission of carrying on in his name the task which he had received from his Father (Jn. 20:21; cf. Mt. 28:18ff.). The commission is comprehensive. However, the passage emphasizes the conferring of the power to forgive sins. Since this is a question of a divine power, the disciples receive the Holy Spirit (Jn. 20:22). In Matthew 28:16ff. the decisive content of the commission is the universal spread of the church among all peoples; in John, however, it is concerned with community of life with Christ and with God, the life of faith in the Christian community.

The story of the encounter of Thomas with the risen Jesus receives its legitimation from the assertion that Thomas was not present when Jesus appeared to the other apostles and did not believe their report. He makes it a condition of his belief that he be able to see the marks of the crucifixion in Jesus' hands and side. Jesus appears to Thomas in order to convince him of the reality of the resurrection. In this way he becomes a divine revealer, to whom faith is the fitting response. Thomas, however, desires proof. He wishes to investigate and to judge for himself. Jesus shows understanding for this desire, but does not force conviction on Thomas. Jesus preserves his own position. It is not reported whether Thomas followed Jesus' summons to examine his hands and to lay his hand in his side. The only answer Thomas is capable of is the confession of faith, "My Lord and my God." Faith opens up for him direct access to the risen Jesus as the revealer of God. He achieves a full certainty which has its roots in the community which, according to John, we have with the Father and his Son (1 Jn. 1:3). It is only in this believing communion with Jesus that the believer "sees" Jesus rightly. It is significant that in the passage about the "little while" (16:16–23) John changes the subject of the seeing. Jesus sees his disciples; that means, he comes to them. The certainty of faith is rooted in the salvific gaze of Jesus. This is true of the first believers and of all who come after them. The testimony of faith of the first witnesses rests in Jesus' testimony about himself. It is this then which remains the criterion for the faith of the church.

The final chapter (Jn. 21) reports an appearance of Jesus in Galilee to seven disciples and the conferring of the office of shepherd on Simon Peter. This represents a piece of tradition which has been refashioned in Johannine thought-forms and further interpreted (cf. the works mentioned above of Kremer and Seidensticker).

## The Origin of the Easter Faith

We turn to the question of the origin of the Easter faith. It cannot be based simply in the psyche of the disciples, as we have shown. But then we must answer the question how it came about. It can be said with certainty that something objective must have happened, something which the disciples came up against, if the Easter faith is to be explained at all. For it represented a complete and lasting alteration of the Apostles. They themselves frequently refer their faith in Jesus' resurrection to particular experiences, namely the appearances of Jesus himself. These in their turn are not a question of some "occurrence," of their being affected by some thing, but a personal reality. It was the appearances of Jesus which provided stimulus and point of departure for the Easter faith. The Apostles called themselves witnesses of the resurrection (Acts 2:32; 3:15; 5:32; 10:39). They take their stand not on the reports of the women, but on their own experience of the living Christ (Acts 1:3). Even the appearances of the Lord led the disciples only reluctantly to faith (Lk. 24:37f.; Jn. 21:1–14), but eventually as a result of these experiences, they become certain that the Jesus who was crucified lives on. Someone who was dead is alive again. They describe the objective process by which this took place in terms of a metaphor drawn from their Jewish environment, "resurrection." P. Seidensticker puts forward the thesis that it was through the experience of the activity of Christ in the church that the conviction arose that Jesus of Nazareth was living on in a transformed spiritual form of being. Through the wonders and signs worked by the Apostles (Acts 3:1ff.; 5:12ff.) Christ bore testimony to himself. His testimony to himself is the testimony of God to the risen Lord (Jn. 1:2; 2 Cor. 13:4). In Seidensticker's view the appearances of Jesus would be secondary to this (cf. Jn. 20:29).

The appearances themselves (Mt. 28:16–20; Mk. 16:9–20; Lk. 24:13–53; Jn. 20:19–29; 21:4–22; Acts 1:4–9) in turn raise several serious problems. These concern place and sequence as well as the event itself. Luke makes no mention of appearances in Jerusalem, while the older gospels, Mark and Matthew particularly, report appearances in Galilee and in part of Jerusalem itself. Obviously there were different traditions. Perhaps the differences may be explained through the redaction-history of the texts. Most important and illuminating is, in any case, the report of the appearances of Jesus in Jerusalem. For precisely this city, in which all hopes collapsed, became through the appearance of the Lord the preeminent place of the Easter faith, and thus the location of the beginning of the preaching about Christ and the building up of the Church. If it is no longer unequivocally clear from the texts who became the first to experience an appearance of the Risen One, this shows that the main thing is not the chronology but the mean-

ing of the appearances for faith in Christ. When Paul declares
that the risen Lord first appeared to Peter, Peter is thereby proclaimed as the principal guarantor of the truth of Jesus' resurrection. What is in question is not so much the sequence of the appearances as the fact that they took place. It is precisely failure
of the resurrection reports to harmonize with each other which
testifies to the primitive and original nature of the tradition. Had
not the original experience of a manifestly bewildering event been
involved, provision would surely have been made for making the
accounts tally. Besides Peter, all the others to whom the Lord appeared were admitted to the role, and given the obligation, of wit-
nessing to the risen Lord.

So far as the appearances themselves as events are concerned,
they must be considered God's revelation in the strict sense of
the word. They cannot be interpreted simply as the expression of
some factor already existing in creation. The appearance of Jesus
after his resurrection consists precisely in this, that the natural
boundary which encloses the mystery of God and of Jesus, who
has now truly advanced into God's transcendence, has been
breached by a miracle consisting in the fact that the Risen One
turns back again, so to speak, and takes on a form belonging to
this side of the veil in order to allow himself to be seen by his
disciples (Lk. 24:37–41).

The empty tomb and the appearances are integrally related: the
appearances explain the fact that the tomb is empty, and the empty
tomb confirms the objective character of the appearances. Generally speaking, contemporary theology does not interpret the
empty tomb as the fundamental source of the Easter faith, although there are a few individual exceptions to this among
theologians. The sight of the empty tomb evoked alarm and confusion but not faith (Mk. 16:8). The empty tomb cannot be interpreted as a literary form, a legend circulated in support of faith
in Jesus' resurrection. If it were a subsequent legendary creation
of the Easter faith, originating in other experiences, or merely a
self-evident inference from the faith in the resurrection and intended to support that faith, then the story of the discovery of the
empty tomb would surely have been told differently, more tri-
umphantly and victoriously. In this context the Pentecost sermon

of Peter may be cited (Acts 2:14–36), in which Peter quotes Ps. 16:8–11. In this psalm, as Peter emphasizes, David prays that God will allow his body to rest in hope and will not allow it to experience corruption. David could not, says Peter, have been prophesying concerning himself, for he "died and was buried, and his tomb is here to this very day. It is clear therefore that he spoke as a prophet who knew that God had sworn to him that one of his own direct descendants should sit on his throne; and when he said he was not abandoned to Hades, and his flesh never suffered corruption, he spoke with foreknowledge of the resurrection of the Messiah. The Jesus we speak of has been raised by God, as we can all bear witness" (Acts 2:30–32). Within the scope of this sermon the passion, death, burial, empty tomb and resurrection comprise one single, indissoluble event. It should not be overlooked, moreover, that all the evangelists narrate the story of the empty tomb, obviously considering the fact important. The most explicit account is John 20:6–9:

Early on the Sunday morning, while it was still dark, Mary of Magdala came to the tomb. She saw that the stone had been moved away from the entrance, and ran to Simon Peter and the other disciple, the one whom Jesus loved. "They have taken the Lord out of his tomb," she cried, "and we do not know where they have laid him." So Peter and the other set out and made their way to the tomb. They were running side by side, but the other disciple outran Peter and reached the tomb first. He peered in and saw the linen wrappings lying there, but did not enter. Then Simon Peter came up, following him, and he went into the tomb. He saw the linen wrappings lying, and the napkin which had been over his head, not lying with the wrappings but rolled together in a place by itself. Then the disciple who had reached the tomb first went in too, and he saw and believed; until then they had not understood the scriptures, which showed that he must rise from the dead.

The value of the Johannine report as history cannot be minimized by classifying it simply according to the overall character of the fourth gospel, which is one of theological reflection.[1] The oldest gospel, Mark's, is plainly based on the report of the empty tomb (Mk. 16:2–8), while his account of the appearances (Mk.

16:9–20) is a later addition. Yet it must be considered that legendary features have become involved in the shaping of the report of the empty tomb.[2]

Regarding the question of the empty tomb as a motive for the disciples' belief in Jesus' resurrection, it must be pointed out that the mere fact of the empty tomb cannot by itself lead to faith in the resurrection or at least certainly does not need to, since it can be easily explained in other ways. The conclusion that the tomb was empty because Jesus had risen, and not for some other reason, is derivable only from the appearances.

According to Mark and Matthew the meaning of the empty tomb was explained to the women by one angel, according to Luke by two. According to John it is Jesus himself who gives the explanation. In the traditional interpretation the "angels" are understood as heavenly beings who "appear" to the women. This explanation is not impossible, but is not necessary (cf. for example Jn. 12:29f.; Gen. 22:11–14; Ex. 3:2–6). It is quite possible to understand the references to angels in the resurrection story as typical indications of a divine revelation. The women achieved an insight which bore the marks of being a message from God and this was clothed in the literary form of the appearance of an angel. This interpretation has much to recommend it. A Vögtle ("Was heisst 'Auslegung der Schrift'?", Regensburg, 1966) has shown that the tradition of the primitive church understood the appearances of the angels not as an actual phenomenon perceived by the women but as an element of biblical style used in the preaching of the early Christian community.

The fact of the empty tomb does not imply that the body was spatially removed. The resurrection consisted, after all, in a re-awakening to a new and spiritualized form of existence. We must assume that the human spirit of Jesus caught up and penetrated anew the dead body so that it became again his body but also completely transparent as the vehicle of his spirit. As the result of this transformation the body no longer existed in space and time and so was no longer perceptible by the human senses. For this reason the question where, in what place, the risen Christ is to be found is meaningless.

If the empty tomb then by itself cannot be a sufficient motive, but only an aid for the origin of the Easter faith, then our considerations bring us to the question of the appearances. Because the appearances are relevations they share the mysterious character of all revelation. This is strengthened by the fact that Jesus is risen as the glorified one. The consequence of this is that his resurrection became known not to all but only to a few—namely, those witnesses elected by God. Through them it was to be made known to others.[3] As is true of any other form of revelation, the appearance in itself does not compel man's belief. But it acts with such power on the disciples who have been permitted this experience that in the surrender of faith they attain certainty as to the reality which has broken into their lives. This is especially clear in the case of the apostle Paul, the course of whose life was so totally altered that he turned from what he had hitherto zealously pursued and took up the cause which he had passionately persecuted (cf. Gal. 1:11–16; 1 Cor. 15:8–9). As for the other apostles, the spirituality, which had begun to develop in them during Jesus' earthly life but was annihilated by his death, now revived—clarified, corrected, transposed to a new level and endowed with an indestructible élan.

Jesus' appearances are distinctly different from the visions described in Scripture and are to be distinguished from them—that is, from those experiences whose point of departure is man's inner self. Jesus' appearances take place not in a dream, not at night, but in the broad light of day. Paul says, with regard to the appearance of Jesus to him at Damascus, that he had visions and other experiences of Jesus which were of a wholly different character, and the other disciples too were well aware of the differences between visions and the appearances of Jesus (cf. 2 Cor. 12:1; Acts 12:9). Their conviction is that in the case of the appearance they are standing face to face with the reality of Jesus, even when they cannot fully understand it. The power of the reality impresses itself in the testimonies that Jesus ate, drank, spoke with the disciples. A new kind of existence is described here in an unreflective way through the only means we have, those of our earthly, experiential existence. It may be that in the words which the risen Jesus speaks, according to the evangelists, we have the reflection of some parting words which were passed over in the accounts of Jesus' last talks with his disciples on earth and now are revealed in their deeper and final meaning through the risen Lord. Considering the weight which the speeches of the Risen One have, such an interpretative rendering would be understandable. They are in their essence and in their content the risen one's revelation of himself by means of words, and cannot be explained simply as the theology of the congregation (cf. Lk. 24:13–35, 44–49; Acts 1:3–8; Mt. 28:18ff.; Mk. 16:14–20; Jn. 21:25).

It is the task of scholarly exegesis to examine whether the passages describing the meal of the risen Jesus with his disciples (Jn. 21:4–13; Lk. 24:30–41f.) or the encounter with Thomas (Jn. 20:27) represent literary forms or intend to report actual events. In the first place they would have to be taken as a concrete form of testimony to the ontological reality of the risen Christ and to his identity with the crucified Jesus (cf. the marks of the wounds). In the second place the events would have to be explained in such a way that the otherness of Christ's body, its new and transformed condition, is not lost sight of. To do otherwise would be to miss the point of the resurrection.

The reality of the appearance is sharply accentuated when the word used is *horan* (*ophtenai*) (cf. 1 Cor. 9:1). In the Greek translation of the Old Testament, the Septuagint, this word is already in use for a divine act of relevation. It means to let oneself be seen or encountered or to be present; but visual perception is not necessarily implied. In other words, the mode of perception remains in many instances an open question. The expression is frequently used to indicate the self-manifestation of God himself: his verbal revelations are frequently introduced with the formula God appeared and said. Hence the choice of this word indicates that the disciples were aware that what they were encountering was the reality of God, the reality of the Lord raised to Kyrios by God, that they were being acted upon by the divinity. It must be emphasized here—and this, of course, holds true with regard to every theological statement—that this "seeing" has an analogical character. A reality is indeed perceived, but it differs from the reality of our exeprience; it is beyond our experience and can be expressed by the term "metaempirical." It is at once historical and suprahistorical, immanent and transcendent. Owing to its meta-empirical character, this reality is not of itself perceptible but must manifest itself, render itself capable of being experienced; hence all appearances of the Lord Jesus are joined with a verbal revelation and thus become personal encounters. The one who appears in the calling of his own calls them into communion with his own life. Accordingly, the response to the appearances is faith, which on its part represents a decision—namely, the decision of surrender to Jesus.

It is of the utmost importance to consider what the disciples experienced in the appearances. It was made known to them that Jesus is the crucified one and the Kyrios, the Son of man and the Son of God; that they have been sent out by him to preach. It is precisely through this experience that their lives are totally transformed (cf., for all the other apostles, what Paul says of himself in Phil. 3:4–11).

The appearances are delimited in time. In some places in Scripture it is indicated that Christ appeared only on one day (Lk. 24:51), in others that he appeared over a period of several days (Jn. 20:26), in others that he appeared over a period of forty days and thereupon the appearances ceased (Acts 1:3).

## THE TEACHING OF THE CHURCH

The testimony of Scripture has found its expression in numerous faith-statements of the church, although generally speaking the central character of Jesus' resurrection is expressed less clearly in the formulas than in Scripture itself. To a certain extent the abundance and diversity of the ecclesiastical formulations reflect the variety of the scriptural declarations. In all the creeds, the Christological part expresses belief that on the third day Jesus rose again from the dead (DS 1ff., 44–45, 189–190).[4] In the oriental form of the Apostles' Creed "from the dead" is omitted and in its stead the expression "in conformity with the Scriptures" is added. This is also true of the Nicene-Constantinople creed (DS 150), which is reiterated in the creed of the Council of Trent (DS 1862–1863). In the creed of Epiphanius it is stated that Jesus suffered in the flesh, was raised and entered into heaven with the same body (DS 44–45). The reality of Jesus' body is often referred to in the creeds, in opposition to the Docetist sublimation or spiritualization of his human nature. The First Council of Toledo, for

example (DS 189–190), around the year 400 (or 447) says that
Jesus was crucified, died and was buried, and arose on the third
day; that afterwards he joined the company of his disciples and
on the fortieth day ascended into heaven. In general the formulations of the creeds do not read that Jesus was raised from the dead
but that he rose from the dead. The Fourth Lateran Council in
1215 (DS 800–803) and the Second Council of Lyons in 1274
(DS 852–858) describe the event in this way. The creeds differ
in this respect from the series of passages in Scripture which speak
not of the active rising of Jesus but of a being raised by the Father
which Jesus passively underwent. The Eleventh Council of Toledo
in 675 (DS 539) had attempted a synthesis of the two ideas when
it declared that Jesus took upon himself a true death of the flesh
and that on the third day he was raised from the dead by his own
power and rose again from the grave. The profession of faith for
the Armenians at the Council of Florence on the fourth of February, 1442 (DS 1336–1338) stated simply and concisely, "He
has risen indeed," repeating the words of Luke 24:34.

## ATTEMPT AT A THEOLOGICAL EXPLANATION

Between the historical Jesus and the risen Christ there is both continuity and discontinuity: the person who died on the cross, was
buried and on the third day thereafter appeared to the disciples
is one and the same. Nevertheless the identity is interfused with
non-identity, for the crucified one has undergone a transformation
which permeates all the strata of his humanity. With its teaching
on this transformation the biblical account of the resurrection is
distinguished from all the myths of the dying and rising gods current in the world-view of "the eternal return." In the death of
Jesus—to use language which, though it is traditional, is imprecise
—his spiritual soul was separated from his body, though in the
experience of death neither soul nor body was released from
union with the person of the divine Logos. It consists in this: that
the absolute Spirit has so pervaded the creature as to make of it a
transparent vehicle for itself. This was effected through the total
self-transcendence of the man Jesus into the dimension of the
divine, which took place in death without the annihilation of what

was truly human in him. The unconditional reception of Christ's human nature into the life of God is in fact the natural consequence of the hypostatic union—that is, the union, residing in the person of the Logos, of the divine and human natures of Jesus. That the glorification did not take place from the beginning of the hypostatic union is the consequence of God's saving intention that the Logos should live a really human life within history and subject to the conditions of history. In Jesus' death the historical form of the life of the divine Logos came irrevocably to an end. The incarnate Logos entered into the suprahistorical reality of God in that he went beyond history and yet continued to exist in the form of life which belongs to the Creator. In the unconditional surrender of the man Jesus to God, creation, especially the world of matter, became completely open for God, so that he could reveal himself unveiled in Jesus without impairing man's freedom.

As a result of this participation of the man Jesus in God's transcendence, spiritually and corporally and hence in all the strata of his humanity, his glorified existence is so different from every form of existence which we meet in experience that it cannot be discovered within our created world. There is no sphere in the cosmos in which the glorified Christ is to be found: man can find him only in faith (Eph. 2:8). The apostle attempts to define the mode of life of the Risen One not only in opposition to an over-spiritualized, anti-physical concept but also in opposition to one that would be excessively empirical. He uses a comparison from biological life in the allusion to the grain of wheat sown in the earth, which must die in order that new life may begin to spring up from it. But chiefly he tries to define the glorification in negative terms: in it the body becomes free of the limitations of matter. The glorified man Jesus becomes incapable of suffering, free of the limitations imposed by time and space, from bodily weaknesses and the possibility of disintegration in death. Yet creatureliness remains, with this consequence, that the risen Jesus as man cannot be omnipresent or even present in a number of places at the same time (DS 602–606; 1636–1637). But in the full sense of the word he is a new creation (2 Cor. 5:17).

It is possible to object, with regard to the declaration of faith concerning Jesus' glorification, that the process of becoming belongs to the nature of matter and that matter exhibits a uniform

structure, so that no distinction between glorified matter and un-
glorified matter can exist. But precisely the becoming of matter
suggests a beginning and an end. If we consider spirit as the meaning of all material being and its events, then no contradiction is
implied in the idea that the goal of the world-reality which we experience lies in the increasing participation of matter in the life of
the spirit, of the taking up of the being of matter into the being of
spirit. This does not, however, mean that matter is changed into
spirit; rather, it is permeated by the spirit and thus made spiritual.
It should be pointed out that matter does not in fact always manifest the same activities. At the beginning of the process of evolution it certainly behaved in ways different from those we have
observed in later phases of world development. Again, matter
appears to change its behavior radically according to temperature,
e.g., with the approach towards absolute zero. For an analogous
explanation it may be pointed out that through the taking up of a
lower being into a higher, the lower is not alienated from its
essence but is only then brought to itself. Finally, the possibility of
glorification is grounded in the creative relation of God to the
world. This relationship is the *a priori* condition for belief in the
glorification of nature. The apostle Paul expresses the transformation of Jesus Christ's human nature in a positive way when he
calls Christ *pneuma*. He explains to the Corinthians that the religious experiences, the experiences of faith, which come to them
are nothing other than the present and saving Christ (2 Cor.
3:17). It is the Spirit of God which so transforms the nature of
Jesus that it becomes the representation and showing forth of
God's glory; the divine glory becomes accessible and perceptible
in it, and the eye which is clear of sight is able to see the glory of
God in the human nature of Jesus. Since the Spirit of God is love,
he necessarily impresses the seal of love on the human nature of
Jesus Christ. The illumination by the splendor of God's glory is
an illumination of love.

SIGNIFICANCE FOR SALVATION HISTORY

In the historical movement of God's self-disclosure the resurrection of Jesus represents the climax. In it God the Father showed

forth his saving power in the highest degree compatible with human nature's possibility of receiving the benefit of the bringer of salvation whom God had sent, through whom and in whom the whole of creation is saved. But at the same time the resurrection is the self-revelation of Jesus as the Messiah sent by God. All the preaching of the apostles receives its authorization from the resurrection (Acts 1:21f.; 1 Cor. 15:13–19). In the resurrection is made visible the goal for which the divine self-disclosure, from the creation of the universe to the coming of Jesus Christ, is intended—namely, glorification. Owing to the intentional and ontological unity between Jesus and the whole of creation and the central position of Jesus Christ in history and in the cosmos, his glorification is the archetype and foundation, the beginning and inchoation, of the glorification of the whole world. He is the head of mankind, the firstborn of creation. The Middle Ages attempted to render intelligible the dynamic significance of the glorification of Jesus for the rest of mankind through the notion that his humanity acts as an instrumental cause. To be sure, one cannot attribute to the resurrection the function of redemptive atonement, which, as we shall see shortly, belongs to the death of Christ. Nevertheless the resurrection is so closely bound up with the death of Jesus that it forms with it one mystery of salvation. Its saving function becomes clearer if viewed in the imagery of victory over sin, death, the devil, and the law. In the resurrection this victory becomes manifest. In fact the resurrection itself represents the act of victory.

From such a standpoint we can view the entire movement of the world in the following manner. To begin with, a process of concentration in salvation history takes place through the ever active creative efficacy of God. Within the world brought forth by God, man appears; within evolving humanity, a people is chosen. Within this people one man is singled out as the bringer of salvation. Within the life of this one man the course of events concentrates on one act, namely, on the resurrection from the dead and the glorification which characterizes it. From this event of highest concentration the development fans out again into multiformity and universality, embracing the Church, mankind, and the whole of creation.

In connection with this history neither the freedom of God nor the freedom of man may be left out of account. It is precisely the freedom of God which determines the whole course of events: by God's free decree of salvation the figures and the event appear at the time appointed, the *kairos* chosen by God. Man's freedom is summoned to the acceptance of God's saving act—that imponderable freedom which possesses the power to say No to God's call. The time between the resurrection of Jesus Christ and his return —that is, the full revelation of his glorified humanity—thus obtains a significance which reaches to the ultimate depths of human destiny.

Until the end of time each generation views Christ in the past, in the present, and in the future: in the past as the one who through his death dies into the fullness of life; in the present as the one constantly active in the Holy Spirit in the work of salvation, as the head of the Church and of the whole of creation which is to undergo transformation, as the one calling mankind into the future, insofar as he invites all individuals, the whole of humanity and the universe itself, to participation in his own resurrected life. As for the continued saving presence of Jesus, he is absent indeed to the eye of the body and to the eye of the spirit in its natural reasoning, but he is constantly present to faith. He works through the Spirit (cf. Jn. 6:63).

Through this gaze of faith which encompasses past and present the Christian hope for salvation is distinguished from Jewish hope. Jewish hope is directed exclusively towards the future; Christian hope has its point of departure and the ground of its anticipation of Jesus' return in Jesus' first coming—hence in the past—and in the reality of Jesus in the present, experienced in faith. The gaze of faith into the past and upon the present shows that the future into which Jesus calls us is already inaugurated: in the risen Jesus it is already in the present.

The connection between the resurrection of Jesus Christ and the resurrection of all mankind and the cosmos, between the glorified Jesus and the new humanity, was often expressed by the Greek Fathers through the statement that man, and even the cosmos itself, has risen in the resurrection of Jesus Christ. The resurrection of Jesus is not an event which rests in itself; rather it is an event which involves us. As the consequence of the Christocentricity of the world men are so much taken up into the existence of Christ that his resurrection already radically includes that of the whole. We also occasionally meet such reflections in the Latin Fathers, particularly Pope Leo the Great.

Scripture refers to the duties of the Christian in the world when, in recording the ascension of Jesus, it stresses the importance of the disciples' not passing their lives in gazing after the ascended Lord. They must, on the contrary, come down from the mountain from which Christ ascended in order to work again in the customary spheres of everyday life. Accordingly the Christian walks as a pilgrim through the world, retaining deep obligations to all of it yet gazing beyond it towards the Lord, who sits at the right hand of the Father and whose return he ardently longs for. Until that great event he seeks in creative love to give the world a form which will be genuinely human.

## CHRISTOLOGICAL PERSPECTIVES

In the resurrection the heavenly Father set the seal of his love on the Messiah who had been put to death by the Jews and the Romans. The resurrection does not follow simply as an extrinsic heavenly act connected with the death of Jesus. It is, to be sure, described in Scripture as a reward, as something earned, but this expression is not to be understood in an external, mechanical sense. The resurrection is much more the final maturation of the hypostatic union. As we have already said, it happened owing to the eternal divine plan of salvation; but in this salvific design the incarnation, the life, the death, and the resurrection were sealed together in one great mystery of salvation. The resurrection means especially the coming to maturity of the movement towards the Father which formed such an essential part of the death of Jesus; it is in this way the fruit of his death. Death and resurrection belong intrinsically together. In his unconditional surrender to the Father's will, Jesus had so totally opened himself to the Father's reality that the Father could make himself fully present in him. In this final, most total surrender Christ summed up in one act the gift of himself to the Father made unceasingly throughout his entire life (Karl Rahner). The Fathers of the Church and the theologians of the Middle Ages expressed the intimate connection between the death and resurrection by saying that Jesus earned the resurrection and that God accepted the sacrifice. In this view the resurrection is understood as the act in which God accepted the sacrifice, an act of creative power. The resurrection is thus a sign and a consequence of that love with which God gave his beloved Son over to death; with which, on the other hand, he set the seal of his acceptance on the Son who had died, as it were, into him—that is, into his eternal will (Phil. 2:6–11; Lk. 24:26).

From this two further questions follow. The first concerns the effective cause of the resurrection. The second concerns the relationship between the resurrection and the ascension.

## RISEN OR RAISED?

The first question arises from the observation that, as we remarked above, while Scripture for the most part declares that Jesus was raised from the dead (Mt. 28:6; Acts 2:32; 3:15; 4:10; 5:30; 10:40; 13:30,37; 17:31; 1 Cor. 15:13–15) it is said several times that he has risen (Mk. 16:6–9; Lk. 24:34,46; cf. Acts 26:23; Rom. 1:4; 6:5). One could make these passages agree with each other by saying that Christ was raised by the Father insofar as he was man; that he has risen in his own power insofar as he is God. If one takes into account the fact that the passages in which the passive form is used predominate, one obtains the original form of the New Testament witness, in which the divinity of Christ, though certainly implied through the general tenor of the statements made about him, is not expressly stated, and the emphasis lies on the idea that God the Father governs the life of Jesus. Through the miracle of the resurrection of Christ, the Father showed the crucified one to be his Messiah and Son (Acts 4:10; 5:30f.; 13:30–37). One can pursue the question here of whether the biblical author wishes only to "appropriate" the resurrection of Jesus to the Father or whether he sees in this action a characteristic act of the Father himself. In any case the saving action of the Father must be so explained that the dogma, discussed earlier, to the effect that in all his actions outside himself, *ab extra,* the triune God acts as one is not infringed. This principle of the

Church's faith applies in the dimension of causal efficiency but not in the realm of formal causality. Because it does not hold good in the realm of formal causality it can be said of the man Jesus, for whose human nature the divine Logos is—as we shall see—the formal cause of subsistence and personality, that as true man he is at the same time the true Son of God, i.e., the Son of the heavenly Father, the first divine person. If the principle of the oneness of the divine activity outside the godhead applied here, the man Jesus would have to be designated as the Son of the three divine persons and the expression "Son of the heavenly Father" seen as only a matter of appropriation. Such a thesis could scarcely be reconciled with the witness of Scripture.

## RESURRECTION AND ASCENSION

As far as the second question is concerned, that of the relation between the resurrection and the ascension, this can be said: Jesus' ascension is attested in Scripture in various ways; it is also the subject of official statements of faith by the Church and is mentioned in all the creeds (DS 1–75). The statement of faith concerning the ascension speaks of two distinct things, the event itself and the transformed condition of life of the risen Lord, participating now in the power and glory of God. According to the Gospel of John, Jesus foretold his return to the Father many times (Jn. 6:62; 14:2; 16:28; 20:17; see also Mk. 14:62; Mt. 26:64). The disciples exeprienced what Jesus had foretold when, as it is described in Acts (1:6–12), he was lifted up before their eyes and a cloud removed him from their sight (cf. Lk. 24:50–53; Mk. 16:19).

The meaning of the ascension does not, like that of the carrying off of Elijah and Enoch described in the Old Testament, lie in a physical transferral to a heavenly place, but in a new participation in the governing authority of the heavenly Father. It is thus a matter of an existential not a spatial context. Whether the physical ascent is a real image of the new suprahistorical existence of Jesus or only a form of expression for a new mode of existence is a question for commentators on biblical theology to decide. In any event the statement of the ascent is not so closely bound up with the world picture of antiquity that it cannot be detached from it.

What is stated is the fact of the risen life, the new creation, the new mode of existence (Acts 2:32–36; 3:18–21). What Acts offers in the form of a picture is vouched for in numerous passages in the rest of the New Testament, especially in the apostolic letters, without any mention of a physical ascent. Christ is attested as the "risen one" who reigns in power and glory, who is enthroned at the right hand of the Father—that is, who shares in the governing authority of the Father (Mt. 22:44; 26:64; Rom. 1:4; 8:34; 1 Cor. 15:25f.). In particular, in the passages in Philippians which we have frequently cited, 2:9ff., the entry of Christ into the heavenly form of existence is described as a process of enthronement, as the conferring of a name above other names, as appointment to the position of Kyrios, Lord—i.e., as the conferring upon him of lordship over the whole of human history and the whole universe (cf. Heb. 1:1ff.; 9:11–13; 1 Pet. 3:18–22; Eph. 1:20–22).

Scripture conceives the exaltation of Christ only as one undivided process. Jesus says from the cross to the robber on his right that today he will be with him in paradise (Lk. 23:43). The passage "Was the Messiah not bound to suffer these things before entering into his glory?" (Lk. 24:26) testifies to the same undivided unity of the two experiences. The same holds true for the text (Jn. 20:22) in which Christ gives the Holy Spirit to the apostles. This presupposes his having gone to the Father. Indeed, according to John's Gospel the glorification of Christ has already begun in the death on the cross (Jn. 3:14f.; 12:23–32; 6:62; cf. also Heb. 2:15; Eph. 2:6ff.). Faith is able to perceive it even in the humiliation on the cross. The following passages point in the same direction: Rom. 1:4; 8:34; 1 Cor. 15:4f.; 1 Thess. 1:10; Mt. 28:18.

In its fullest sense the resurrection embraces the ascension. The ascension is not a new element in the life of the risen one or in his manner of existence but only the end of his appearances before his return, his parousia. Throughout forty days Jesus spoke with his own with regard to the concerns of the kingdom of God (Acts 1:3). But then the appearances ceased. Only at the end of the world will Jesus again show himself as the glorified one: thus the ascension must be designated as that act through which the end of the appearances of the risen one was fixed.

In the theology of the Greek Church Fathers the resurrection and ascension are very often seen as a single process in the manner which Scripture itself suggests.

The statements of faith concerning the ascension inevitably lead us back to the question of where the risen Christ is to be found. It would be naive to suppose that somewhere in the cosmos a kind of space is set aside to which Christ has repaired, since he needs conditions which specially favor his glorified mode of existence. This would be to misapprehend the event of the resurrection and ascension completely. What is meant in speaking of the ascension is the reaching of a fullness of life, specifically a life which differs essentially from all earthly life of our experience in that it is freed from the limitations of the forms of existence which we know.

We must go a step further and emphasize that the ascension of Jesus Christ does not represent an entry into a heaven already prepared. If Scripture occasionally expresses itself in such formulations, it is nevertheless clear what is meant. It was precisely in the resurrection and ascension that Christ created a heavenly form of existence, for himself as well as for all of his brethren and indeed for the entire cosmos. "Heaven" is life in the glory of God; or, better, participation in the glory of God, the participation of man and the cosmos in the tripersonal exchange of life of God himself. Manifestly, then, "heaven" is a fulfillment of the whole man, body and soul, and it is moreover life in community.

## JESUS THE SAVIOR

Through the risen Lord it becomes clear what is to be understood by salvation. It is life in the condition of "glorification," a glorification which permeates all the levels of creation, not only the spiritual but the material as well. Matter as well as spirit is destined for a new, never-ending form of existence, not its present state of subjection to self-will but a glorified state, participating in the life of the spirit and indeed of the absolute Spirit. It is precisely in that state that the directedness of matter towards personal being will be realized most completely. The glorification of the world, as we have said, has already begun with the resurrection of Jesus Christ. It is the inchoation and pledge of our own resurrection

(Acts 13:37; 1 Cor. 15:20ff.; Phil. 3:10f.; 1 Jn. 1:25). Participation in the resurrection of Jesus Christ is not only an event of the future but becomes the saving present as often as a man allows himself to be grasped by the Lord in faith, allows himself through baptism to be transformed into a new man according to the archetype of Jesus (Rom. 6:1–11; 8:11; 5:14ff.). Indeed being a Christian means, according to Paul, "being in Jesus Christ." But this means to stand in the saving, effective power of Jesus Christ. In the Letter to the Colossians this participation is described as a present state in the following way: "In baptism also you were raised to life with him through your faith in the active power of God who raised him from the dead" (Col. 2:12). Ephesians expressed the same thesis: "And in union with Christ Jesus he raised us up and enthroned us with him in the heavenly realms" (2:6). These passages testify that one who believes in Christ is already risen; they justify those statements of the Church Fathers that see the resurrection of the whole cosmos already consummated in the resurrection of Jesus Christ. On the other hand, to be sure, the resurrection of men and the cosmos is represented as an event of the future (Rom. 8:10ff.; 2 Cor. 5:4). In the Second Letter to Timothy (2 Tim. 2:18) the sacred writer evaluates the assertion that the resurrection has already taken place as "empty and worldly chatter," vehemently protesting that on the contrary the future will excel the present. For him it is the future that is decisive. According to this letter, in the one who binds himself through faith and baptism to Christ a life-power becomes operative which in the resurrection on the day of judgment will be able to make itself felt in its fullness. The believing Christian is always governed by the resurrected Lord (Gal. 2:20), but the life he lives in Jesus Christ remains hidden until Jesus' coming (Col. 3:4). One who shares in the resurrection of the Lord must consequently go through the earthly pilgrimage and suffer his own cross. Only in death does the transformation which begins with baptism attain to its fullness; yet meanwhile the risen Lord is present in the believer really and dynamically.

The New Testament letters, particularly those of the apostle Paul, are a constant summons to men already participating in the resurrection-life of Christ to live their daily lives as people bound to Christ. Thus the admonition to live a life appropriate to the bond with Christ belongs essentially to the resurrection proclamation. The one who has entered through baptism in a special way into the realm of Jesus' activity belongs no longer to himself but to the Lord. What such a fulfillment of life looks like in the concrete can be seen in principle by looking at the life of Jesus; hence life in conformity to the bond with the Risen One becomes an imitation of the historical Jesus. An imitation of Jesus pushed to its most extreme consequence is shown to us in Scripture in the fate of Stephen. In conformity with the archetype of the risen Christ and in Christ's power he traverses the way of death to attain to glory (Acts 7:59f.). In the direst extremity, the situation imposed on Stephen, in which it is no longer possible to make a contribution in creative love to the shaping of a world worthy of human beings—and indeed as the result of a radical opposition of the world—nothing is left to the man who believes in Christ but to withdraw from the world and die into God.

## POSTSCRIPT: THE TESTIMONY OF THE EPISTLE TO THE HEBREWS

The Letter to the Hebrews calls for special comment. Grown in the soil of Pauline theology but as an independent tree of a special kind, it does not deny the primitive Christian tradition of the resurrection of Jesus, but it makes reference to it in only one passage, and even then in a formalized way (Heb. 13:20). The unknown author attempts to cope in a different manner with the stumbling block represented in the eyes of Jews and Gentiles by the outrage of the death on the cross—the assertion that it took place "outside the gates" underscores the disgrace (Heb. 12:2; 13:12f.). On the one side, in the author's view, stands the execution of Jesus (12:2) and on the other the Old Testament cult-institution attested to in Scripture. He undertakes to explain in greater detail and as a fundamental reality an idea only suggested in Paul, John, and the synoptists. What he essays is a new explication of the faith of the congregation through presenting the descriptions of the Old Testament cult as prophetic declarations of that which has taken place with and around Jesus. In images derived from Old Testament cult usage, whose actual meaning is not always easy to discover (at times it is not more than a matter of guesswork), he shows that the Old Testament models were brought to fulfillment in Jesus, and specifically in the death on the cross and in his continuing sacrifice in heaven. The death on the cross and the continued sacrifice in heaven belong together in his view, are coordinated in the closest possible relation; but the emphasis lies on the heavenly sacrifice of Jesus. The exaltation attested by Paul is represented in the Letter to the Hebrews by the image of the entry of Jesus into the Holy of Holies, where he has taken his place forever at the right hand of God (10:12; 12:2). He is crowned with honor and glory (Heb. 2:7,10). The readers of the Letter to the Hebrews, in danger of growing weak in their faith, are called upon to direct their gaze to the apostle and high priest of the religion we profess, Jesus (Heb. 3:1). They are to realize that through the blood of Jesus the way to God has been laid open for them to enter freely, that they now have a great priest set over the household of God (10:21), namely, the high priest of the good things to come. Jesus lives forever to make intercession for the faithful (7:25). Christ has entered into heaven to represent us in the presence of God. The position of honor which Jesus now holds at God's right hand is, of course, not yet the final stage of the glory due to him. A concluding act is yet to come which the Paraclete will initiate.

And as it is the lot of men to die once, and after death comes judgment, so Christ was offered once to bear the burden of men's sins, and will appear a second time, sin done away, to bring salvation to those who are watching for him (Heb. 9:27–28).

## Notes

[1] Cf. C. H. Dodd, *Historical Tradition of the Fourth Gospel* (Cambridge, 1963).

[2] E. Gutwenger, "Die Geschichtlichkeit der Auferstehung Jesu," in *Zeitschrift fuer Katholische Theologie*, 88 (1966), pp. 257–282.

[3] Cf. Thomas Aquinas, *Summa theologica* III, 55, 1.

[4] DS: H. Denzinger, *Enchiridion Symbolorum*, ed. Adolf Schönmetzer (Freiburg: Herder, 1965[33]). Quotations from this work are in the English translation contained in *The Church Teaches*, trans. the Jesuit Fathers of St. Mary's College, Kansas, with a preface by Gerald Van Ackeren, S.J. (St. Louis: Herder, 1955).

# ◄ 4

## *The Death of Jesus*

### THE RESURRECTION AND THE DEATH

From the resurrection the New Testament authors look back to the suffering of Jesus and the whole of his public life: the movement of their thought is directed towards the interpretation of these events in the light of the resurrection. What precedes the death on the cross serves to make it understandable that the result was execution. This thesis is not weakened by the observation that not all the events reported by the New Testament authors fit into this pattern; it is the overall tendency that is meant. The separate phases in the one mystery of salvation do not merely follow each other but are so interwoven that the glorification still bears the mystery of the crucifixion in itself (cf. the stigmata) and, inversely, the crucifixion is already permeated by the glorification. But they are also so interwoven that the events preceding the crucifixion are not self-contained; they are, so to speak, open-ended in relation to the crucifixion and the resurrection, not in the same sense that every human life is directed towards death, but in the sense that in all its specific details the saving life of Jesus in which he constantly offers himself to the Father in full, free surrender contains in itself the nucleus of that total surrender of self to the Father which took place on the cross and which for its part reached its final goal in the glorification. In all these considerations it should not, of course, be overlooked that it was through his very

existence, through the structure of his whole being, and not merely
through his actions, that Jesus reopened the way to God and thus
to salvation.

In the present discussion the passion will be spoken of first, and
then the life of Jesus which went before it. In this approach the
historical event of the passion, insofar as it is one element in the
course of history, need not be described; however, its salvation-
meaning—i.e., its function for the movement of mankind towards
the final and absolute salvation-future—must be analyzed.

## THE TESTIMONY OF SCRIPTURE

That the death of Jesus was a salvific act is not to be inferred from
the circumstances in which it took place. They were in no way
unique. Death on the cross, the most terrible and disgraceful form
of execution, was frequent during that period. That Jesus' death
was salvific we must learn through the kerygma, the preaching of
the apostles, and the words of Jesus himself. We shall discuss first
the witness of the synoptics and Acts, next that of the apostle
Paul, then the witness of the Letter to the Hebrews, and finally the
testimony of the remaining writings.

### The Synoptics and Acts

The fact is important that death did not come to Jesus as a fate he
was unable to avoid; he went to meet it quite consciously, with his
eyes open. According to the testimony of the synoptics he prophesied it three times: after the avowal of his messiahship (Mk.
8:31); later, when he set out on the last journey to Jerusalem
(Mk. 9:31); and finally, on the way to Jerusalem (Mt. 20:17;
cf. Jn. 3:14ff.). We are led deeper into the meaning of his death
when Jesus says that he has come not to be served but to serve
and to give his life as a ransom for many (Mt. 20:28). In Paul's
farewell speech in Ephesus, Luke reports him as saying, with the
same import, "Keep watch over yourselves and over all the flock
of which the Holy Spirit has given you charge, as shepherds of the
Church of the Lord, which he won for himself by his own blood"
(Acts 20:28). The disciples had difficulty in really grasping what

Jesus was saying with regard to his death; only on that supposition is the despair into which they were plunged by it comprehensible. Immediately before taking leave of them at the Last Supper, Jesus explained that his body would be given up for the sins of men and his blood shed for the forgiveness of sins, that the New Covenant would be made in his blood (Lk. 22:19f.; Mk. 14:22ff.; Mt. 26: 26f.). The passages in Acts in which the death is described as the fulfillment of Old Testament prophecies may also be mentioned. These are the speeches of the apostles Peter and Paul which were mentioned earlier in connection with the resurrection of Jesus.

## Paul

Along with the resurrection the death of Jesus forms the core of the Pauline kerygma. Paul preaches Christ crucified to the Corinthians and the Galatians (1 Cor. 2:2; Gal. 3:1; 6:14), rejecting the temptation to talk "worldly wisdom" in view of the lack of understanding with regard to the Lord's crucifixion on the part of both Jews and Greeks. To be sure, he strives to counteract the scandal which the Jews see in Jesus' death and the folly which the Greeks see in it by testifying to the death as an entry into new life, the life of Easter (1 Cor. 15:5–8). Moreover he refers, and rightly, to the message of the Old Testament, presenting himself as another witness to the fact that Christ has died for our sins in conformity with the Scriptures (1 Cor. 15:3). The character of the death as a sacrifice freely undertaken emerges when Paul reminds the Corinthians of a tradition originating with the Lord himself, which they have heard earlier on from Paul's lips (1 Cor. 11:23ff.), the words of the Eucharist, according to which Jesus' body is a sacrificial body, his blood sacrificial blood. He is the paschal lamb which has been slain. Paul sees in this fact, that the one sacrificed on the cross has entered into his life, the turning point in his personal history and in the history of the world. The personal spiritual power which ruled Paul always is that which was established by God, when all men had sinned and been deprived of God's glory, as a propitiatory sacrifice (*hilasterion*) for our sins, through faith in Christ's blood, so that God's justice should be proved and ours should be created (Rom. 3:23ff.). He has given himself as the ransom (*antilytron*) for all.

Sin can no longer corrupt anyone who believes in him who raised our Lord Jesus Christ from the dead, in him who was given over to death for our sins and raised up for our justification (Rom. 4:24f.). Those who believe in him bear the seal of the Holy Spirit; they are called to live in love, abandoning all malice. They are to live in Christ, who gave himself as a sacrifice, a fragrant offering, to God (Eph. 5:2). In Paul, too, the dimension of salvation history comes to the fore when the death of Christ is brought into relationship with the paschal lamb. Jesus is the true paschal lamb in whose death on the cross all earlier sacrifices find their fulfillment. Through this, Jesus' death on the cross presents itself as one element in the course of salvation history. To the Jews it was utterly incomprehensible; yet, had they had a fuller comprehension of their own history, he would not have incurred their mortal enmity.

Paul, like the synoptic tradition, frequently states that Christ has died for men. In the New Testament the short word "for" sometimes means "for the benefit of," sometimes "in place of," and as a rule the two meanings are closely connected. In the Second Letter to the Corinthians a kind of juridical representation is expressed in the text "One man died for all and therefore all mankind has died" (2 Cor. 5:14). As far as the closer connection of meaning between this and Jesus' sacrificial self-surrender is concerned, Paul describes it with the phrase "for our sins." Jesus Christ gave himself for our sins (Gal. 1:3f.). He died for our sins (1 Cor. 15:3), i.e., because we have sinned and he wanted to expiate these sins.

*Hebrews*

As has already been stressed, the author of the Letter to the Hebrews set himself the goal of quickening his readers' faith by trying to present the death on the cross, a source of scandal to both Jews and Gentiles, as an element in God's comprehensive plan of salvation. He realizes this intention in that he was able, through a typological treatment of sacrifice in the Old Testament—a concept undoubtedly familiar to his readers—to explain the death on the cross in terms of fulfillment. In the background stands the tenet of faith that the fundamental structure of man's relation to God is correctly described in terms of Old Testament sacrifice. Man needs the priest

(as mediator and victim) in order to attain to God. That the whole
Old Testament is a foreshowing of the New belongs to the divine
plan of salvation. After the breaking of the old covenant by the
human partner, God, as the prophet Jeremiah testifies (31:31–34),
will set up a new covenant. It will be a characteristic of this new
covenant that, owing to the total renewal of the people through the
forgiveness of sin, the Law will be inscribed in their hearts, making
any external influence unnecessary. This vision had become of decisive significance for the entire Old Testament. The Septuagint had
already clearly emphasized the unique superiority of God through
the choice, obviously based on theological considerations, of the
Greek word *diatheke* (testament) as the usual translation of the
Hebrew word *berith* (covenant), for the Greek word makes the
higher position of the divine partner to the covenant substantially
clearer. Paul had plainly stressed the contrast between the old (2
Cor. 3:14) and the new covenants (2 Cor. 3:6), and the Letter
to the Hebrews follows his precedent when—no longer thinking of
the Law but rather of the cultic element—it places the two testa-
ments over against each other. Drawing upon the fundamental conception of Jeremiah, Hebrews describes the first covenant, ratified
by Moses in the sprinkling of blood, as defective, aging and rendered
obsolete by the new (Heb. 8:8–13). The new, the second, covenant
is the higher; it is eternal; it is established in virtue of greater divine
promises, and its power to sanctify and save is procured through the
death of Jesus Christ. In the old covenant the law of blood was in
force: "Indeed, according to the Law, it might almost be said, everything is cleansed by blood and without the shedding of blood there
is no forgiveness" (Heb. 9:22). However many sacrifices there may
have been under the old covenant, they were still ineffective in attain-
ing their end: God, and so salvation. But Jesus is priest in a new
way. He is holy, innocent, without stain of sin and separated from
sinners, raised high above the heavens. Unlike the high priests of the
old covenant he was under no necessity of offering each day a sacrifice for his own sins and then for those of the people (7:26ff.);
"for this he did once and for all when he offered up himself. The
high priests made by the Law are men in all their frailty; but the
priest appointed by the words of the oath which supersedes the Law
is the Son, made perfect now forever." His dignity as Lord enables

him to press forward through all earthly things to God himself, opening the way to God for men. Nevertheless for him also the law governing the Old Testament sacrifice, that "everything is cleansed by blood and without the shedding of blood there is no forgiveness," held true. But the blood which Christ shed was his own blood; in this sense he is at once victim and priest (Heb. 9:11f.,24). The blood of Christ, who through the Holy Spirit offered himself as an unblemished sacrifice to God, will cleanse our consciences of dead works to serve the living God (9:14). Christ has appeared once and for all at the climax of history to destroy sin by the sacrifice of himself. He was offered once to take away men's sins (9:28). Jesus has offered a single sacrifice for sins (10:12); through one sole offering he has perfected for all time those who are thus consecrated (10:14). We have been sanctified through the offering of the body of Jesus Christ once and for all (10:10). With Jesus' salvation-creating act, whose uniqueness and definitiveness are stressed again and again, the divine work for the salvation of men is brought to completion: salvation has come; forgiveness has been guaranteed (10:17f.). Precisely the thing that enables Jesus to accomplish what the Old Testament sacrifice could not—namely, his dignity as Lord —might create an obstacle to the effectiveness of his saving death, for it might seem to alienate him from men so that they would be unable to relate to him. But such an alienation has been rendered impossible by his having become true man, like his brethren in all things (2:17); and, having himself undergone suffering and temptation, he can help others in their trials. He has himself entered into the situation of those lost in catastrophe (*Unheil*), to make his way with them back to salvation. The bringer of salvation had had to sustain himself in a situation similar to that required of the men of faith: "In the days of his earthly life he offered up prayers and petitions, with loud cries and tears, to God who was able to deliver him from the grave. Because of his humble submission his prayer was heard: son though he was, he learned obedience in the school of suffering, and, once perfected, became the source of eternal salvation for all who obey him, named by God high priest in the succession of Melchizedek" (Heb. 5:7–10). Jesus' suffering and death are therefore not simply a sacrifice, a material sacrifice in the sense of the old cultic law in which reconciliation with God could be understood only in terms of material blood offerings: they are a full activation of the will, a pledge of the entire man, and specifically of a man who had considerable opposition of an inner sort to overcome. This victim offers himself, and if salvation was won through suffering, who can evade the challenge which is presented again and again by belief in this to each individual who suffers? [1]

## The Gospel of John

According to John's Gospel, what Paul bore witness to had been heard from the mouth of John the Baptist by those who were contemporaries of Jesus. On the day after the emissaries from Jerusalem had come to question him openly concerning his preaching, he pointed to Jesus with the words: "Look, there is the Lamb of God; it is he who takes away the sin of the world" (Jn. 1:29). This called to mind for those versed in Scripture the description which Isaiah had given of the Messiah: "All we like sheep have gone astray; we have turned every one to his own way; and the Lord has laid on him the iniquity of us all. He was oppressed, and he was afflicted, yet he opened not his mouth; like a lamb that is led to the slaughter, and like a sheep that before its shearers is dumb, so he opened not his mouth" (Is. 53:6f.). Here the Messiah is foretold as God's servant who bears our sicknesses and takes our pains upon himself (Is. 53:12). Jesus is the paschal lamb of the New Covenant, slain for the sins of the world (Rev. 5:12; cf. Acts 8:32). Hence those who believe in him are without sin; but if they nevertheless, in their weakness, commit sin, they have an advocate with the Father, namely, Jesus Christ the righteous. He intercedes for us without ceasing, for he is the expiation of our sins, and not only ours but those of the whole world (1 Jn. 2:2). In this we are certain of the love of God, that he sent his son a propitiatory sacrifice for our sins (1 Jn. 4:10). Like the Pauline writings, John's Gospel proclaims Jesus as the Passover offering. In the book of Revelation of John, Christ is named twenty-eight times as the "Lamb that was slain." He is the unblemished sacrificial lamb and the true sacrifice in which the Old Testament sacrifices attain their meaning.

*First Peter*

What we read in the First Letter of Peter rings like an echo from
the Pauline writings. The principal passage on the subject is
1:17–21, wherein the Gentile Christians are admonished to live,
conscious of their redemption and the high price paid by their
Redeemer, in thankfulness, joy, and reverence before God. The
receiver of the ransom is plainly God the Father. By it men are
set free from a futile way of life, that is, a way of life without
God. The concept of the atoning power possessed by the sacrificial blood has entered here into the action of ransom (cf. also
1 Pet. 2:22ff.).

## THE DEED OF GOD

The redemption proceeds from God. To see in the idea of redemption an appeasement of the divine wrath would be to lapse
into mythology. When such expressions are found in theological
literature or in the faith-declarations of the Church, one must
seek to disentangle the meaning from the form of expression. It
is not God who has undergone conversion: on the contrary, the
conversion is effected in man through God's redemptive action,
rendering him capable of entering into conversation with God and
prepared to do so. The redemption is a free act of God. Most
particularly, God revealed in the saving death of Jesus his love
and his righteousness; in Jesus' death he made them real, actual,
present (1 Jn. 3:16; 4:10). Through Jesus God renewed his invitation to men, whom he willed to save, to enter dialogue with
him. He undertook to overcome from within sin's power of destruction in the hearts of men.

When anyone is united to Christ, there is a new world; the old order
has gone, and a new order has already begun. From first to last this has
been the work of God. He has reconciled us men to himself through
Christ, and he has enlisted us in this service of reconciliation. What
I mean is, that God was in Christ reconciling the world to himself, no
longer holding men's misdeeds against them, and that he has entrusted
us with the message of reconciliation. We come therefore as Christ's
ambassadors. It is as if God were appealing to you through us: in

Christ's name, we implore you, be reconciled to God! Christ was innocent of sin, and yet for our sake God made him one with the sinfulness of men, so that in him we might be made one with the goodness of God himself (2 Cor. 5:17–21).

It is God himself who through Christ has established peace between men and himself, and among men: this is the blessed reality in which the Colossians live. "Formerly you were yourselves estranged from God; you were his enemies in heart and mind, and your deeds were evil. But now by Christ's death in his body of flesh and blood God has reconciled you to himself as dedicated men, without blemish and innocent in his sight" (Col. 1:21f.).

Why God ordained that sacrifice on a cross should be the means of salvation remains, of course, a difficult question, wrapped in impenetrable mystery. We can only grope for the answer in what follows. As we have already noted, a close connection exists in Scripture between sin and man's subjection to death; suffering and death are understood as manifestations of the sinfulness of man. Even though the eventual exhaustion of man's life-forces is inherent in his nature, nevertheless, had he not sinned, he would have been spared, owing to his loving relationship with God, from that bitter experience of death which he must suffer in consequence of turning away from God.

Originally man's relationship with God was to have been such that man as a person would have been completely master of himself; thus he would have integrated the realm of nature into that of the person (the "gift of integrity") and would have had to experience neither suffering nor death as something foreign, overpowering, obstructing and oppressing him; he would have been able to bring into his possession and have at his disposal his entire nature—not only his body but the spirit bound up with his bodily activity. Through the love penetrating him from God and returning from him to God he would have integrated into his relationship with God, in totally free self-fulfillment, the exhaustion of his vital forces in death, and all those painful influences as well, from without and from within himself, which precede death and prepare for it. (This is referred to as the gift of "supralapsarian" grace, intended for man before original sin.)

Through sin, that is through the abandonment of love and the isolation which this occasions, man lost the capacity for this integration. Suffering and death now stand in opposition to his self-fulfillment and self-possession. Now death is experienced not only as the separation of body and soul but as a process through which man as a subject who is at his own disposal becomes powerless. Nevertheless he must take a position with regard to death and suffering, for they always involve a demand that man should acknowledge that it is the power of sin which has robbed him of his power of integration. He must accept and acknowledge this impotence as the consequence of sin.

Within this view of life and death lies the redemptive death of Jesus. In the fact that Jesus dies something happens which is part of human nature. But this is not to be understood as "pure nature," *natura pura* (there is no such thing in the concrete); on the contrary, it is nature under the power of sin. For although Jesus had no share in original sin, the human nature which the eternal Word took as his own was human nature in that fundamental condition which was effected through the first sin and the inherited sin of men: he took on "flesh" (Jn. 1:14f.; Rom. 8:3f.). This means that he took upon himself and lived out a human life with its implications of suffering and death. The death and the suffering which led to it were inherent in the insertion of his life into history and in the authenticity of this life: with the first moment of earthly existence he was destined for death, since his life ran its course not outside of but within human history. To be sure, this explanation leaves still unanswered the question of why he had to die the terrible and shameful death on the cross, but to that it is possible to give the following reply. Precisely in this death, which Jesus suffered as the representative of the whole of humanity, the deprivation of all self-directedness and all self-possession which takes place in every death was epitomized. The nailed hands and feet express this total powerlessness over the self. Jesus had anticipated in total self-surrender this extremity of powerlessness, and thus he was able to express on the cross and acknowledge before the whole world that God is the only Living One, the only giver of life. The powerlessness resulting in death implies not only that man cannot help himself in the face of death but that no one else can help him: he is thrust into lone-liness. Jesus entered into this agony of loneliness in which no one could (or might) help him. It had two aspects. The first men wanted to be free of God: Jesus took it upon himself to embrace this element in the form of an experience of isolation from God. Sin isolates, for it imprisons man in his own ego, a law unto himself. Jesus submitted himself to this element of sin also in his abandonment by all but his nearest and dearest friends—and even these could only stand as witnesses to how he died in three hours of agony. What it all comes down to is this: death exposes man, who wanted to become like God, in his totally ungodlike impo-tence. This element of death Jesus likewise took upon himself to an extreme degree, not only in the manner of his death but in the reaction of others to it—in the derision of passersby and by-standers, who came from both the lowest and the highest social and political strata (death as a scandal to the "world"). This death was salvific because through Jesus' unconditionally willed acceptance of death as the form in which sin expressed itself, men, of whom he was the representative, were brought to the judgment of themselves, willingly confessed their sin, gave glory to God, and were thus enabled to return to peace with him.

That which took place in the death of Jesus was the peak and culmination of what he had acted out during his whole life. Viewed purely as a history, his life remained unfinished; indeed, seen from outside, it was wrecked on the wood of the cross. He renounced self-development and the honor which is the normal harvest of a successful life.

Add to this one further element: the sinner, who insofar as he lacks the power of integration cannot attain to total possession of himself, seeks to exercise his innate desire to order and to rule in relation to things and his fellow men. In so doing he risks treating men as things and possessions, of using them to the point of using them up or casting them away when they have ceased to be useful or have become a hindrance to him. Jesus took it upon himself to be put to death by men, whose brother he longed to be, and thus to undergo the ultimate expression of sin's power.

The man Jesus was capable of undergoing this death, the dread-

ful issue of humanity's sin, as something positively willed and not
an unavoidable blow of fate, because through God the Father's
gift of himself to him and the acceptance of this gift by Jesus'
human will, Uncreated Love was with and in him; hence he was
able to yield himself to the Father without reserve within the
conditions of his human situation.[2]

God himself decided upon this death in an imponderable eternal plan, because of the sinfulness of man, as a way of revealing
himself, and also as a way of revealing how he sees man. In the
death of Jesus as the representative of sinful men the situation
of the autonomous man who has turned away from God presents
itself. Jesus' death on the cross is a divine showing of the condition of sinful man—forsaken, relinquished by God, his vital forces
rendered impotent. That Jesus himself had to experience abandonment by God (Mk. 15:34; Mt. 27:46) was not merely an
appearance but a reality whose dark mystery is incomprehensible
to us. Precisely the experience of abandonment by God expresses
the fact that Jesus, though himself wholly free from sin, nevertheless died the death of the sinner, and indeed in the most extreme manner. It is precisely in dying as a sinner that the sinner
experiences his complete loneliness. That Jesus in his obedience
took this final and most dreadful experience also upon himself we
learn from his words: "Father, into thy hands I commend my
spirit" (Lk. 23:46). For the final loneliness was borne by him
with the uttermost love, so that the desert of loneliness became
the source of a most intense community. Of the crucified one it
can be said, "Ecce homo," and indeed in the sense of "Ecce
homo peccator."

## THE JUDGMENT OF GRACE

Through the cross of Christ, God passed judgment on man. That
is to say, in a divine, sovereign act of justice and holiness he
made manifest the situation into which man fell through sin. In
Christ's death on the cross the abyss of sin and the existential
lostness of the sinner, and at the same time the holiness and
righteousness of God are revealed.

This revelation has that quality of hiddenness that characterizes every divine revelation: it will be seen only with the eyes of faith. Only one who looks towards the crucified Jesus in faith is able to interpret the cross as a disclosure of the holy God and sinful man. Here stands harshly revealed the issue of that movement, now carried *ad absurdum,* wherein men at the dawn of their history aspired, in rebellion against God, to decide the nature of "good" and "evil" for themselves—that is, to take the ordering of their lives into their own hands.

As devastating as the judgment of the cross was, it is nevertheless a judgment of grace. God passed this judgment only once, he sent his only-begotten Son to the cross. Only this man was able, owing to his nature, to reveal the abyss of sin, because he alone was empowered to carry out God's revelation of himself as holy and righteous.

In the second place, the goal of the death on the cross is not death but new life. This cannot be attained simply through the giving up of that old life which had fallen into sin; it is possible only through a renovation from within. God holds man responsible; man must answer for his acts, must bear the consequences of his decisions. Jesus, through his death on the cross, does this in the name of all men. How man is to answer for his sin God has already laid down from the beginning of his eternal plan of salvation: through Jesus' death on the cross. In free obedience to God and in love for his brethren Jesus embraced the fundamental human situation of sin and death, and in this he acknowledged that only God can grant man salvation and life. Thus the possibility was created for God to give himself to man without trivializing man's deeds and without forcing his own salvation upon him.

The death on the cross is therefore an expression, through God's mercy, both of his holiness and his justice. We can call it the sacrament of our salvation. If Jesus is the original sacrament of salvation, then he is so as the crucified one. In the light of these considerations Jesus' death on the cross appears as the result not of an arbitrary decision but rather of a divine decision whose nature is determined by the nature of sin itself. In the death on the cross Jesus showed forth God, the abysmal depths of sin, and the direction in which sinful man is finally driven.

This element undergoes, moreover, a special elucidation in this, that in the slaying of Jesus the powers of destruction, hate, and falsehood are overcome through the love which he carried to its uttermost consummation. Hence in Jesus' death on the cross the dominion of love is established. In it the Reign of God takes a decisive step forward.

## THE DEED OF JESUS

Scripture states frequently that Jesus gave himself up to death in obedience and love (Mk. 10:45). He was not offered up like a thing but was ready, by his own decision, to yield up his life. He had assumed the eternal divine plan of salvation into his own will unconditionally. The action of the man Jesus did not replace God's action but put it into effect. Jesus knew himself to be charged with the destiny of men, which could be reversed only through the carrying out of God's eternal plan of salvation. Obedience ruled his entire life: it was summed up in his death on the cross (Jn. 10:17). The death must not be isolated from the life which preceded it. Jesus, the second Adam, brought salvation through obedience as the first Adam, through disobedience, brought about the irruption of ruin and death into human history (Rom. 5:18). Jesus' act of obedience was an act of love, as, inversely, his love was obedience. This love of Jesus was experienced in a personal manner by Paul (Gal. 2:19f.). It is compared in Scripture to the love of a bridegroom for his bride. In death Jesus won for himself the Church as his bride, his wedded wife (Eph. 5:25). It was love which impelled him to sacrifice himself (Jn. 10:11; 15:13). Because in him love had proved itself to the uttermost, love will never again be silent (cf. 2 Cor. 5:14). The one who was rich has become poor for our sake so that we might be rich through his poverty. In this precisely his act of love consisted (2 Cor. 8:9). This poverty advanced by stages: by it he divested himself of his divine glory and was obedient even to death on the cross (Phil. 2:5–8). At the deepest level this love is rooted in the eternal love of the Father (Jn. 3:17): it is an epiphany of the limitless love of God himself (Rom. 5:1–11). There is no room in it for self-will, for self-assertion, or for any claims with regard to God (Heb. 5:7–10).

It is evident that the decisive thing in the sacrifice on the cross is not the degree of Jesus' suffering but his inner dispositions. This remains true even though, in terms of the foregoing considerations, death, and indeed specifically death on the cross, must not be understood as incidental but as an expression of obedience and love based on the fundamental human situation; and the most intense degree of pain serves to manifest the highest degree of obedience and love. Hence on Golgotha Jesus was absolutely open to God's creative love.

The death of Jesus, which so to speak established the possibility for God to communicate to the man Jesus the fullness of everlasting life evidenced by the resurrection, and so also to all who are united with Jesus in the bond of faith, did indeed conquer sin and death. Nevertheless this conquest did not restore the original power of grace; rather, it has enabled man, once and for all under sentence of death, to take a stand in regard to it in a way which was impossible before—namely, in faith, hope, and love for the crucified one. Hence he can escape from death; not, to be sure, from the event itself but from the finality of its power. Through his communion with Christ, it is possible for suffering and death to embody for him the same salvific meaning as does the death of Christ: unconditional surrender to God, not in virtue of a natural decision but in virtue of the profound working in him of God's grace through Christ. Through its participation in the death of Jesus the death of the individual receives a sacramental meaning.

## THE EFFECTS OF JESUS' DEATH

The word "salvation" can be understood from a great variety of aspects. For different people it can mean peace, or love, or a political order worthy of man, right social order, a free economic order, good health, education, knowledge, moral upbringing—in short, the securing of our existence in the most diverse areas. None of these points of view is excluded in the biblical proclamation of salvation, but they are sustained by one state of salvation which embraces these truly important benefits and contains them in itself. In first place stands—to express it negatively—the conquest of sin in the sense of the abandonment of God; to express it positively, unity, reconciliation, peace with God, which in turn presents itself essentially in the unity and peace of men among themselves: for without love of neighbor there is no love of God. Peace and community and the fundamental elements of what is termed salvation in the Christian sense, and indeed peace with God as well as peace and community among men themselves. But love of neighbor does not only involve the encounter between individuals; today it is at work, making its presence felt, in a social order full of the human benefits created by technology and industry and in the human solidarity which gives life to these things. In this sense the benefits we have mentioned stand within the sphere of the Christian message of salvation, not insofar as they are bound up with definite forms of human communal life but insofar as they propagate and indeed make possible an existence worthy of man which in its turn depends on the right relation of man to God and the relationship of men to one another that is sustained by the right relation to God. Peace is the fundamental category from which all other benefits of salvation derive.

## The Overcoming of Sin

Jesus stated with the greatest emphasis that his mission was to re-establish the right relation of men to God and of men to one another. He is actuated by this purpose when, during his life, he proclaims the "reign of God." Included in this proclamation is the statement that men's hostility to God must be overcome. The forgiveness of sins pronounced by Jesus (Mk. 2:5) lies in the dimension of the reign of God which he proclaimed. Through the saving word of forgiveness the sinner is so radically renovated in the very depths of his being that he is able with trust and confidence to call God "Father." This does not mean that the sinful act and the objective consequences it involves, which may be immense, will be eradicated from history. Such a notion would be highly unrealistic. What is meant by the forgiveness is that man ceases to be a castaway. Through the forgiveness of sins a barrier is removed, so that the dialogue between God and man is resumed. Jesus, standing in the place of the Father they cannot see, has communion with sinners.[3] He enters into the community of the table with them. He becomes the friend of tax collectors and sinners (Mk. 2:15f.; Lk. 5:30; Mt. 9:10; 11:19). He takes men into the community in which he himself dwells with the Father (Lk. 19:1f.; Jn. 15:10; cf. Jer. 31:31–34). In numerous turns of phrase Paul gives praise to the peace wrought by Christ with God. Again and again he expresses the desire that his readers may possess it (e.g., 1 Cor. 1:3; Eph. 6:23; Gal. 6:16; cf. Heb. 13:20). Peace, according to his understanding of it, is a condition of final fulfillment, salvation and holiness (Rom. 5:1; Eph. 2:15). If God reconciled us to himself through the death of his Son while we were still his enemies, what high expectations may we not have of his love, now that we have attained reconciliation with him through our Lord Jesus Christ (Rom. 5:8–11; 2 Cor. 5:18ff.)?

## The Overcoming of Death

Another of the benefits of salvation is deliverance from death. As we have seen, the Old Testament hope for the reign of God comes up against a barrier, death itself. Perhaps one might say, with Erich Przywara, that the structures of destruction and restoration characteristic of the Old Testament were a foreshadowing of the event on Golgotha and present an analogy of faith (*analogia fidei*) between the old and new covenants.[4] The fact of death itself has not been abolished through Jesus, but he has conquered death insofar as its connection with sin is concerned. This is to say that Jesus rendered accessible to men a new way of experiencing death. To a certain extent the ontology of death was changed. In Jesus, man can die into God if he submits himself to God in faith, hope, and trust. In this death he matures into a full and final life, namely the life of the resurrection. Through participation in the cross of Christ death attains a sacramental, a grace significance, and so likewise does the suffering which leads to it. It becomes the way and the instrument for the fulfillment and perfection of life, in a power and fullness which surpass all human possibilities, all that might be hoped or longed for. We shall give fuller consideration to this point later on.

A further benefit of salvation proclaimed by Paul is deliverance

from the Law. By the "Law" Paul means the legal prescriptions
of the Old Testament. The Law itself was holy, just, and good
(Rom. 7:12), but it was in two ways an occasion of sin. Because
of the Law the human passion for self-assertion against God's
commandments flared up (Rom. 7:8ff.). Moreover, men learned
from it to deceive themselves, to act as if it were possible for a
man to work out his salvation by his own powers simply by fulfilling the prescriptions of the Law (Gal. 2:15–21; 5:4).

## Liberation from the Law

Deliverance from the Law through Jesus Christ does not mean
entering a state of lawlessness. But the bond to the letter of the
Law was dissolved through the bond to the person of Christ. The
eternal commandments of God continue in force, but they make
themselves heard in the voice of Jesus Christ. No longer is the
fulfillment of an impersonal law required of man, but loving surrender to God through Jesus Christ (Rom. 6:14; Gal. 5:18).
Fulfillment of the law becomes encounter with God and our fellow
men. Paul is never weary of proclaiming Jesus' redeeming act
as an act of deliverance. It is deliverance in the sense of making
men capable of the right use of freedom. The liberty into which
men are brought is not freedom to act arbitrarily but the freedom
of love, to be exercised in conformity with the ten commandments
as they apply in the given situation. It is not a negative principle
of prohibition; it is positive and creative. This holds true even
when love, as is the way of great gifts, is experienced as a burden.
This freedom will be complete only in its final perfection, for love
too waits for its fulfillment at the end of time. The destructive
power of hatred, of egoism, of tyranny, of falsehood, binds man
in such a way that he is unable to do what is truly worthy of a
human being. The man delivered by Jesus Christ into true freedom is aware of being bound not externally by a multitude of
regulations but internally by the love which holds sway in him.
For him the commandments are directions for putting love into
practice in his human circumstances of time and place and in
the diversity of his human encounters (Jas. 1:25).

## The Breaking of Demonic Power

Scripture sees a further benefit of salvation in the victory over Satan's kingdom (Jn. 16:11; 12:31). Satan sought to subject Christ, like all others, to his power, beginning with the temptations in the desert and continuing until the sentence of death passed by Pontius Pilate. According to Scripture, Satan, as the personal power of malice and hatred, is the initiator of all the enmity towards Jesus. Satan had to learn by experience that Jesus was not like other men; he could not deflect him by cunning or deception from his salvific course; he could not drive him into reciprocating his hatred or duplicity. It was necessary for him to resort to force, and so he put it into the minds of the authorities that they must rid themselves of Jesus. Satan, though vanquished, still has power to bring about great evils and much destruction, but the man who believes in Christ need have no fear of Satan.

The powers opposed to salvation have been so disarmed by Jesus Christ that the man of faith can look confidently upon the dangers of life. All these benefits of salvation are closely interconnected. Of fundamental and decisive importance is the reconciliation, the peace with God; in it is the guarantee of the peace of men among themselves (Mt. 22:37–40; Mk. 12:30f.; Lk. 10:2–7; cf. Dt. 6:5; 10:12; 11:13; 13:4).

## JESUS' DEATH AS AN EVENT OF RESTORATION

Jesus brought salvation because, in a manner conforming to the situation of mankind under the necessity of death, he thrust his way through the confines of sinful human nature into true transcendence; he made the transition into the life of glory at the side of the living God. Through him, with him, and in him the whole of humanity called by God has attained the same release. Through him men have drawn near to God and have been received by him; received not in a passive sense, as if God had simply been holding himself in readiness for them, but in an active sense, in that without destroying his freedom as a creature God has brought about man's return to himself. In this breakthrough into transcendence the human activity is effected by the activity on God's part.

In the development of theology the saving value of Jesus Christ's death on the cross has been interpreted in manifold ways as the result of the variety of indications in Scripture. All theologians are agreed that Christ exercised a representative function. Without becoming the progenitor of the new humanity in the biological sense he has become its head in the spiritual sense, the creator of its salvation. Although this is not the only factor, the diversity of the interpretations of Jesus' saving death is largely conditioned by the encounter of the Christian faith with the modes of thought of a particular time and place. Greek thought, at the time of its encounter with Christianity, was concentrated on the question of being; accordingly the Greek Fathers understood the redemption as the restoration of the broken order of being and life. They were able to build the structure of their thought on the scriptural witness that through Jesus sin and the other powers of destruction had been vanquished, so that the unifying forces of love and obedience were once more at work in mankind.

When the Christian message made its way into the Roman Empire with its stress on legal order, and then into the Germanic society with its preoccupation with the idea of honor, it became necessary for Christian thought to take these conceptions into account. This process was initiated by the lawyer Tertullian, systematized by Anselm of Canterbury, completed by Thomas Aquinas, and critically examined by John Duns Scotus. The fundamental concept is this: the relation between God and man is seen in terms of an analogy with the earthly legal order. Insofar as God as Creator can make laws binding man, and man as creature owes obedience to God, the concept is valid. The God-world relation in itself contains legal elements. In this view sin was conceived as a violation of the lawful order. The Germanic influence manifests itself in the definition of sin as an offense against the honor of God. The restoration of the broken legal order is effected through satisfaction—that is, some act which serves as recompense for the breach of order—and through atonement—that is, suffering voluntarily assumed as penance for sin.

Insofar as he dispossessed himself, surrendered the possibility of developing his natural powers to the full during his life, accepted the limits set to his effectiveness by the Father, renounced the honor which was his due, Jesus' life can be characterized as atonement, set over against the passion of men for autonomy. It can likewise be characterized as satisfaction, insofar as he acknowledged God in love and obedience as unconditional Lord and accepted the limitations of human nature as created and subject, moreover, to the world-power of sin.

In theology the expressions "adequate" and "superabundant" atonement and satisfaction are used in the interests of greater precision. Jesus made not only adequate but superabundant atonement and satisfaction because the measure of his love and obedience was not only equal to but surpassed human egoism. In Jesus a power of love and truth was operative which surpassed all the forces of evil and falsehood (cf. 1 Pet. 1:18f.; Rom. 5:20). Anselm of Canterbury, carrying the development of these ideas further, introduced into theology the concept of an "infinite" offense against God, an idea which has survived into our own time. Sin, in this view, since it is an infinite offense against God, can be adequately redressed only through the satisfaction made for it by the God-man, for only an act of his has infinite value. According to Aquinas, the sacrificial suffering of Christ is a superabundant satisfaction; it carries its value in itself prior to its acceptance by God (though for Christ's satisfaction to be effective, of course, God's acceptance of it is necessary). John Duns Scotus rightly objected that the thesis of an infinite offense against God is untenable because a creature cannot do anything which has infinite value either for good or evil. If the infiniteness of the offense is seen in the fact that the infinite God is the object of the sinful act, then by the same token one must call a human act done in God's grace infinite, since its object is likewise God. It can be said with justice that the wide acceptance of Anselm's thesis in Catholic theology has been unwarranted. It depends on too many doubtful elements and is best rejected.

In its thesis of the propitiatory sacrifice made by Jesus Christ on Golgotha, Scripture provides points of departure for the doctrine of satisfaction and atonement. Hence it can be said that the teaching on this point developed by theology is sufficiently founded in Scripture to justify its acceptance by the Church into the official declaration of faith. Nevertheless the statements of the Church's teaching office should be carefully examined to determine the degree to which the doctrine belongs to the actual content of the Church's faith. The Council of Trent included a reference to the mystery of satisfaction through Jesus' death on the cross in its teaching on original sin, justification, and the sacrament of penance; however, this mystery was presented not *per se* but only in connection with the other statements of faith. One may well maintain, therefore, that the council's reference to it is not in itself a formal statement of faith but merely an inclusion of a subject lying in the general area with which the council was concerned. But it should be noted, all the same, that this thesis that the sacrificial death of Jesus has the character of satisfaction and atonement belongs to the content of the ordinary proclamation of the faith in the Church (see DS 1689; 1513; 1522f.; 1528f.; 1566; 1576; 1582; and see, in addition, the letter "Miserentissimus Redemptor" of Pope Pius XI, 1928).

In the theological analysis of the subject, and occasionally in the Church's doctrinal statements as well (see the Council of Trent, DS 1513 and 1528), Jesus' suffering is brought into relation with merit and reward. It is possible to understand "merit" either as an achievement worthy of reward or as the reward itself. If manifold misconceptions are to be avoided, it is of decisive importance that "reward" should be taken here as meaning not something added to an action from outside but a value inherent in it and arising out of it. Through his death Christ attained to a state in which the divine glory, hitherto hidden in him, was revealed; his body was transfigured, his whole intellectual and spiritual being so permeated with joy that no anxiety, no fear, could any longer touch him. The "merit" or "reward" here is the transition from the condition of humiliation into the fullness of life which rightly belonged to the structure of his being, into the glory of his resurrection and ascension. Christ "merited" this glorification through suffering and death because such was the Father's will (Lk. 24:26,46; Rom. 5:19; Heb. 2:9). These and other passages in Scripture provide starting points for the doctrine that what Jesus merited for himself he merited for us as well.

The Letter to the Hebrews, in a passage characteristic of such texts, offers striking testimony to the conquest of sin, death, and Satan through the death of Jesus Christ:

But in fact we do not yet see all things in subjection to man. In Jesus, however, we do see one who for a short while was made lower than the angels, crowned now with glory and honor because he suffered death, so that, by God's gracious will, in tasting death he should stand for us all.

It was clearly fitting that God for whom and through whom all things exist should, in bringing many sons to glory, make the leader who delivers them perfect through sufferings. For a consecrating priest and those whom he consecrates are all of one stock; and that is why the Son does not shrink from calling men his brothers, when he says, "I will proclaim thy name to my brothers; in full assembly I will sing thy praise"; and again, "I will keep my trust fixed on him"; and again, "Here am I, and the children whom God has given me." The children of a family share the same flesh and blood, and so he too shared ours, so that through death he might break the power of him who had death at his command, that is, the devil; and might liberate those who, through fear of death, had all their lifetime been in servitude. It is not angels, mark you, that he takes to himself, but the sons of Abraham. And therefore he had to be made like these brothers of his in every way, so that he might be merciful and faithful as their high priest before God, to expiate the sins of the people. For since he himself has passed through the test of suffering, he is able to help those who are meeting their test now (Heb. 2:9–18).

In this text salvation is portrayed as the conquest of death and of the one who had it at his command—that is, Satan—through the death of the bringer of salvation. The atonement, which Jesus accomplishes through the sacrifice of himself, in that it breaks the power of sin, destroys death. The text may perhaps be para-phrased as follows. There is one who leads us to salvation. He goes along a way on which his followers—sons, brothers, children —are able to go because he has gone before them. This road leads to death, but through death into heaven. Thus the death of one who, coming from God, took to himself a human nature and lived the life of man becomes objectively the decisive breakthrough in the developmental process in which mankind and the universe are being brought to fulfillment; death has lost its hold on the world. The certainty of this revolutionary event changes man's situation radically. He becomes free of the fear of death—for the bondage peculiar to the pre-Christian or non-Christian consists in the consciousness permeating everything of a certain and absolute end which issues in darkness impenetrable to the mind. The Letter to the Hebrews expresses the existential doubt characteristic of the modern mind in its attitude towards life and the fact that the Christian message makes possible the radical conquest of this doubt.[5]

## SALVATION FOR ALL MEN

The redemptive act of Jesus Christ embraces all men in its effects, and indeed the whole creation. The first to receive its influence were those who had been removed from life before the Christ-event but had hitherto been unable, owing to the reign of the powers of evil and destruction until then, to enter the freedom of companionship with God. They were now set free by Jesus, insofar as they had not conclusively turned away from God. This is what is meant when it is said, in 1 Peter 3:18f., that Jesus went to the imprisoned spirits and made his proclamation to them (cf. also 1 Pet. 4:6; Eph. 4:8f.). In this phrase later Christians found the point of departure for the belief that Christ's soul descended after death into Limbo (see the creeds since the fourth century, the Fourth Synod of Nicea; DS 429; Synod of Sens in 1140; DS 395).

The world-picture of antiquity is used here to make it clear that Jesus really died, insofar as death always meant, to the ancients, a descent into the underworld. At the same time it is emphasized that Jesus' redeeming power reaches all the men who died in the preceding centuries and millennia of human history. They were able to hear the same joyful message that the robber on the cross heard before his death (Lk. 23:43).

A second group that was reached by the saving death of Christ is represented by those who, according to the testimony of the gospels, were raised from their graves at the death of Jesus and appeared to their relatives. It must be asked whether these resurrections meant only a temporary return to life, like the raising of Lazarus or of the young man of Naim or the daughter of Jairus. Even then, they would reveal the opening of a new epoch.

In contemporary theology the raising of these dead is sometimes understood as a participation in the resurrection-life of Jesus himself. The difficulty of this interpretation lies in the implication it contains that some of the persons redeemed by Jesus attained the life of glory before Jesus himself. This objection is not disposed of by stressing the close connection between the ascension and Easter or by seeing the nucleus of the resurrection-life already contained in the death of Jesus. It is not to be doubted that Jesus was really dead for a period of some time and that he regained life only on the third day, as Scripture says.

The new epoch expresses itself in the fact that the curtain of the Temple (Mt. 27:51) that had concealed the Holy of Holies was torn in two. A new Holy of Holies, Jesus' risen life won through suffering, has superseded it.

We must stress the fact that all men, and indeed the whole of creation, were affected by the redemption achieved by Jesus Christ. Here arises the difficult problem of the relation of the Old Testament people of God to the people not belonging to him. Jesus knew himself to be sent to the lost sons of the house of Israel (Mt. 15:24) and accordingly he seldom went into Gentile territory (Mk. 7:24–30). The Old Testament people of God, however, were to be the vehicle of salvation to all men. This was already promised in the Old Testament (e.g., Is. 2:2ff.; 45:14–25), where the pardon of non-Israelites is stressed more than once. In the New Testament there is also frequent testimony to the pardon of Gentiles in the pre-Christian period (Mt. 12:38ff.; Lk. 4:16ff.; and especially Heb. 7:1ff.). Jesus is the Lamb of God who takes away not only the sin of his people, but of the world (Jn. 1:29; cf. 11:20–23). He is propitiatory sacrifice for the sins of the whole world (1 Jn. 2:2). He gave himself as ransom for all (Rom. 3:22ff.). He has died for all, so that the living no longer live for themselves, but for him who died for them (2 Cor. 5:15; Rom. 5:18ff.; Mk. 14:24; Mt. 26:28; Lk. 22:19f.). Thus the risen one gave his disciples a commission to proclaim the good news to all peoples (Mt. 28:19; cf. Mk. 13:10). (On the question of how the adherents of the great world religions are reached by the redemptive work of Christ, see what has been said in the first volume of this work.)

What is in principle true of the saving action of Jesus Christ, its application to all men of all times, was realized when the Old Testament people of God did not acknowledge Jesus as the promised Messiah but rejected him. This became the historical occasion for the proclamation of the message of salvation to the Gentiles. Of course, the Jewish people are not excluded from salvation. The death of the Son of God is not charged only to those of whom Peter says, "You killed him who has led the way to life" (Acts 3:15). The believer does not see in the execution of Jesus a process of the sort that occurs often enough in the history of the world; he sees in Jesus' death the power of sin at work. According to God's impenetrable judgment and purpose, the power of sin was permitted—indeed, was forced—to do its worst in Christ. The death was owed because of sin, that is, the entire human race is responsible for it. Thus not only the Jew, but every human person, must say before the cross: *Mea culpa.* The Jewish people carried out something for which the whole of humanity is responsible. And what the Jewish people did they did not do as a whole people, nor did they do it alone. They did not act as a people, for in the first place it was the leaders who wanted to do away with Jesus; others, unable to withstand their propaganda, gave their consent. Jesus' phrase "They know not what they do" manifests God's own appraisal of the situation. Nevertheless they retain, of course, the degree of responsibility which puts them in need of forgiveness. Jesus' prayer "Father, forgive them" will prevail over the shout of a people easily misled and unaware of what they were about: "His blood be on us, and on our children" (Mt. 27:25). The Jewish people did not do it alone, for the Roman occupation authorities were essentially involved: without their consent the execution could not have taken place.

For Paul the refusal of his people to believe is an unfathomable mystery, but he is nevertheless convinced that the chosen people remains chosen. This distinction will remain with it forever: God loved it as his son and his glory rested upon it; he made the covenant with it and gave it the Law and the promise; to it the prophets belong, and above all Jesus Christ according to the flesh, in his human nature (Rom. 9:15). Moreover, there is a sense in which it is a devout remnant, for not all its members have refused to believe. So irreversible is God's election of this people, in the view of the apostle, that their very unbelief becomes the instrument of salvation to the Gentiles. For owing to the rejection of faith in Christ by the majority of Jews a new people had to be created— the Church, the New Testament people of God—for the fulfillment of the eternal covenant. This new people arose out of the devout remnant of the old to which those called out of paganism were joined; they now know themselves as the true children of Abraham, as the spiritual Israel (Rom. 9:11). The hour will come, says Paul, when God's saving purpose will be fulfilled in the people that received the Old Testament revelation: when the full number of Gentiles, the number determined by God, has entered the Church, then the whole of Israel will be converted. The consummation of the world will begin with the turning of Israel to Christ. Therefore the consummation of the world at the end of time cannot come before Israel as a whole gives itself to Christ: as salvation came in the beginning from the Jewish people, so the final salvation of all mankind depends upon their conversion. Hence the preservation of the Jews as a people has reference to the end of time, and Christian hope for the future must include the hope for the deliverance of the Jewish people; otherwise it will be lacking in what is essential to it.

Here is evident a deep bond between Christian and Jew. The Christian, to be sure, sees Christ as the fulfillment of the Old Testament promises, but for him too the promise is fulfilled only in principle; the final fulfillment will take place only with the second coming of Christ, of which the first was a pledge and an assurance. This hope for the second coming of Christ receives the chief emphasis in the Christian life. The vision of the Christian is directed more into the future than into the past, and this he has in common with the Jewish people, which still lives in expectation of the promised Messiah. The difference in the two outlooks consists in this: the Christian hope for the future rests on the reality of Jesus, in whom the promise to Abraham is fulfilled, whereas the Jewish hope continues to rest upon the word of promise given to Abraham.

The universality of the redemption cannot be interpreted as a

natural process which comes to pass according to certain fixed
laws. It is the ordinary practice of theology to distinguish between
objective redemption—i.e., the action accomplished by Christ—
and subjective redemption—i.e., the appropriation in faith on the
part of man, who needs redemption, of the saving death and resurrection. Christ died as the representative of all, but his representative function becomes efficacious for salvation only for those
who acknowledge him as their intercessor before God. This is an
event which belongs to the life of faith. In this view the action of
Jesus Christ is conceived not as a complex of events in history,
lying open to men's gaze, but as the reality entering into the tex-
ture of human history and guiding its course with unflagging
dynamism. This is a power which seeks to reach men, to shock
them and so to impel them to surrender themselves to Christ (see
the doctrine of the Church). The design of salvation involves the
participation of all men in Jesus' death and resurrection. As long
as men do not share in the death and resurrection of Christ,
Christ's action is wanting in something—namely, the fullness that
will come when all the saved have died and risen in Christ: only in
the absolute future will the totality of Christ's work be revealed.
So far as the reordering of the world through Christ is concerned,
man remains free, he himself bears the responsibility for his salvation. It stands prepared for him in Christ, but only the man who
reaches out towards Christ will take possession of it. Through his
death and resurrection Christ created a new historical situation.
No man can stay outside it or remain indifferent to it: each must
take a stand with regard to the Christ-event, whether to reject
belief in it or to accept it and live with the life of Christ. One who
does not set himself in opposition to the current of salvation flow-
ing from the death and resurrection of Christ (the life of grace)
grasps in faith the Jesus who has advanced through death into
transcendence, and will be borne along by the same movement.
Even though those who believe in Jesus are bound together in a
great community, the congregation of the saved oriented towards
the end of time—the Church—it nevertheless remains the decision
of each individual whether the saving work of Jesus can become
effective in him.

As Jesus accomplished his saving action through the ceaseless donation of himself during a whole human life and not through an isolated action, so those who are united with Christ go their way of salvation through the fulfillment of their earthly task within the conditions of earthly history. What we said earlier concerning the reign of God applies equally to human salvation: it consists in precisely this, that God—Love—is operative in a man through Jesus Christ. Christ's saving grace is given in a hidden manner: the public manifestation of salvation is reserved to the future. For this reason the hope of those who submit themselves in faith to Christ is directed towards the future. Paul declares, "We have been saved, though only in hope" (Rom. 8:24). This hope involves the future salvation of the whole man, and not of the soul alone; and moreover, the future salvation of humanity as a whole, and not only of the isolated individual. Since the death and resurrection of Christ the whole creation is caught up in a current sweeping with extraordinary force towards the future, for the Christ who made the transition through death to glory looks back upon men from the future, calling them to himself. In the midst of this great pilgrim community we see the Church, the pilgrim people of God, which constantly summons not only its own children but all men to join it in its journey into the future.

Nor is the material world excluded from this movement into the future. Paul writes:

For the created universe waits with eager expectation for God's sons to be revealed. It was made the victim of frustration, not by its own choice, but because of him who made it so; yet always there was hope, because the universe itself is to be freed from the shackles of mortality and enter upon the liberty and splendor of the children of God. Up to the present, we know, the whole created universe groans in all its parts as if in the pangs of childbirth (Rom. 8:19–22).

In our time the question has often been raised of whether other heavenly bodies apart from the earth are inhabited, and if so, whether the inhabitants have been redeemed by Jesus. The problem must be treated with great sobriety and realism. Certainly there is no need for faith or theology to cling to the idea that no other planet is inhabited by rational beings, and should the existence of such beings be proved by science one day, we should have to say that Christ, who is the head of the universe, is their head also. But we could not say what function he had as head in their case because divine revelation is silent concerning this matter (Col. 1:15–22; 2:10).

It can also be asked what relation exists between Christ and the angels. The angels could not be redeemed by Christ because the good angels are in no need of redemption and the evil ones are incapable of receiving it. Nevertheless grace has come even to the angels through Christ. He is their head, since everything has been created for him (Col. 1:16). "Through him God chose to reconcile the whole universe to himself, making peace through the shedding of his blood upon the cross—to reconcile all things, whether on earth or in heaven, through him alone" (Col. 1:20; cf. Eph. 1:10).

## Notes

[1] O. Kuss, *Der Brief an die Hebräer*, 2nd ed. (Regensburg, 1966).

[2] This is drawn in part from F. T. Dutari, "Zum Theologischen Ver-staendnis der Gnade des Kreuzes der Natur," in *Zeitschift fuer Katholische Theologie*, 88 (1966), pp. 283–314.

[3] D. Sölle, *Stellvertretung: Ein Kapitel Theologie nach dem Tode Gottes* (1965).

[4] *Alter und Neuer Bund: Theologie der Stunde* (Vienna-Munich, 1965).

[5] O. Kuss, *loc. cit.*

# ‹ 5

## *Jesus' Salvific Activity Before His Death and Resurrection*

### CHILDHOOD

It was from the standpoint of the Resurrection that the disciples looked back on the death of Jesus; in the light of the Easter experience it took on a new significance for them. But this raised the question what it was that brought about the terrible debacle of Golgotha. Their answer was that the public actions of Jesus (lasting at least two to two and one-half years) were his path to the cross; more than that, that his words and deeds had always had a salvific character. On closer inspection this could be seen in the many wonders that he worked, of which all the Gospels, but especially Mark, give witness. Jesus' life before his entrance into the public arena was not at first included in the preaching of the early church and is mentioned neither in the letters of Paul nor in Mark. It was only in the Gospels of Matthew and Luke, which took on their final shape around the year 80, that this became a matter of interest (Mt. 1f., Lk. 1f.). Both of these Gospels provide us with an account of Jesus' childhood, as a sort of preliminary, accounts which have many elements in common and also many differences which are explainable from their theological orientation. Matthew's account is written very much with the Old Testament in mind. But even in Luke the original Palestinian-

97

Aramaic form can be discerned, although Luke apparently made some use of the language which we find in an inscription dating from the year 9 B.C., found at Priene in Asia Minor about 1890, which celebrates the Emperor Augustus as savior.

The linguistic form of the childhood narratives shows marked differences from that of the rest of the Gospels. Angels, for example, although they are not entirely absent from the life of Jesus, do not play a large role in it (Mt. 26:53; Mk. 1:13; Lk. 24:4); but in the childhood narratives they are constantly coming and going as heavenly messengers (Mt. 1:20; 2:13; Lk. 1:11–20; 1:26–38; 2:9–14). "In Luke 1:11, the angel is described as 'angel of the Lord,' which is obviously a translation of *Maleach Yahweh*. The concept of the *Maleach Yahweh* is a product of developing theological reflection in Israel. Earlier no difficulty was felt in saying that Yahweh spoke to men and dealt with them, but later God becomes more of a background figure. Now he has messengers to men, angels. In Luke 1:19, the archangel Gabriel says to Zachary, 'I am Gabriel; I stand in attendance upon God.' This is clearly anthropomorphic language, providing God with a court and a throne. It is also an expression of conceptions prevalent in Judaism at the time, which speak of 'angels of the face' as those especially near to God who are allowed to behold his face. . . . The figure of the angel is an expression of God's power and glory among men. If the New Testament narratives have the life of Jesus accompanied by angels, the point is that Christ is and brings about the presence of the reign of God" (K. H. Schelkle, *Wort und Schrift,* Düsseldorf, 1966, p. 60f.).

The childhood narratives have been interpreted in very diverse fashion, as legendary inventions and also as historically accurate accounts. But we do them justice only when we take into consideration their basic theological intention and view the literary form as serving this.

As parts of the Gospels they are, like the rest, testimonies of faith. Matthew's concern is to show that in the conception, birth, and life of Jesus the promises of the Old Testament were fulfilled. For Luke the childhood of Jesus is already the beginning of his passion.

As regards the literary form, they are an instance of the midrash, common enough at the time. This consisted in taking a text of Scripture or an event reported in Scripture and providing it with an edifying decoration. The kernel in each case is taken from Scripture but is given a free, often poetic elaboration, is developed further and applied to the religious life (cf. M. Dibelius, *Die Form-geschichte des Evangeliums,* 3rd ed., Tübingen, 1959). The decisive thing is the salvific significance of the birth and the childhood of Jesus and of the events connected with these. The salvific meaning of the statement of Jesus' virginal conception and birth will be treated later. The point of the genealogies (Mt. 1:1–17; Lk. 3:23–38) is to testify that God is the Lord of history. They are not intended as an account of the family tree. God directs the whole of human history in such a fashion that it culminates in Jesus. He is its goal. The explicit mention of sinners in these genealogies shows that God achieves his intention even by means of human failure. It is the grace of God, and not matter for human glory, that human history moves towards Jesus, the Messiah, the Savior. The genealogies are an important means of making a theological statement. This remains true even though not all the details in them can be historically verified.

The stories of the angels' song on the meadows of Bethlehem and of the summoning of the three Wise Men by a star have also to be interpreted as a theological statement in the form of a midrash. They announce the universality of the salvation that Jesus brings, to both Jews and Gentiles. As regards the star especially (Mt. 2:1–15), it would not correspond to the intention of the text to see the historical core of Matthew's story in the great conjunction of Jupiter and Saturn. The text is obviously not concerned with an astronomical event but with a wondrous apparition which has nothing to do with astronomy (cf. Mt. 2:2,9). In order to represent the significance of the Christ-event, even for the Gentiles, the Gospel seems to have used a form already used in the non-biblical world. For example, Aeneas is led from Troy to Latium by a star (Vergil, *Aeneid,* II, 694ff.). According to the commentary of Servius on *Aeneid,* X, 272, a comet appeared when Augustus became emperor and the people were filled with joy. Such literary connections show that, despite the gulf between the New Testament and profane humanistic literature, there is a continuity in the process of salvation history.

It can be reasonably said of the infancy narratives that here

the new transparency shows itself which was created by the entrance of God, out of his transcendence, into human history and
into the world. Even if the world closed itself against God by
rejecting his son, still the transparency of creation established by
God in the Incarnation will not be destroyed. It is understandable
that it became especially evident around the Son of God become
man and at the beginning of the new historical epoch he introduced.

Further, the infancy narratives give expression to the salvific
meaning of Jesus by following the story of Moses in describing the
course of his life and thus indicate that Jesus is the new Moses.
The liberation of Israel from slavery in Egypt is an anticipation,
a preliminary representation, a "type" of the redemption of man
from the slavery of sin by Jesus.

A further purpose of this "pre-history" is to point to Jesus as
the son of Abraham, especially as the son of David, as the new
and true David and King (cf. Mt. 9:27; 15:22; Rom. 1,3ff.).

Finally the "pre-history" serves to announce the passion to
come. In the light of Golgotha, meditation on the events that surrounded the beginning of Jesus' life revealed features already there
which eventually led to his death. The child is rejected by Herod
(Mt. 2:3) and Archelaus (Mt. 2:22). According to Matthew
2:3, the entire city of Jerusalem is shaken by the news of the
birth of the Messiah. If it is understandable that the half-pagan
Herod always feared for his throne and so persecuted any likely
pretender, still it is curious that the people of Jerusalem, believing
in Yahweh, should be shaken by the announcement that the long
expected Messiah has come. Here it is clearly the case that the later
rejection of the Messiah is projected back to the beginning.

In the words of Simeon too (Lk. 2:34f.), Jesus' passion is announced: "This child is destined to be a sign which men reject.
. . . Many in Israel will stand or fall because of him and thus the
secret thoughts of many will be laid bare." Long before these
words were put together Paul had preached the same message to
the Corinthians (1 Cor. 1:23).

Karl Rahner supports this view (in H. Vorgrimler, ed., *Exegese
und Dogmatik,* Mainz, 1962, p. 43): "If the individual parts of
the Gospels have had a normal history before becoming part of the

Gospel (as the history of literary forms has rightly taught us), then we must be prepared to find, on comparison of the individual parts with each other, that they will not always have exactly the same historical literary form. We must reckon with the possibility, for instance, that it is not as certain from the historical point of view of fundamental theology that Jesus was ever in Egypt or that he was crucified in Jerusalem. None of this is in any way directed against the authority of the accounts—for these accounts themselves by their very nature admit of such a question."

The theological interpretation which we find in the "pre-history" is put into poetic form in the three canticles of the infancy narrative, the canticle of Mary (Lk. 1:46–55), of Zachary (Lk. 1:68–79), and of Simeon (Lk. 2:29–32). These already existed very probably in Luke's Aramaic source and represent a reflection, in the spirit of Old Testament poetry, on Jesus as the promised Messiah.[1]

Following the model of some Old Testament figures, Luke gives him as being about thirty years old, considered the ideal age, when he began his public life, (Gn. 41:46, Joseph; 2 Sam. 5:4, David; Ez. 1:1, Ezechiel; cf. W. Grundmann, *Das Evangelium nach Lukas,* Berlin, 1961, p. 112).

## THE MIRACLES OF JESUS

It must be emphasized at the outset that it would not be doing justice to the salvific deeds of Jesus before his death to reduce these to the miracles reported in the Gospels and to set aside the everyday life which surrounded them. The total activity of Jesus, including that of his childhood and of his "hidden" life in the family circle at Nazareth, has significance for the history of salvation. The reason for this is not difficult to see, at least in the light of faith. In Jesus, God's Son, the eternal Logos is at work and so the entire life of Jesus bears the character of a loving and obedient dialogue with God. It is a continual act of devotion to God and of alliance with him. Since the life of Jesus is a life for others, all others, and there is nothing he does which is not done in the name of mankind, in him and through him, mankind in principle returns to God and so comes to participate in salvation, in union with

God. Quiet and unassuming devotion to God took up the largest part of the life of Jesus, and the acts of power which stirred men are compressed into a short period, and even within this period, although they excite sensation, are still isolated events in Jesus' day-to-day life. The facts tell us that salvation comes to man in the first place not in the great deeds which move and shake the world, but in the continual, mostly soundless flow of ordinary everyday life. It is in this that obedience, devotion, and love for God occur, existence for others and the sacrifice of oneself for one's neighbor. The remarkable deeds which go down in history bring to light and advance with power what has been at work and has grown in silence. Jesus' deeds of power must be seen as part of a life of obedience and of love; on the other hand the focal point of his life expresses itself with a special force in his acts of power.

Among the salvific deeds of Jesus two groups stand out: his familiar conversations with sinners, who are often his companions at table, and those acts which the Gospel of John calls "signs." These last were treated earlier from the epistemological point of view. Their christological significance will be discussed later. For the moment we are concerned with their soteriological meaning, that is, their significance for man's salvation.

Jesus' personal friendship with sinners needs to be emphasized (Mk. 2:13–17; Mt. 9:9–13; Lk. 5:27–32). Jesus calls a tax collector to be one of his closest disciples, even though "tax collectors and sinners" seem to form one group (Mt. 11:19; Lk. 19:1). The reason is that the right to collect taxes was leased out to the highest bidder, who became the chief tax collector of a district, and in order to recoup his payments, almost necessarily had to force his employees, the "tax collectors," to dishonesty, exploitation, and deceit. The profession of tax collector could scarcely be exercised without dishonesty and injustice.

In addition, the tax collector is continually dealing with the Gentile; he serves the unbeliever, the Roman, the Herodian. Jesus' word tears the tax gatherer loose from his servitude to money. Jesus shares his meals with these "tax gatherers and sinners" (Mk. 2:15–17; Mt. 9:10–13). In this act we catch a glimpse of the turning-point of history. The Pharisees, in their concern for the commands of God and the holiness of their people, will not share their table with any who stand in suspicion of transgressing the law. It is not Jesus' intention to excuse those who sin, but to bring them the grace of God. His call to follow him is a recall to the peace of God. In the sharing of a meal with Jesus, reconciliation with God takes place so tangibly that the sick of soul feels himself well again. The deeds of Jesus are God's search for those who wait for him without knowing that they wait for him. He resembles a physician who heals, whose task it is to help the sick and wounded. Those who are well do not need the doctor. Clearly it is the Pharisees, the pious and the just, who are meant here. Jesus does not object to their health. He means it earnestly, not ironically, when he calls them just; they really do know about God and they take his commandments seriously. But now it is their task to help, to have mercy on those who sin. Jesus says this with a quotation from the Old Testament (Osee 6:6) which only Matthew mentions, and then repeats in 12:7. This statement is important for an understanding of Jesus' struggle against the Pharisees. They have really received something from God and from his justice; but instead of helping the others who are "poor" and "sinners," they stand on their pride, they judge and condemn and insult Jesus, who forgives sin and overcomes demons (Mt. 9,3ff.), and whose dealings are often described by the simple statement: he has mercy, he is moved to pity (Mt. 9:36), just as God's own dealing with man is described as mercy (Mt. 18:27). The most important example of the injunction in Matthew 9:13 is the parable of the Prodigal Son (Lk. 15), both in its characterization of the Pharisee (the elder brother) and also of the merciful love of God for the prodigal.[2] The issue at stake in Jesus' familiarity with sinners is the call of God, encounter with the God who gives himself in grace and thereby saves the reign of God.

Jesus' acts of power, his miracles, possess a similar salvific meaning. They bring about an encounter with God through an encounter in faith with Christ. We do not need to treat further here the question of the possibility of miracles (see above, pg. 101). As regards the factuality of Jesus' miracles, they are so interwoven with his life that without them he would not be the one who, according to the Gospels, he is. Certainly we have accounts of miracles from the non-biblical world and in Judaism. These accounts usually follow a particular pattern. The accounts of miracles in the Bible frequently use this pattern also. This does not mean that they are purely legendary stories, but only that the actual events were interpreted in the customary manner of the Evangelists and with the stylistic forms that the time offered. The miracle stories are an expression of theological reflection. The norm for this theological reflection is the risen Lord. With him mankind enters a new epoch, the final form of which is not yet visible. Jesus' deeds of power are seen in the light of his resurrection. They are indications, signposts, pointing to the new aeon. It is possible to characterize this epoch as the time of the reign of God, that is, of God's dealings in power and grace with man and of man's resultant salvation. The miracles serve the reign of God and thus the struggle against man's catastrophic situation. They are an attack on those forces of destruction which grasp at the inmost core of the human person: sin, Satan, sickness, death, human need in all its forms. We cannot pick and choose among the miracles reported in the Gospels and allow certain ones, such as the healings of the sick, and reject others, for example, miracles in the world of nature. For the reign of God announced by Christ and introduced by him is meant to bring the whole man and the world which belongs to him to salvation. On the other hand, if we grasp this purpose of the miracles, the limits which Jesus drew to this activity become understandable. He did not work just any miracles "at the drop of a hat," but only such as served the purpose of his mission, the founding and the furthering of the reign of God and man's right relationship to God. It is no objection, therefore, against his miracles if he heals sicknesses but does not replace amputated limbs. Still less does it speak against the purpose of these acts if it is only here and there that he attacks the powers of destruction. His miracles are only eschatological signs. They are meant to point to the possibility of a new existence, the existence of the risen Jesus and beyond this to the final transfiguration of mankind.

The factuality of Jesus' miracles must be considered from such points of view. Jesus' miracles differ from those reported from the non-biblical world both through the manner of their occurrence and through their meaning. Jesus does not work any miracles for show, for punishment, to bestow rewards, or to make a profit. He does not allow himself to be pushed into the role of a mere wonder-worker, either by his opponents (Mk. 8:11f.), or by the people seeking material help (Mk. 1:35–38). He does not use magic formulas. The power which produces these effects is simply and solely his will, or, if you wish, the will of God, which is active in Jesus and is expressed in his word (cf. A. Vögtle, *LThK X²*, p. 1258).

Historical reality is especially tangible in the case of those miracles that fit only into the pre-Easter period and which therefore cannot be considered as symbolizations of Jesus' universal salvific meaning, as if invented by the early Christian community in the style of legends. In point of fact the miracles of Jesus belong to the earliest preaching of the Apostles. Indeed in the mission sermons they occupy a central position. Peter, for example, in his Pentecost sermon links up Jesus' deeds of power with his death and resurrection: "Men of Israel, listen to me: I speak of Jesus of Nazareth, a man singled out by God and made known to you through miracles, portents, and signs, which God worked among you through him, as you well know. When he had been given up to you . . . you used heathen men to crucify and kill him" (Acts 2:22f.). In the house of Cornelius, Peter preached as follows: "I need not tell you what happened lately all over the land of the Jews. . . . You know about Jesus of Nazareth, how God anointed him with the Holy Spirit and with power. He went about doing good and healing all who were oppressed by the devil, for God was with him" (Acts 10:37f.). The brief summaries which the Gospels give on Jesus' activities support this. Healing and teaching are described in a popular manner as the characteristic activities of Jesus. "He went round the whole of Galilee, teaching in the synagogues, preaching the Gospel of the kingdom, and curing whatever illness or infirmity there was among the people" (Mt. 4:23). In chapters 8 and 9 of Matthew Jesus is described as a Messiah of deeds.

The preaching of the Apostles has its ground and foundation in Jesus' deeds and also in his conception of himself. In words which are without doubt authentically his own, Jesus points to his deeds of power and links them with his message about the reign of God. Of course, the way such original words of Jesus are judged will depend upon the interpretation of his figure as a whole (see chapter 2). In Luke 10:13ff. Jesus cries out (cf. Mt. 11:21–24): "Alas for you, Chorazin! Alas for you, Bethsaida! If the miracles that were performed in you had been performed in Tyre and Sidon, they would have repented long ago, sitting in sackcloth and ashes. But it will be more bearable for Tyre and Sidon at the Judgment than for you. And as for you, Capernaum, will you be exalted to the skies? No, brought down to the depths!" The inhabitants of Chorazin, like those of Bethsaida and Capernaum, rejected God's offer, made in wonders and signs. They remained unbelieving (cf. E. Neuhäusler, *Anspruch und Antwort Gottes,* Düsseldorf, 1962). The city of Chorazin is not mentioned again in the entire post-Easter tradition. It was no longer a matter of interest for the Christian community after Easter. The text is a testimony of the "historical" Jesus about himself. In the deeds of power of which Jesus speaks the reign of God breaks into human history. They are great and public signs of the grace of God. For this reason Jesus is shaken by the cities' unbelief. They turned their back upon God who has come to them in grace, and called down judgment upon themselves.

Even the passage about Beelzebub, which represents one of the earliest traditions (Lk. 11:17–23; see Mt. 12:25ff.), is a statement which can only fit into the pre-Easter period and therefore comes from the mouth of a historical Jesus. Of especial interest is the statement: "If it is by Beelzebub that I cast out devils, by whom do your own people drive them out? If this is your argument, they themselves will refute you. But if it is by the finger of God that I drive out the devils, then be sure the kingdom of God has already come upon you" (Mt. 12:27f.; Lk. 11:19ff.). Jesus' opponents do not deny his miracles but his divine authority. They do not recognize that his driving out of the devils is the coming of the reign of God. This is their unbelief.

Apart from these testimonies about himself, there are passages which, analogously to Jesus' *ipsissima verba,* reveal his deeds of power as *ipsissima facta.* In the view of F. Müssner they are those statements directed against the Pharisees and the Essenes. The chief of these is the account of the healing of the leper (Mk. 1:40–45). "Once he was approached by a leper, who knelt before him begging his help. 'If only you will,' said the man, 'you can cleanse me.' In warm indignation Jesus stretched out his hand, touched him, and said, 'Indeed I will; be clean again.' The leprosy left him immediately, and he was clean. Then he dismissed him with this stern warning: 'Be sure you say nothing to anybody. Go and show yourself to the priest, and make the offering laid down by Moses for your cleansing; that will certify the cure.' But the man went out and made the whole story public; he spread it far and wide, until Jesus could no longer show himself in any town, but stayed outside in the open country. Even so, people kept coming to him from all quarters." The phrase which occurs in the western text, "in warm indignation," does not mean indignation over the power of death, but indignation against the false legalism which governed the treatment of lepers in Israel. Leprosy was viewed as a punishment of God. From the cultic ritual point of view, the leper was unclean. He had to go about in torn clothing and cry to all who drew near him: "Unclean, unclean." He was an outcast and resembled a dead man. He was excluded from the temple worship and was not allowed to enter the Holy City. Jesus' encounter with the leper was a symbolic expression of his entire religious program. He lets the leper come to him, he even touches him and brings the presence of God to one shut out from the temple. By stretching out his hand he takes the sick man under the protection of God, and by touching him he enters into union with him. The actual healing, however, takes place through a word of power. Jesus' indignation is directed against the self-righteousness of his contemporaries (including the Essenes). He is angered over the blindness of men who practice pious self-deception and miss the true nature of the reign of God. The same is true in the case of the Sabbath cures.

The historicity of Jesus' deeds of power is closely bound up with their meaning as signs of the close proximity of the reign of God. They are expressions of a new epoch, in which the reign of God will be dominant. This can be seen in many ways. The proclamation that the reign of God is at hand (Mk. 1:15) is immediately actualized by the cure of a possessed man in the synagogue of Capernaum (Mk. 1:23–28). The Sermon on the Mount (Mt. 5ff.: the Messiah of the Word) is followed by an account of ten miracles (Mt. 8ff.: the Messiah of the Deed). Jesus' preaching and healing go together and are expressions of the reign of God, which breaks through with him. The breakthrough of the reign of God is revealed concretely in the destruction of the reign of Satan.[3]

The events in Gerasa represent a special manifestation of the power of the demons and the irresistible salvific force of the reign of God (Mk. 5:1–20; Mt. 8:28–34; Lk. 8:26–39). The demons, torturing the people they infest, beseech a new dwelling-place in the swine nearby. They receive permission and destroy the swine. This is an expression of Satan's resistance to God's creation and Jesus. But he is dethroned and can no longer enslave God's creation.

The cure of the lame man in Capernaum is particularly illuminating (Mk. 2:1–12; Mt. 9:1–8; Lk. 5:17–26). When the man was let down through the roof of the house in front of Jesus, "when Jesus saw their faith, he said to the paralyzed man, 'My son, your sins are forgiven.' Now there were some lawyers sitting there and they thought to themselves 'Why does the fellow talk like that? This is blasphemy! Who but God alone can forgive sins?' Jesus knew in his own mind that this was what they were thinking, and said to them: 'Why do you harbor thoughts like these? Is it easier to say to this paralyzed man, "Your sins are forgiven," or to say, "Stand up, take your bed, and walk"? But to convince you that the Son of Man has the right on earth to forgive sins'—he turned to the paralyzed man—'I say to you, stand up, take your bed and go home.' And he got up, took his stretcher at once and went out in full view of them all, so that they were astounded and praised God. 'Never before,' they said, 'have we seen the like.' " This scene shows that Jesus attacks the problem of human need at its root, which is the separation of man from God (cf. Gen. 2). Jesus wanted to make it clear that it was this which was the primal source of human suffering. We have no reason to think that the sick man was more of a sinner than anyone else, but in him we are shown that man is far from God, and that that fact is the root of the evil that he suffers. On the other hand the incident shows that forgiveness is not simply something which remains interior to man, but it affects man in his totality, in his very bodiliness, and brings him back as a complete person into the realm of God's glory (E. Schweitzer, *Das Evangelium nach Markus,* Göttingen, 1967, p. 32f.).

"According to Jesus, the sick whom he heals and the dead whom he raises are not people who have been struck by God for their sins, they are the victims of the Strong One, and a Stronger One now snatches them from him (cf. Mk. 3:27). In his miracles then, Jesus already brings creation back incipiently to salvation, and so the Kingdom of God, which is present in him in power, manifests itself in his miracles. This salvation embraces not only man's soul but also his body and by that fact the whole of creation" (F. Müssner, *Die Wunder Jesu,* Munich, 1967, p. 52). Since in the biblical view Satan's hostility to creation shows itself in the catastrophes of nature, we have no right to exclude the "nature miracles" from Jesus' preaching of the kingdom of God.

Jesus' miracles and the kingdom of God then belong closely together. The miracles are a confirmation of the dynamic power of his proclamation of the kingdom and this in its turn gives them their meaning and purpose.

It remains true that the miracle stories are frequently stylistically fashioned after the model of similar stories outside the Bible, or have undergone interpretation and selection and been fitted to the needs of the early Christian community as testimonies of faith. The story of Jesus walking on the lake of Genesareth (Mk. 6:45–56; Mt. 14:22–33; Jn. 6:16–21) is an account of a historical event, but we cannot be sure precisely what that event was. The core of the incident is probably that Jesus came to the disciples' rescue when they were in difficulties on the water in some manner which occasioned him to use the phrase "It is I," so that it impressed itself on the disciples (Müssner, p. 65). Something similar can be said of the multiplication of the loaves (Jn. 6:1–13; Mt. 14:13–21; Mk. 6:34–44; Lk. 9:10–17). No doubt the account is reminiscent of the Old Testament story of the manna and the quail in the desert, but it forms so much a part of the story of the activity of Jesus that we have no sufficient grounds to doubt its authenticity. It is also reminiscent of the Last Supper. "Nevertheless the story remains the account of a real meal which was an important symbol at a particular point in Jesus' life. . . . The author wishes to tell us that Jesus is Lord even over external needs, that hunger, like sickness and death, is not his lasting enemy. . . . Jesus is in command of the situation, even when the mob is excited, hungry, and ready to rebel. . . . Nevertheless the miracle which he works to help them is not something which

anyone has a right to presume or to demand" (Schweitzer, p. 177).
We see how important the multiplication of the loaves was to the
evangelist Mark from his remark about the disciples after the
storm on the lake, "They were completely dumfounded, for they
had not understood the incident of the loaves; their minds were
closed" (Mk. 6:52).

For an event to be seen as a miracle, faith is essential: the effect
on man of any revelatory act of God is constitutive for the revelation itself. Mark reports: "He left that place and went to his
home town accompanied by his disciples. When the Sabbath came
he began to teach in the synagogue; and the large congregation who
heard him were amazed and said, 'Where does he get it from?'
and, 'What wisdom is this that has been given him?,' and, 'How
does he work such miracles? Is not this the carpenter, the son of
Mary, the brother of James and Joseph and Judas and Simon?
And are not his sisters here with us?' So they fell foul of him.
Jesus said to them, 'A prophet will always be held in honor except
in his home town, and among his kinsmen and family.' He could
work no miracle there, except that he put his hands on a few sick
people and healed them; and he was taken aback by their want
of faith" (Mk. 6:1-6). The point of the miracle is that it constitutes an encounter between the compassionate God and man
who needs help. But God does not impose himself: it is only when
man opens himself freely to God that God gives himself to man in
a deed of power. But then in that case the dawning faith of the
receiver can grow to fullness. A person who observes a miracle,
but without faith, is capable of ascertaining the fact of the event,
but is not capable of seeing it as a miracle, that is, a sign of the
reign of God.

An event never imposes itself as a miracle: it can be an occasion for hardening of the heart as much as for conversion. A
striking example of this is the healing of the possessed man. Everyone present saw the event, but Jesus' adversaries interpret it as
devil's magic. Jesus' act, therefore, was not so unambiguous that
it could force people to recognize the kingdom of God. That he
cast out devils in the power of God and not in the name of the
prince of devils revealed itself only to the eyes of faith. The incident in Nazareth which preceded this shows that Jesus was re-

jected precisely because of his words and his deeds of power. Likewise in the Gospel of John it is the resurrection of Lazarus that leads to the definitive rejection of Jesus.

If Jesus' miracles are signs of the presence of God, they are also signs of the reign of God still to come: they have eschatological significance. They are partial projections of the absolute future, reaching their culmination in the resurrection of Jesus. All human projections of the future are included in God's projection, but radicalized, transcended, and brought to fruition in it. It is this dynamism which gives Jesus' miracles their significance. This dynamic power is destroyed if they are reduced to mere "significance" by demythologization, or are interpreted in a simply existential fashion, or if the historical event behind them is dismissed as unimportant.

Miracles are initiatives of God in salvation history, leading creation towards its final completion. Their significance is universal: they are promises in act, motives for hope. It is true for miracles, as for the entire Christ-event, that what is important is not their actuality in the past so much as their dynamic power for the future.

## Notes

1 Cf. K. H. Schelkle, *Wort und Schrift* (Düsseldorf, 1966), pp. 59–75; J. Gewiess, "Die Marienfrage Lk. 1:34," in *Biblische Zeitschrift* NF 5, 1961, pp. 221–254; J. Gnilka, "Der Hymnus des Zacharias," in *Bibl. Zeitschrift* NF 6, 1962, pp. 215–238; A. Vögtle, "Die Genealogie Mt. 1: 2–16 und die matthäische Kindheitsgeschichte," in *Bibl. Zeitschrift* NF 8, 1964, pp. 45–58, 239–262; NF 9, 1965, pp. 32–49; id., "Das Schicksal des Messiaskindes," in *Bibel und Leben* 6, 1965, pp. 246–279; id., *LThK* VI, 2nd ed., 1961, pp. 162f.; E. Krafft, "Die Vorgeschichten des Lukas: Eine Frage nach ihrer sachgemässen Interpretation," in *Zeit und Geschichte* [Festschrift R. Bultmann] (Tübingen, 1964), pp. 217–223; J. Schmid, *Das Evangelium nach Lukas*, 4th ed. (Regensburg, 1960); W. Trilling, *Fragen zur Geschichtlichkeit Jesu*, 2nd ed. (Düsseldorf, 1967).

2 See J. Schniewind, *Das Evangelium nach Matthäus* (Göttingen, 1964), pp. 119ff.; cf. E. Schweitzer, *Das Evangelium nach Markus* (Göttingen, 1967), pp. 35f.; J. Schmid, *Das Evangelium nach Markus*, 4th ed. (Regensburg, 1964).

3 Schmid, *loc. cit.*, 3rd ed. (Regensburg, 1954), p. 457.

# ◄ 6

# *The Salvific Words of Jesus*

We have already spoken of the word of Jesus, in the first volume of this work, on the notion of revelation, and above, where we treated of the saving death of Jesus. It is only through his word that we learn that his acts were in fact salvation-bringing acts. By its own saving dynamic his word relates the event of salvation to the whole of the divine revelation. Previously, however, we discussed Jesus' saving acts together with his saving word; in the following his words will be treated as a power in their own right.

The word of Jesus possesses a twofold function: the dynamic function of bringing salvation, and the function of instruction. Both are only two sides of the one function of the Word which is the self-disclosure of God.

## GENERAL CHARACTERIZATION

It is by his word that Jesus sets up the Reign of God. It is by his word that he forgives sin, restores the dead to life, heals the sick, stills the storm, multiplies the loaves. His work is thus an exercise of his saving power. And by his word he interprets his death as a saving death.

In his acts God both reveals himself and gives an authentic interpretation of man; so also he reveals himself in the word of Jesus, and at the same time he offers us an authentic interpretation of man, so that when we hear the word of Jesus, we can say,

*Ecce deus,* and also *Ecce homo.* The decisive thing in the word of Jesus, however, is that it is a call to salvation, that is, to peace, to unanimity, to dialogue with God.

As far as the form of the words of Jesus is concerned, he employs many modes of expression known in his time (parables, teaching, examples, sayings, aphorisms). But important above all is the fact that his hearers received the impression that he taught with authority.

The comparison has often been drawn between the teacher Jesus and the unknown "teacher of righteousness" of the Qumran community, which lived near the northwestern corner of the Dead Sea from the middle of the second century before Christ until 68 A.D., with a short interruption, and which at the beginning of the Jewish War (66–70) hid its library in the neighboring rock-caves. It was the opinion that the "teacher of righteousness" had anticipated essential points of the Apostolic Christ-faith up to and including the doctrine of the Trinity. It has since been shown that these theses are arbitrary and untenable. Nevertheless, there are some common elements. The "teacher of righteousness" claimed possession of a prophetic spirit. He had received his interpretation of the Law from God himself. For this reason he demands unlimited obedience from his adherents. The differences, however, are fundamental. He views himself only as an expounder of a revelation of God which was already given and closed, and the abolition of the ritual laws would have been utterly impossible for him. But Jesus dared to declare precisely ritual purity as religiously worthless. Above all, there are no parallels to the I-statements or to the Amen-formulae of Jesus.

Jesus' consciousness of his sovereignty surpasses all the demands of the Law. It is obvious that Jesus was much more than a Jewish scribe. Thus Matthew never has the disciples address Jesus with the words "prophet" or "rabbi" (cf. Mt. 26:25, 49), but as *Kyrie,* Lord (Mt. 26:22). He apparently wants to stress that Jesus is not a teacher in the Jewish sense, but Lord, indeed the divine Lord, since *Kyrios* is the name of God in the Greek translation of the Old Testament. Jesus appears as teacher only in the eyes of strangers and in conversation with strangers who do not know who he actually is.

## THE REVELATION OF THE THREEFOLD PERSONHOOD OF GOD

### *The Question of Method*

A most important part of the content of God's self-revelation in the word of Jesus is that of the threefold personhood of God. Of course Jesus at no time or place ever said: "God exists in a threefold personhood." Something of this sort would have been completely impossible, because it would have been either incomprehensible or blasphemous to the strict monotheism of his contemporaries. The self-disclosure of God in the Old Testament has as its aim precisely that God be acknowledged as the one and exclusive God. The temptation fermented again and again in the Old Testament people of God to turn toward heathen gods. So the disclosure of God's triune personality, after monotheism was secured, had to ensue in a very cautious and progressive manner. However, already in the apostolic age and even in Jesus' preaching, as well as through the reflection of his disciples, it began to take shape, and indeed so clearly that development into the full form of the Church's later trinitarian faith was possible. This development should not be viewed as a straightforwardly logical one. The disclosure of the threefold personality of God took place in a very stratified world of conceptions and images, and it sums up in itself many strands of revelation. When a large idea moves into the future, single elements press forward, recede again, are covered up by others, attain more and more clarity, until the final form of that which was meant from the beginning comes forward. Even if the New Testament authors had a deep understanding of Jesus Christ, they still lacked the requisite tools for conceptualization, especially the categories of person and nature which later became decisive for the doctrine of the Trinity. They had to express the mystery which suggested itself to them with insufficient linguistic resources. In the post-Apostolic period, the dynamic of the human spirit in a dialectic with philosophical movements, and under the guidance of the Holy Spirit, reached a form of the Trinitarian faith which was not at all evident from the outset as the only possible one, but which, in the to and fro of the movement of the confession of faith, was nevertheless deemed fitting concerning God, Christ, and Holy Spirit.

When we set about interpreting the revelation of God as trinity, it must be stressed from the start that here too it holds that God has revealed himself not in order to increase our store of information but for our salvation. God has revealed himself not as triune personality in itself, but for us, even though he is that for us only because he is it in itself. If God is tri-personal, then it follows that salvation, which consists ultimately in dialogue with God, takes place in the fact that we share in the intra-divine dialogue of the three persons.

This becomes still clearer when we ask ourselves how we are to begin the inquiry. Two possibilities present themselves: one is analytic and systematic, the other is salvational, historical, genetic. That is to say, we can start from the later teaching of the Church as we find it in the councils and feel our way back from there over the single steps of the development to the origins of the doctrine in Scripture. It appears, however, to accord more with the methods of scholarship if we begin with the witness of scripture, keeping the official teaching of the Church in mind, of course, as the final form which the doctrine took. It may be that theology will discover that the resources at its disposal cannot show that the Church's teaching follows directly from the Scripture. In this case the Church, i.e., the community of faith, and the teaching office of the Church must deal with the problem by other means.

### The Mystery

As the New Testament looks towards the future, requiring further development, so it also looks back towards the past, namely, to the Old Testament, and asks whether there are traces there of that which emerges in the New Testament. We would expect this in principle, since the Old Testament was the preliminary stage and the preparation of the New. It is of special importance that behind the Old Testament witness to God stands a personal metaphysics which differs from the "object" metaphysics developed by the Greeks. That is to say, in the Old Testament God manifests himself as a personal God. He blesses, he judges, he acts, he calls, he comes towards men, he is near to them, he gives them salvation, and he does all of this in absolute freedom. God's personhood includes, as our earlier analysis has shown, the fact that God in himself is somehow dialogical. For personhood, or the subjectivity of being, can be understood dialogically. As long as the trinitarian life of God is not made accessible, however, it remains totally unknown how we are to understand the dialogical character of absolute Being, God. The question can be raised, whether there are only logical distinctions in God or real ones. Is the dialogic element in God to be understood only according to the analogy of a human soliloquy, or by analogy with the I-Thou relationship between created persons?

The trinities we find in the non-biblical realm are of no help to us in trying to answer this question, neither the Jewish-Hellenistic triads (Philo), nor the triad-conceptions of the great world religions. With the first, it is a matter of the attempt to explain the creation of the world by means of an intermediate being between God and creation, without having to involve God in the mechanism of the world. With the latter it is fundamentally always a matter of three mythologies where the gods themselves are personifications of natural powers and occurrences. Even if a metaphysical analysis of the concept of being leads us to conclude that absolute being has a dialogical character, still the trinitarian life of God is totally inaccessible to us. That God is trinitarian is a mystery in the strictest sense in its "That" as well as in its "How." The trinitarian faith, the incarnation of the Logos, and the self-communication of God to his creatures form the heart of the Christian mystery of faith. All that human intelligence can do here is to try as far as possible to understand what is meant so as to eliminate compelling objections.

### *"Mission" as a Key Concept*

The key concept for the understanding of the New Testament doctrine of the Trinity is that of "sending." [1] What precisely is to be understood by "sending" will be explained later. To begin with it may suffice to employ the concept in a general sense. The word "sending" is a formula for the saving movement of God towards men and for his nearness to men. In the Old Testament God sent the prophets, for example Moses, and specifically through his Word or through his Wisdom or through his Spirit.

It was a completely new manner of sending when God sent his own Son into the world and into human history. In the Son God himself is present. Through this sending he became an acting subject within human history. If all sendings serve the dialogue of God with men, then through this sending of his Son an encounter between God and man was created according to the mode in which men conduct a dialogue among themselves. This sending shows a close unity of God and the Son sent by him, but on the other hand, it shows there is a distinction between them. When the Son sent by God broke back again through the boundary between the transcendent and the immanent spheres of reality, he, together with the Father, with God, sent the Holy Spirit. In the Holy Spirit God is present within human history between the resurrection (glorification) and the return of Jesus Christ.

Immediately and above all, the saving action of God expresses itself in these sendings of "missions." The New Testament witnesses to a divine activity of sending in three stages. That is, it points directly not to an ontological trinity, but to a functional one. In this functional Trinity, however, the ontological also comes to light. Justice would not be done to the meaning of the sending, if the functional Trinity it indicates were understood only as three phases in which the one God has revealed himself. It is indeed always the one God who devotes himself in a saving way to the world, but he devotes himself to it in accordance with the inner distinction which reigns in himself. It becomes clear then that the one God attested to in the Old Testament, who sends his Son and together with the Son sends the Holy Spirit, must in the light of the New Testament be understood as the Father, who has a Son, and together with the Son bestows the Holy Spirit. What happens in the sendings is a revelation of the differentiation in absolute Being itself. Absolute Being itself, in consequence of its spirituality, which has a substantial and essential dialogical character, is differentiated in itself. The differentiation, which appears in the sendings, is therefore not only a differentiation for us, but also a differentiation in Being itself. This differentiation in absolute Being itself becomes a differentiation for us. Through his revelation God gives himself through the Son in the Holy Spirit to men.

In the theology of the third and fourth centuries these three are designated as hypostases. Usually this word is translated as "person." However, the things which characterize a person in our sense of the term are an individual mind and will. And it is precisely these which cannot be predicted of the hypostases in God (Councils of Lyons and Florence, cf. DS 172, 415, 441, 501, 531, 542, 851, 1330). To speak of three persons in God in the normal sense of the word would be the equivalent of saying that there are three Gods. The terminology, current since Tertullian and Augustine and the Cappadocians, is dangerous. It can be used only if its strictly analogous character is borne in mind. This means that the factor of dissimilarity which is part of analogy must be especially stressed here.

We can say: there exists in God a diversity, without the unity of God thereby being disturbed; and furthermore, that this diversity in the sense of triplicity is essential for absolute Being. Absolute Being cannot be conceived as a block of being, out of which three elements extend outward. Rather, being itself is differentiated in itself. Since true Being is the being of spirit, we can provisionally form an idea of the differentiation, if we consider that knowledge implies an antithesis between the I and the Thou and also a union of the Thou and the I. Hence, God is essentially trinitarian. This trinitarian characteristic is not an incidental addition. From his essence God cannot live other than as trinitarian. In this view we find that the numerous trinities in the world of our experience take on a new light. They are all reflections of the essentially trinitarian structure of absolute Being.

Later theology attempted to interpret the differentiation, which must be so understood that the unity of God is not lost, in terms of the key word "relation," originating from Greek philosophy. We turn now to the data concerning the Trinity in Scripture.

## THE TESTIMONY OF SCRIPTURE

### *The Old Testament*

Because the Old Testament is a preparation for Christ, a shadow of the future (1 Cor. 10:11; Gal. 3:24), we find, on the one hand, that the Old Testament has allusions to the multi-personhood in God, though without any clear development, and also that even these allusions themselves could not be understood as such by the Old Testament faithful; it is only in the light of the New Testament that they are capable of being understood as allusions to a Trinity.

Throughout the entire Old Testament the fundamental idea emerges that God is absolute mystery, which no one can see without dying, but that God nevertheless has revealed Himself to the fathers and has associated himself with them in historical actions. This approach of God to man is mediated through the Word, through the Spirit, through Wisdom. But Word, Wisdom, Spirit are at any given time God Himself acting with saving power. Where Spirit and Wisdom no longer hold sway, there, according to the interpretation of the prophets, God had abandoned his people. When he nevertheless turns in his mercy again towards the people, he again sends a prophet in the fullness of the Spirit, who will deliver his Word. The prophets promise repeatedly a future saving presence of God in his people, which will surpass God's modes of being present up to then. The nature of this mode of being present remains hidden, however. It is in the New Testament that we see the mode in which God fulfills the promises he gave through the prophets. He makes himself present in his Son and in the Holy Spirit within human history. Thus not only single expressions, like Word or Wisdom or Spirit, but the total movement of the Old Testament revelation itself is a preparation for the revelation of God as tri-personal or at least as multi-personal.

In the New Testament itself we can discern two forms of witness to the Trinity, namely, in the words of Jesus and in the interpretation of his words, deeds, and person given by the apostles. What Jesus himself says is itself divine revelation. But the apostles' exposition also has the character of revelation, because their interpretation of Jesus takes place under the guidance and enlightenment of God. The apostles are not only receivers but also bearers of revelation.

### The Synoptics and Acts on the Son

The names given to Jesus in the New Testament are important, but will be mentioned here only briefly. They will be treated more fully in the following section on the being of Jesus. We cannot separate our understanding of Jesus from our conception of the Trinity; however perhaps it will be sufficient for the moment if we present the indications available in Scripture for the divinity of Jesus Christ only insofar as is necessary for a grasp of the historical development of the doctrine of the Trinity. In many ways the development of Christology and of the doctrine of the Trinity go hand in hand. For the sake of an ordered presentation, however, the two lines of development need to be handled separately.

Jesus considered himself the Son of God in an altogether special and exclusive sense. The Gospels make this point chiefly in a passage derived from the earlier collection of Jesus' sayings, which brings out the distinctive yet most intimate relationship between the Father and the Son: "I praise you, Father, Lord of heaven and earth, that you have hidden this from the wise and understanding but revealed it to babes. Yes, Father, for thus it was well-pleasing to you. Everything has been delivered to me by my Father, and no one knows the Son except the Father, and no one knows the Father except the Son and anyone to whom the Son chooses to reveal Him" (Mt. 11:25–27; Lk. 10:21–22). Here it is the historical Jesus who speaks of himself, not just the post-Easter proclamation of the early Church. Jesus knows that he possesses the fullness of the Spirit (Lk. 4:18). In him the reign of God has come and is present (Mt. 12:28; Lk. 11:20). He is the one who is decisive for the salvation or the non-salvation of men (Mk. 13:13). Whoever denies him is liable to judgment (Mt. 11:20–24). He has dominion over sickness, death, and sin. The cures that he performs are signs of his power to forgive sins (Mk. 2:1–12). He is the authentic interpreter of the Law (Mk. 2:23–28; 3:1–6). The expression "Son," of course, according to its formal intrinsic value, would not guarantee an essential relationship of Jesus to God. This, however, is vouched for through the nature and manner in which Jesus depicts his Sonship. He attributes to himself a fullness of power and an authority which, in the faith of his hearers, belongs to God alone (Mk. 11:27–33; 12:1–12). In view of this situation, the question arises of precisely how Jesus is related to the one God of the Old Testament faith. The New Testament itself gives no direct answer to this question. It does however provide a good deal of material that was capable of further development.

### The Synoptics and Acts on the Holy Spirit

The entire New Testament teaching regarding the Spirit, including that of the Synoptics and Acts, rests upon that of the Old Testament. Acts has even been termed the Gospel of the Holy Spirit.

In the Old Testament the "Spirit" is identified with God. The word signifies the saving operations of God in the world. The Spirit is God, and a divine power. Since this power manifests itself by bringing forth and preserving life, the Spirit is regarded as the original ground of being (Gen. 1:2; 2:7; Pss. 104:29f.; 33:6; Job 12:10; 34:14f.; 2 Macc. 7:23). It is the Spirit of God that acts powerfully in history (Ex. 33:14–17). He inspires and guides the bearers of revelation. He enlightens the prophets and drives them to speech and action. The Spirit is the power that unites God with those whom he has taken into his concern. Frequently the Spirit is also designated as the ground of sanctification for individual believers. The gifts of the Spirit will become the possession of all in the Messianic kingdom. The teaching of the Old Testament regarding the Spirit thus has an eschatological character. The Spirit of God in no way appears in the Old Testament as a person. However, in the course of time the concept undergoes more and more personification. The New Testament faith in the Spirit differs from that of the Old Testament above all in this, that according to the witness of the New Testament, the Spirit hoped for in the Old Testament as the eschatological saving gift is poured out upon the believers in a wonderful manner and the promise is thus fulfilled.

The Spirit plays a decisive role in the life and work of Jesus (Mt. 1:18, 20; 12:18,28; Mk. 3:29; 13:11; Lk. 2:26ff.; 10:21, etc.).

In the baptism of Jesus the Synoptists see the descent of the Spirit upon the Messianic servant of God (Mk. 1:10f.; Is. 11:2f.; Acts 10:38). Upon him rests the Spirit of the Lord in accordance with the promise of Scripture. With the help of the Spirit Jesus breaks the dominion of Satan (Mt. 12:28; Lk. 11:20). Whoever understands Jesus' work as satanic offends against the Holy Spirit (Mt. 12:31f.; Lk. 12:10). Jesus' resurrection is understood as a breaking through into the sphere of the Spirit. More than once he promises the Spirit, for example, "When you are brought before the synagogues and state authorities, do not begin worrying about how you will conduct your defense or what you will say. For when the time comes, the Holy Spirit will instruct you what to say" (Lk. 12:11f.). He promises the Spirit to his disciples before the ascension (Acts 1:8). In the power of the Spirit the disciples are to be the Lord's witnesses, in Jerusalem, in Judea, in Samaria, and to the ends of the earth. On Pentecost the Spirit was in fact sent to the entire congregation of believers gathered in Jerusalem (Acts 2:1–5). From that time on it is the Spirit who guides and directs the Church (Acts 5:3,9; 16:6f.; 21:10f.).

It is interesting that in the speeches in Acts two operations of the Holy Spirit are distinguished. On the one hand there are deeds which burst out from the person filled by the Spirit, breaking through all customary order and upsetting all expectations. On the other hand there is a calm, orderly behavior towards individuals and the community, born out of love. The Spirit is communicated through baptism and the laying on of hands. It plays a leading role in the sending out of the disciples, the "mission" (Acts 13:2–4). More than once special activities are attributed to it (cf., e.g., Acts 7:55; 8:15, 17; 10:19,44f.; 14:9). The question, however, is whether it can be maintained on the strength of such activities that the Spirit is a person in his own right, or whether it is only a matter of personification. The latter would seem to be correct. However, the later ecclesiastical explanations of the personhood of the Holy Spirit represent an authoritative interpretation of the activities described in the Synoptic Gospels and in Acts. In any case, it must be said that the Synoptic texts are open to such an interpretation, and that although they do not themselves plainly teach the personhood of the Spirit, they do make such a teaching possible.

## The Synoptics on the Threefold Personhood of God

The divine triad is mentioned explicitly in two places in the Synoptic Gospels: the manifestation following the baptism of Jesus, and the solemn mission of the apostles preceding the ascension. At the baptism of Jesus, the Father, Jesus himself as Son, and finally the Holy Spirit, who descended in the form of a dove from heaven, are named (Mt. 3:13–17; Mk. 1:9–11; Lk. 3:21f.; cf. also Jn. 1:32–34). It does not follow from the wording alone, however, that an ontological Trinity is meant. The expression "Son" (of God) is often employed in the Old Testament and also in the non-biblical realm to indicate a special relation of man to God, that is, in a functional sense. As far as the Holy Spirit is concerned, the passage describes that bestowal of the Holy Spirit which was promised in the Old Testament for the Messianic time. However it is legitimate to see in the reference to the Spirit more than an allusion to a function or role of God. Such a function or role presupposes an ontological state of affairs. That which took place in Jesus' baptism had exemplary meaning for Christian baptism. According to Jesus' instructions it is to be conferred in the name of the Father, the Son, and the Holy Spirit. According to the Gospel of Matthew (28:19f.), the resurrected Jesus says to the disciples: "All authority has been given to me in heaven and on earth. Go therefore and make disciples of all people, and baptize them in the name of the Father and the Son and the Holy Spirit and teach them to observe all that I have commanded you. And lo, I am with you always to the end of the world." Since this text represents an early baptismal formula, and since, in addition, the primitive Church, according to the uniform witness of Acts and Paul, carried out baptism in the name of Jesus, it must be asked whether the wording of this text comes from the resurrected Jesus himself, or whether in it instructions going back to the Lord himself are clothed in a formula taken from the usage of the time. If the latter should be correct, we have in this form of the command to baptize a particular stage in the development of the primitive Christian baptismal confession. It would in no way contradict the "truth of the Gospel" if in the text a phrase spoken by Jesus before the crucifixion were reflected in a formulation coined by the cult and redaction. The primitive com-

munity shows in any case through the careful and general reception
of baptism after Pentecost that it was convinced it was thereby fulfilling a commission of the Lord, even though we can no longer
establish the wording of it with certainty.

As far as the content of the passage is concerned, Father, Son,
and Spirit appear as the source of the new life bestowed in baptism.
The one baptized is united with them, and becomes bound to them.
The revelation of the Trinity is given here, then, not for its own
sake, but for the sake of man's salvation. The text bears the appearance of expressing the metaphysical Trinity: Father, Son, and
Spirit are united by repeating "and." They are placed on the same
level of being. Of course, the a-personal grammatical form for the
third member of the triad (*pneuma* = neuter gender) presents a
difficulty. But since the word stands equally beside the other two,
it accords with the thought expressed in the formula, if the third
member, in spite of the grammatical difficulty, is understood just
as personally as the first two members. The New Testament was
clearly not concerned with this. When, however, the Church later
attributed "personal" existence to the Holy Spirit as well as the first
and second members, the Father and the Son, this is a legitimate
conclusion from the formula.


*Paul*

The entire theology of Paul has a trinitarian structure. But in his
case also it is not primarily a matter of a trinitarian doctrine, but
rather of the proclamation of a trinitarian mission through Christ.
In the Letter to the Ephesians he writes, "Through Him, namely
Christ, we both (Jews and Gentiles) have access to the Father in
the one Spirit" (Eph. 2:18). Only through Christ are we joined
with God, but this union with God takes place in the Holy Spirit,
The Holy Spirit appears here to a certain degree as the sphere or
realm in which a man lives who is united through Christ to the
Father. Here the structure of Christian existence expresses itself.
Paul is not interested in a Trinity in itself, but only in a Trinity for
us. This does not mean that he proclaims only a functional Trinity.
Much as the functional Trinity, i.e., the triune personal saving
action of God, stands in the foreground of his thinking, so for him

the functional Trinity is still the form of expression to the inaccessible ontological Trinity.

Paul's letters contain many passages referring to the Trinity through which one infers an ontological Trinity; in some of them it is quite clear. The plurality of the trinitarian formulae indicates that Paul, in a still incomplete conceptualization, not very clearly developed, wants to bring to expression a reality which he himself has repeatedly experienced, but for which the necessary conceptual material is not yet available. For this reason the Pauline formulae are often of great diversity and undecided meaning. They are not easily brought into an ordered system. Precisely this shows how important it is for Paul to explain afresh again and again the reality which he has experienced. He has it at heart to summon his listeners to shape their life out of the reality which he proclaims.

The following passages express a divine triad and need to be taken into account: Romans 1:1–7; 5:1–5; 8:3f.; 8:8f.; 8:11; 8:16f.; 8:10–30; 14:17f.; 15:16–19; 15:30; 1 Cor. 2:6–16; 6:11; 6:15–20; 12:3–11; 2 Cor. 1:21f.; 3:3–6; 3:10–17; 4:13f.; 4:5–8; 12; 13:13; Gal. 3:1–5; 3:11–14; 4:6; 5:21–25; Eph. 1:3–13; 1:17; 2:22; 3:5–7; 3:14–17; 4:4–6; 4:30–32; 5:18–20; Phil. 3:3; Col. 1:6–8; 1 Thess. 1:6–8; 4:2–8; 5:18f.; 2 Thess. 2:13f. Of these triadic texts the most important would seem to be 1 Cor. 12:3–11 and 2 Cor. 13:13.

First of all, we shall deal with the Pauline teaching concerning Christ so far as this is needed for the present question. Christ is the likeness of the invisible God (2 Cor. 4:4; Col. 1:15). (Cf. "the reflection of his glory and the stamp of his substance" [Heb. 1:3].) The word "likeness" designates not merely the mirroring of God through Christ. In the conceptual sphere in which Paul uses the word, it means something like appearance, or shining out, invisible reality, in which it participates. It is in fact reality itself insofar as this appears. The likeness is indeed also the beloved Son of God (Col. 1:13). When the world was not yet, he existed in that type of being which belongs to God. For this reason he is God as the Father is, as Paul says in the Letter to the Romans. The Father sent him, his Son, into the world, in order that he might ransom us from sin and bring us the Sonship of God. In him God thus reconciled us again with himself and received us as his children (Eph.

2:12–18). Through faith in Christ we have peace in God and in the Lord Jesus Christ (1 Thess. 1:1).

The Christ whom we apprehend in faith exists in a glorified state. In his glorified mode of existence he is active as Head of the Church. As such he is the source of life for all, as the first Adam was the source of sin and death (Rom. 5:12–21). Through incorporation into the communion of the Church the individual man is united with Christ and gains participation in the glory of Christ. Through communion with Christ we become sons of God, since Christ is God the Father's own Son and he extends his Sonship, so to speak, over us. As we belong to Christ, so Christ belongs to God (1 Cor. 3:22f.). The subordination of all believers under Christ and of Christ under God, so that God will be all in all, will attain its consummation after the judgment of the world. Christ is also the Head of the whole creation. It is of special significance that Paul applies that word to Christ with which the Septuagint translated the Old Testament *Yahweh,* namely, the word *Kyrios,* Lord. Jesus is the Lord (Rom. 10:9). He is as such also the Judge (1 Cor. 4:4f.). He is the Lord to whom everything belongs for himself. The glorified Christ is the vivifying Spirit (1 Cor. 15:45). He possesses the Spirit not through participation, but out of his own nature and being. For this reason he can be the life, power, and wisdom of the believers (1 Cor. 1:24). All of these statements of Christ's sovereignty receive a special significance through the fact that Paul sees clearly the the human weakness of Jesus, his humiliation, his obedience to death on the cross (Phil. 2:5–11).

We turn to Paul's doctrine of the Spirit. The word Spirit (*pneuma*) is employed by him in a sense that has very many levels of meaning. It forms a central concept in his letters. It governs and colors his entire witness to Christ. We do not need to dwell on those texts in which Paul speaks of the human spirit. The texts in which the word Spirit is used of God designate God himself as well as God's communication of himself, his presence and his transforming influence on men. Like Acts, but much more fully, Paul describes a twofold effect of the Spirit, the uncommon and extraordinary, which manifests itself in astonishing exclamations and sounds uttered by those affected by the Spirit, and also the day-to-day effect, above all in mutual love, by which the operation of the Spirit becomes chiefly manifest. As for the first form of the Spirit's activity, Paul certainly criticizes the overestimation of such gifts of the Spirit, but he does not reject them completely. He gives a criterion to judge them by: the building up of the congregation, or proper faith in Christ. Because of the danger of disorder which could be brought about by the excessively emotional or enthusiastic gifts of the Spirit in the congregation, Paul summons the Corinthians to strive for the better gifts of the Spirit. These consist, however, not only in those relationships which form the everyday life of the Christian in the likeness of Christ, but also in unexpected charismatic endowments, but just in such endowments which differ from the enthusiastic outcries. It belongs to this charisma, for example, when the Spirit drives a Christian in the gathering to call out, "Father." The mystery of Christian existence discloses itself directly in such gifts of the Spirit. In the Letter to the Galatians he states: "You are sons; God has indeed sent His Son into our hearts, who calls: Abba (Father)" (Gal. 4:6). Similarly, it is said in the Letter to the Romans (8:15), "The Spirit you have received is not a spirit of slavery, leading you back into a life of fear, but a Spirit that makes us sons, enabling us to cry Abba (Father)." It may be supposed that in the congregational gatherings or on other occasions, the Christians suddenly cry out, "Father," as if grasped by a foreign power, and so expressed in an epitome, the faith filling them. In this outcry of the new key word for the designation of the divine nature and the relation of men to one another, the person grasped by the spirit experiences a direct confirmation of his own position in relation to God. For the Spirit himself testifies to our spirit that we are sons of God (Rom. 8:16). It can be assumed with certainty that at the conversion of the Galatians (Gal. 5:18) special activities of the Spirit of a charismatic kind appeared, which brought the truth of the Gospel of salvation through faith alone concretely home to those present, leaving them in amazement (Gal. 3:5). In the Holy Spirit the divine Word fills and moves the messengers of Christ too in their innermost heart. The Spirit is the foundation of their new and transformed existence. He plays a decisive role in the establishing of the Christian community. To the degree that the Spirit is effective in the baptized a new pattern of behavior emerges in them. It becomes visible that the believer truly possesses the *pneuma*. In this dimension too, as in all his statements of faith, Paul joins the imperative with the indicative. Since the Christians have received the Spirit, they must live out of the Spirit. They are to realize what has been given to them. In particular, participation in the suffering of Jesus Christ is the strongest concrete evidence that a man is a member of the body of Christ and permeated by the resurrection powers of this body, that is, by the Christ who has been made Spirit. For Paul the possession of the Spirit means salvation. This salvation is, however, only a preparatory one. The Spirit is the pledge, as it were, the down payment or first installment of salvation (Rom. 8:23). He is the guarantee of full salvation in the future. The possession of the Spirit thus has an eschatological significance.

If we inquire about the relation of the Spirit to God, two answers present themselves. The Spirit is the Spirit of God. He belongs to the being of God and proceeds from God, in order to impart himself to the faithful and in this way to refashion and renew their existence (1 Cor. 2:10–14). Through the Spirit the love of God is poured out into the hearts of men (Rom. 5:5). The same Spirit is called, however, the Spirit of Jesus Christ (Phil. 1:19). Union with Jesus is effected in that element which Paul calls the Spirit. The Spirit, who is perceptible and recognizable in the ecstatic who cries out: "Abba" (presumably in the worship of the congregation), is the Spirit sent by God; but he is at the same time the *pneuma* of the Son of God. For an understanding of Paul's theology here, it should be remembered that he learned to know Christ from the beginning as Spirit, as *pneuma;* he never knew Jesus as a man walking about on this earth. This is the new mode of existence into which the Son of God, who in the flesh is of David's descendants, has entered since his resurrection from the dead. Jesus Christ's crossing over into the transcendence of God makes it possible for him to communicate himself to individuals and the congregation in the way that it is described by Paul. The expressions "Spirit of Christ" and "Spirit of God" are quite interchangeable. "But that is not how you live. You are on the spiritual level, if only God's Spirit dwells within you; and if a man does not possess the Spirit of Christ, he is no Christian. But if Christ is dwelling within you, then although the body is a dead thing because you sinned, yet the spirit is life itself because you have been justified. Moreover, if the Spirit of him who raised Jesus from the dead dwells within you, then the God who raised Jesus Christ from the dead will also give new life to your mortal bodies through his indwelling Spirit" (Rom. 8:9–11). The Spirit sent by Christ has brought the decisive liberation. It is the new order of salvation that is determined by the Spirit, because the Spirit leads into the realm of life of Jesus Christ.

If we further ask whether the Spirit is an impersonal power of God, whether he is thus fundamentally God himself, or whether he represents a distinct acting subject, attention may be called to the fact that, according to the witness of the Apostle, the Spirit dwells in man as Christ himself dwells in us (Rom. 8:10,16; Eph. 3:17); that the faithful are a temple of the Holy Spirit, as they are a temple of God; that they are justified in the Spirit and in Christ (1 Cor. 6:11), sanctified in the Spirit and in the Lord; that the Spirit groans in man, that he, like Christ, intercedes for man (Rom. 8:27–34); that he is sent by God into the hearts of men, as the Son is sent (Rom. 8:9–11). He dispenses his gifts as he wills (1 Cor. 12:4–11).

As clear as these passages appear to be, however, their demonstrative power is diminished by the fact that at other times Paul makes other personifications. The power of sin, for example, is also a reality which dwells in man, which determines the planning, aspirations and thoughts of man. Sin reigned royally in death. Death itself also exercised a tyranny over man, even though it is no longer lord over man. In addition, the question can be posed whether according to Paul the Spirit is not identified with the glorified Christ, in which case Paul's conception would not be a triadic but a dyadic conception of God. In fact it is said of the glorified Jesus himself that he has become Spirit. The Corinthians apparently had special experiences of the Spirit, and they inquired about this mystery. Paul gives them the answer, "Now the Lord is the Spirit" (2 Cor. 3:17). In the resurrection Christ actually attained a spiritual, a pneumatic mode of existence. Jesus is the last Adam who became vivifying Spirit (1 Cor. 15:45). It is not likely, however, that Paul simply identified Christ and the Spirit, in the sense that the Lord is in all respects nothing other than the Spirit and vice versa. Paul very frequently and very clearly distinguishes between Christ and the Spirit. Perhaps one may say that Paul sometimes makes a dynamic identification, insofar as the glorified Christ is active in the Spirit. Even when the Father, Christ, and the Spirit are distinguished, this does not lead to three subjects of activity, autonomous and acting side by side. The unity of God is not negated by the differentiation that Paul made. Rather, the Father acts at any given time through Christ in the Holy Spirit. However, it must be stressed that we do not have from Paul any conceptually developed doctrine of the Trinity, as was later arrived at by the Council of Nicea.

The passages 1 Corinthians 12:4–11 and 2 Corinthians 13:13 come closest to the doctrine developed later. In the first text the Spirit, Lord, and God are named. "There are varieties of gifts, but the same Spirit. There are varieties of service, but the same Lord. There are many forms of work, but all of them, in all men, are the work of the same God." The enumeration of the different gifts of grace closes: "But all these gifts are the work of one and the same Spirit, distributing them separately to each individual at will."

The second passage reads, "The grace of the Lord Jesus Christ and the love of God and fellowship in the Holy Spirit be with you all." Jesus Christ, God, and the Holy Spirit are named together. That God and the Lord are two cannot be denied. The third member is joined to them equivalently. It means participation in the Holy Spirit. Thus the genitive-objective is employed for the Spirit, while the genitive-subjective is used for God and Lord. This difference does not, however, warrant the opinion that in the first two cases two persons in the sense of later Church doctrine are spoken of, but that the third refers only to an a-personal reality. Participation in the life of the Holy Spirit establishes the connection of the believer in Christ with the exalted Lord and with God the Father. Thus in the Pauline formula not only a triad, but the inner union of the three is attested. They stand in such close relation that none merely lives next to the others, but rather all three live in each other, and the one is active through the others.

Perhaps one may also refer to Romans 5:1–5, as well as Romans 15:30f. and Ephesians 1:13–15. All of these texts are starting points for further developments and lead naturally to them.

Finally it can be said that it was the abundance of charismatic expressions of the Spirit which engendered and kept alive a sense for the totally new, the unexpected, the over-powering, the over-throwing. There is no special pattern to this in the Pauline letters. The occasional warnings of the Apostle to those grasped by the *pneuma* are not intended to harm or annihilate the spiritual life flourishing, but to secure the right place for it within the individual and communal existence and to exclude false forms. Indeed, in the middle of his warnings Paul emphatically stresses, "Do not quench the Spirit" (1 Thess. 5:19). For this would mean exactly that the congregation moves far from Christ. There is no fixed and exclusive form for the communication of the Spirit. Rather, the Spirit acts freely and unrestrictedly. Meanwhile, it would be an unjustified reduction of the Pauline doctrine of the Spirit to see the working of the Spirit only in uncommon phenomena. The Spirit works much more in the daily life of the Church. For the tasks which continuously and variously present themselves in the congregations, he allows the powers necessary at any given time to arise out of the midst of the congregations, which remain bound to the authority of the Apostle. The miracle of the Spirit, which so manifested itself everywhere, strengthens the awareness and the joy of faith, threatened from many sides, and the certitude of the faithful. Paul, with his congregations, stands in a tradition that has firm testimony in the Old Testament and which is found already in the pre-Pauline congregations (cf. perhaps the Pentecost report in Acts). Paul sees that which was promised in the Old Testament has become reality. He conceives the Spirit as the characteristic power of salvation for the interim period between the resurrection and the return of Jesus Christ. In his view, if salvation is present anywhere, it is because the Spirit is there. The Spirit rules the entire realm between God and man. He transforms man, to whom he is given, into something new, something divine.

From the especially extraordinary gifts of the Spirit, which are visible to all, Paul finds and points out the path to the knowledge of those gifts of the Spirit which bear and form the life of the community, especially of that gift important and lasting above all, love, which determines and forms the ethical life of the congregation.

Through its doctrinal decisions the Church has brought no foreign elements into the Pauline doctrine of the Spirit, but rather explicated what Paul expresses in a preconceptual manner. He was not particular about sharp conceptualization, but about the proclamation of the reality, ultimately inexpressible in concepts, which has been mediated through Jesus Christ (O. Kuss, "Der Geist," in *Der Römerbrief*, Regensburg, 1959, pp. 540–595).

### John on the Son

In the Johannine writings God's self-disclosure as one triunely personal has advanced to the farthest point. From the whole of the Gospel of John we single out in the first place the song of entry, the prologue. And here again we turn our attention to the expression *Logos* (Word). The first verse (Jn. 1:1) reads, "In the beginning was the Logos, and the Logos was with God, and the Logos was God." The expression "in the beginning" intends to bring to expression not a beginning of existence, but rather the being of the Logos before history. "Through him" is indeed everything else created. The prologue tends from the beginning towards the Incarnation and makes the unheard of assertion, to the praise of the incarnate Logos, that he existed without the "life of the flesh" before every creation. He is described in the first clause as individual subject. Through this he differs essentially from the Jewish-Hellenistic speculation of wisdom, from the Logos teaching of the Jewish-Hellenistic philosophy of religion of Philo, and more than ever from the Gnostic theses of powers of creation which issue and emanate from God successively. As Jesus has a post-history, so he has also a prehistory. He lives in personal communion with God, as is assured in the second clause. The glory which he has surely had with the Father is founded in his communion of life with God (Jn. 17:5). In the third clause it is plainly declared of the Logos that he is God. He is God just as that One with whom he exists in the closest communion of being and life. In this assertion the word "God" is not employed as a generic concept; the nature common to the Logos and God is what is being expressed. This is important, for only the fullness of the God-nature which the Son receives from the love of the Father gives the guarantee for the fullness of his power to reveal and save. Thus this assertion too is directed towards the activity of the Logos in the world, towards his life and salvation-function for men. The God-nature he has in common with the Father is the foundation for his power to save, hence the word "God" is not used as an expression of function, but of nature, a nature which is of course in the service of a soteriological function.

As the whole of John's Gospel has its roots in the Old Testament and in late Jewish theology, so the Logos concept must be traced back to Jewish-Christian ideas, but it cannot be traced back to Gnosticism. The Johannine Logos has nothing to do with Greek philosophy, which sought a uniform understanding of the world and of being, into which the reality of man could be inserted. In Stoic philosophy particularly, the Logos represents worldly reason and the rational moral conduct of men. On the other hand its connection with the Old Testament Word of God theology can easily be seen. In the Old Testament the Word of God has a creative and world-preserving power, it is a force bringing new life and salvation. Jesus himself uttered words of incomparable dignity. Whoever hears his word and receives it faithfully, hears the Word of God, but it is not because he declares the Word or the words of God that he is called Logos in the strict sense. It is rather that his words have unconditional value and power because he *is* the Logos—the divine bringer of revelation and salvation. Later Jewish theology usually preferred the concept "wisdom," in place of "word," though without eliminating "word" from its vocabulary. In rabbinic Judaism statements are made about the Torah that are similar to those in the prologue concerning the Word. In this school of thought the original Word of God was increasingly explained as referring to the Torah.

As a possible source for the Johannine Logos we must take into account the Jewish philosopher of religion, Philo. With his Logos doctrine he wanted not only to bridge the gap between a purely spiritual God and the material world, but also to explain activity and will in the human soul. Thus he gives the Logos divine attributes: to him belongs a cosmic function and at the same time he has a share in the salvation of men. Philo identified divine wisdom with the Logos, and thus related Biblical-Jewish and Hellenistic-philosophical thought, because he wanted to open a way from the Old Testament-Jewish thought world to the Hellenistic world.

It may be said that he does open up a mental world of Jewish Hellenism, in that he unites wisdom speculation with the Logos.

All the same, he probably did not directly influence John's Christian Logos hymn. Though this originated in an intellectual milieu similar to Philo's, it was a milieu that from the very beginning received its own character from Christian faith. The difference lies above all in the following factors: for Philo the Logos is an intermediate power between God and creation; his divinity is only figurative and the saving function which he assigns to him consists only in this, that the Logos governs the world and especially the souls of the wise: he is not a historical bringer of revelation and salvation to whom one must submit in faith.

A dependence of the Johannine Logos on Gnostic myth is frequently maintained (R. Bultmann), but in spite of some similarities (cf. the Mandean liturgies and the Odes of Solomon), the difference, indeed the opposition, is so great that one cannot assume a dependence. The old Gnostic myth was concerned with cosmogony: it sets out to explain the origin of an evil material world; it rests upon a dualism. The Word itself is a good force, which has redeeming power for men, who are redeemed through knowledge. The "Word" is another expression for the *Gnosis* which reveals to man the good essence which forms the core of his being, and the home and goal of his spiritual self. It might be surmised that John took the expression "Logos" from Gnosticism for its apologetic value, although he gives it a totally different meaning which is, quite simply, opposed to Gnosticism. But since the word Logos was also present in the Old Testament and in Jewish-Greek thought, it is much more probable that John took it from this intellectual sphere.[2]

In the further development of John's Gospel the word Logos is no longer used, the more familiar "Son" takes its place. We find Logos again in the First Letter of John and in his Apocalypse. In the latter (19:11–13) John describes seeing heaven opened and a rider coming forth whose name is "Faithful" and "True," who judges and rules with righteousness, whose eyes are like a flame of fire, and who wears many diadems. John adds, he is called the Logos of God. With this designation, which sounds like an echo from the Book of Wisdom, the judicial function of the Word is suggested (cf. Rev. 1:18).

The designation "Son" instead of "Logos" brings out the personal self of the Lord as well as his God-nature; his distinctness from the Father and union with him are brought out in ever new forms and images. The Son is older than the oldest generation, older indeed than the whole world. He exists before all (Jn. 8:23,38; 17:5). He owes everything to the Father (Jn. 13:3; 16:15), yet at the same time he is one with the Father in action and in being. The Father is in him and he is in the Father (Jn. 14:10f.). He is Lord and God. This is eternal life: to know God and the One he has sent, Jesus Christ (Jn. 17:3). The unity of Father and Son is the ground and archetype for the unity of Christians with one another (Jn. 14:20). The I-statements of Jesus form the high point of his revelation of God in John's Gospel. It cannot be denied that he attributes to the Son a preexistence with the Father and that he applies to him the predicate "God," however the relationship of God to the Son designated God may have been understood. On this precise question the Gospel gives us no details. On the one hand it proclaims the uniqueness of God, as do all the New Testament writings, but on the other it ascribes divinity to the Son.

## John on the Holy Spirit

John's Gospel offers the most mature doctrine on the Spirit in the New Testament. This is, of course, connected with the fact that the author interprets the historical Jesus in the light of his experience of the Lord after his resurrection in a way that is in advance of the other evangelists. It is just as self-evident for the author as for the other New Testament writers that the glorified Lord is identical with the historical Jesus, indeed John places an exceptionally strong emphasis on this. He begins with the teaching on the Spirit in the Old Testament and late Judaism. According to the Old Testament, the Spirit is to bring about a transformation of men at the end of history which will enable them to carry out God's will easily and fully (Ezek. 11:19; 36:25ff.; Is. 44:3). From the evidence of the Apocrypha and rabbinical literature, this idea appears to have been extraordinarily prevalent at the time of Jesus.

What is attested of the Holy Spirit in John's Gospel has its foundation in the beginnings of the Christ-faith itself. Jesus promised to send the Spirit and the promise was fulfilled on Pentecost (Acts 1:6–8; 2:1–11), and continues to be fulfilled in the descent of the Holy Spirit on those who believe and are baptized (Acts 2:38; 8:17f.; 19:6).

Jesus is himself the bearer of the Spirit (Jn. 1:32f.). This is why his entire activity is imprinted with the Spirit (is charismatic). Thus his words are spirit and life (Jn. 6:63), and true worship is to be worship in spirit and truth—that is to say, the worship established by Christ himself. John's Gospel, like Acts, attests that the risen Lord will pour out the Spirit on those who believe and will be the gift which establishes the Church. According to John 7:37–39, the Spirit will not be given before the Lord is glorified. His glorification and return to the Father are necessary before the Spirit can be sent; his coming presupposes the completion of the saving work of Christ. The coming of the Spirit in no way suggests a second revelation, following on that given by Jesus; his task is to keep the work of Jesus always present to his Church and to lead men into deeper and deeper participation in it.

At the hour of parting when the disciples were downcast because of the hardships, temptations, and threats they expected, the Lord comforted them with the promise of the coming of the Spirit. The Father as well as Jesus is called the dispenser of the Spirit (Jn. 14:16f.); the Father will send him at the Son's request and in his name. It is also said that Jesus will send him from the Father, or simply that the Spirit will come (Jn. 15:26). It is of great importance that Christ gives his followers the promise that he will send them "another Paraclete." "Paraclete" is a Greek word which means "Advocate," "Helper," or "Counselor"—not "Comforter."

The following texts from St. John's Gospel give Jesus' teaching on the coming of the Spirit:

I will ask the Father, and he will give you another to be your Advocate, who will be with you forever—the Spirit of Truth. The world cannot receive him, because the world neither sees nor knows him; but you know him, because he dwells with you and is in you (14:16f.). I have told you all this while I am still here with you; but your Advocate, the Holy Spirit whom the Father will send in my name, will teach you everything, and will call to mind all that I have told you (14:25f.). But when your Advocate has come, whom I will send you from the Father—the Spirit of truth that issues from the Father —he will bear witness to me. And you also are my witnesses, because you have been with me from the first (15:26f.). Now I am going away to him who sent me. None of you asks me "Where are you going?" Yet you are plunged into grief because of what I have told you. Nevertheless I tell you the truth: it is for your good that I am leaving you. If I do not go, your Advocate will not come, whereas if I go, I will send him to you. When he comes he will confute the world, and show where wrong and right and judgment lie. He will convict them of wrong, by their refusal to believe in me; he will convince them that right is on my side, by showing that I go to the Father when I pass from your sight; and he will convince them of divine judgment, by showing that the Prince of this world stands condemned (16: 5–11).

In John's first Letter the glorified Lord is himself called Paraclete (Advocate): "My children, in writing thus to you my purpose is that you should not commit sin. But should anyone commit a sin, we have one to plead our cause with the Father, Jesus Christ, and he is just. He is himself the remedy for the defilement of our sins, not our sins only but the sins of all the world (1 Jn. 2:1f.). Accordingly there appear to be two Paracletes, Christ in heaven and on earth the Spirit, who works in the Church of Christ as helper and counselor.

In these texts, the point at issue is not directly the nature, but rather the function of the Holy Spirit. Within the Church he makes the work of Jesus Christ present and opens up men's understanding of it. Consequently he is the principle of tradition in the Church and as principle and guarantor of Christian tradition, he is, so to speak, effectively united with the successors of the apostles. In consequence of this, it can be said that in a certain sense the Holy Spirit has a history, though not of course to the same extent that this is true of the Logos. The Logos has a history insofar as he is the principle of subsistence of the man Jesus, the Holy Spirit only insofar as he is the principle of tradition within the Christian community.

The Spirit is distinct from Jesus: he is sent by him, or by the Father, nevertheless he stands in the closest relation to the Lord,

and the Lord to the Spirit. Jesus Christ is himself present in the
Spirit. He had indeed to leave his disciples, but in place of his
bodily presence with them he became present in another way,
in the Spirit, and this means a greater openness and nearness than
any earthly presence could.

Since the Spirit constantly bears witness to Christ, refusal of
faith, the rejection of God's offer of salvation, becomes the real
sin. Sin shows itself in the refusal of belief in God's revelation
and in the salvation history accomplished by him, as well as in
the proclamation of God's revelation in the Church: either means
that a man is shutting himself off from God's love. The witness
which the Holy Spirit bears through the Church brings vindica-
tion and victory to Jesus and the Church, and at the same time,
a condemnation of unbelief. Of course, it is only faith that sees
and acknowledges this; unbelief sees only defeat in the death of
Jesus, in which the unbelieving rejoice: they think Jesus is no
longer here, because they cannot see him. Similarly, unbelief does
not see or recognize God, and this is the worst judgment that can
befall unbelief, that it should delude itself, complacently convinced that God does not exist, because the One sent by God
can no longer be seen. It is precisely in this that unbelief has
already been judged. Salvation is founded on faith in Jesus Christ
now and for the whole future: whoever refuses to accept him
remains in a state without salvation.

Now we come to the last question, which is the decisive one—
whether the Spirit is to be understood in Johannine theology as
a function or as a person. The function of the Holy Spirit is of
course attested, in the first place, but it is the expression and
action of a subject identical with neither the Father nor the Son.
This does not mean that the Holy Spirit is set apart from the
other two; nor is there anything suggesting this to be found in
the doctrine of the Trinity: such a conception would be a grave
misunderstanding. Although he is distinct from them, the Holy
Spirit exists in the closest connection with the Father and the
Son. The phrase "diversity in unity" is true here. The Holy Spirit
has the same relation to the Father as the Lord. In all this the
idea of sending is of special significance: it is used most of all
of Christ (see Jn. 3:17; 3:34; 8:42; 10:36). But what is said

of Christ is said in the same way of the Holy Spirit. In this the personhood of the Spirit appears more clearly than in the Synoptists or the thought of Paul. It may be mentioned, as a purely linguistic point, that in spite of the Greek neuter noun (*pneuma*) in the texts cited, the masculine demonstratives *autos* and *ekeinos* are used of the Spirit.

## THE HISTORICAL DEVELOPMENT OF THE DOCTRINE

In the course of history two forces have operated to bring about a further development of the Scriptural witness to the threefold personhood of God: the inner dynamism of the human spirit itself, and the encounter with non-Christian philosophies, especially Neoplatonism. Because Scripture does not give us a full conceptualization of the tri-personal life of God, many questions were left open which required answers. These were frequently given in concepts and thought-forms borrowed from Greek thought. This led to a differentiation of the ideas as Christians used them from the same ideas in Greek philosophy. Thus a problem had to be faced—how to translate the contents of the Scriptural witness into the conceptualizations of Greek thought without the original doctrine being altered, reduced, or added to, and so to reshape the Greek thought that it could become an effective vehicle for Christian concepts. The sharper the contradictions were seen to be, the more delicately the conceptual material had to be refined. This appeared to be an overwhelming task, especially because it seemed to endanger the principal item of the Old Testament revelation, monotheism. It is not to be wondered that it took centuries for an intelligible solution to be found or that many attempts fell by the way.

The word "Trinity" is already found in the apologists of the second century (*trias* in Theophilus of Antioch, *trinitas* in Tertullian in North Africa). For the purpose of an overview we can observe that we find belief in the Trinity expressed in the following places: in the liturgy of baptism (Didache 7; Justin, 1st Apology, 61; Irenaeus, *Against Heresies,* III, 17, 1; Tertullian, *On Baptism,* 13; Origen, Com. on Rom., 5,8; Cyprian, Epistle 73,18), in the Apostles' Creed, in the professions of faith of the second and third centuries. A particularly clear expression of it is the private confession of faith of Gregory Thaumaturgus (died c. 270). It is also clearly stated in the early doxologies. It is worth noting that in all these formulations the economic or salvation-history conception of the Trinity is combined with the metaphysical one.

The results of recent investigations show that it was the concept of sending or mission which formed the point of departure for a clarification of the doctrine of the Trinity. At first this idea contributed to the rise of subordinationism: the one sent appearing to be subordinate to the one who sends. Several biblical phrases such as "The Father is greater than I" (Jn. 14:28) appear to point in the same direction. An expression of this tendency is found in the explanation given of Old Testament theophanies, which are usually attributed to the Logos. The Father remains invisible, but the Logos becomes visible, he alone can show himself and thus mediate between the invisible God and the visible world. It is often said of the Logos that he has been brought forth from the Father so that he could create the world. In such ideas as these we can see Hellenistic influence. For a long time (until well into the third century) it remained hard for theology to distinguish clearly between the sending of the Logos —his world and redemption functions on the one hand—and his generation, his eternal divine origin, on the other. What seemed to be meant by the biblical concept of sending became emphasized through the influence of Stoic philosophy, especially the Stoic conception of emanation and return, the subject of which is the Logos, pantheistically understood. These kinds of subordinationist tendencies are found in almost all Church Fathers and writers of the second and third centuries: Justin, Athenagoras, Theophilus, Tertullian, Hippolytus, Novatian, Origen, Eusebius. This was almost inevitable. The "subordinationism" found in these theologians must be seen as the first unsuccessful attempts to bring monotheism into harmony with the true Sonship of God of Jesus Christ. Theologians tended more and more to explain the sending as a form of expression of an inner metaphysical structure of the divine life. We must make a distinction between their real concern for the truth and the imperfections in their solutions.

Transposing these into the inner-divine realm brought out the antinomy between unity and triplicity more and more clearly. It is easily understood that a series of attempts emerged which had later to be ruled out as heretical. These represent rationalistic simplifications of the problem—at one time the triplicity, at another the unity, at another the equality of the three persons was denied. But each of these attempts shows an important and justified concern, though they ended in undialectical one-sidedness.

The opposite of this concern for the monotheism fundamental to Christian revelation and faith is represented in the views that we list together under the name monarchianism. These were expressed in a dynamic (Ebionite) and a modalist (Sabellian, patripassian) form. According to the first, taught mainly by Paul of Samosata in the third century, the Father is one God and Christ is a man in whom the power of God dwells in a special manner. Similar explanations appeared in the writings of the Socinians in the sixteenth century. The second form, modalism (a word which originated in the seventeenth century and specifically out of the philosophy of Spinoza), considered God, insofar as he continues in his invisibility, as the Father; insofar as he became man, the Son; and insofar as he saves men, the Holy Spirit. Sabellius (third century), the most significant advocate of this thesis, taught that the Father, Son, and Spirit are not three real ways of existence of the one God, but only three ways in which God reveals himself (*modi*), three functions of the one God. Since according to these conceptions the Father himself suffered, the tendency was sometimes derisively called "patripassianism" (founder, Noetus of Smyrna). According to this thesis, God is triune only as God for us, not as God in himself. Similarly, Immanuel Kant sees in the Christian doctrine of the Trinity a symbolization of the divine power, wisdom, and goodness. Through Schleiermacher the dissolution of belief in the Trinity gained impetus in Protestant theology.

The second danger is exaggeration of the distinction. It attained its most extreme form in Arian subordinationism. The foundation for this could have been either the real ambiguity involved, or the Judaic idea of angels, or the Neoplatonic conception of "the One." Arianism went beyond the subordinationist tendencies of the period, not only in what it actually taught, but also—and this is decisive—in its intention. While the Fathers of the Church wanted to teach the equality of the persons but had no auspicious source for explaining it, in Arianism a doctrine was consciously and deliberately invented, using unsuccessful attempts at explanation. Arius put forward the thesis that God became Father through the fact that he brought forth the Son for the purpose of the creation of the world. The Son is a creature, since he is created out of nothing, though to be sure, a creature who differs from all others. He can also be called God, but only in a moral sense, insofar as he can be said to participate in God's nature and life. The adherents of Arius later divided into strict Arians, Anomoeians, and Homoiousians. With the teaching of the Council of Nicea, which condemned them, and with the Neoplatonic conception of the three essential hypostases, they share the thesis of the strict oneness of God, and of a certain triad of supreme principles, as well as their reciprocal connection through procession or emanation; the equality they rejected, though not all with the same intensity.

The Council of Nicea, in 325 (DS 125), defined that the Son proceeds from the nature of the Father and is of the same substance as the Father (*homoousios*). For the first time, the creed which it advanced confessed the Son as true God, begotten, not made. In the second part of the document it rejected the main points of Arius: that the Son was created in time out of nothing or out of another substance (*hypostasis*) or essence (*ousia*) than the Father, and that he is changeable. As the key concept for the presentation of the correct faith it employs the word "homoousios," which was borrowed from the Gnostics. It is to be observed that the Council, in spite of the strong emphasis on the metaphysical doctrine of the Trinity, brings forward in the same breath the "economic" or functional doctrine of the Trinity, in that it names the Father the All-sovereign and Creator of the visible and invisible, and says of the Son that through him all is created, that he became man for our salvation, suffered and died, and on the third day arose again from the dead, and will come again to judge the living and the dead. In this, the Council differs somewhat from the purely essentialist doctrine of the Trinity found in the creed attributed to Athanasius.

The fourth and fifth centuries were occupied with the struggle to obtain acceptance of the Council doctrine. At first, the relation of the Son to the Father was at stake, the relation of the Holy Spirit to these two was not yet reflected upon, but about 360 the Holy Spirit too was included in the discussion and the *homoousia,* i.e., identity of substance or oneness of substance, was expressed of him too. The protagonists of the struggle were above all Athanasius and the Cappadocian Fathers (Gregory of Nazianzus, Gregory of Nyssa, and Basil). Athanasius and Didymus were the creators of a theology of the Holy Spirit and prepared the definition of the Council of Constantinople in 381 (DS 150). Treatment of the Trinity in the early church reached its highest point in the West, in the theology of Augustine (*De Trinitate*).

In the struggle surrounding the Council of Nicea we find two different conceptions, the so-called Greek and Alexandrian-Latin. Up to a certain point these two different conceptions of the Trinity can also be called the salvation-historical and the metaphysical. The difference, of course, should not be exaggerated, but is, nevertheless, characteristic. In the conception represented by the Cappadocian Fathers in the East and by Ambrose in the West, the persons, especially the person of the Father, stand in the foreground of interest. In the Alexandrian-Latin, represented by Athanasius, Augustine, and his successors and adherents, it is the one substance which is the center of attention. There can be no doubt that in this the Neoplatonic doctrine of the One exerted a great influence. The temptation of the so-called Greek conception has always been subordination; the temptation on the other side is Sabellianism. But mostly it is a matter of no more than a temptation. In the first conception it is the oneness of God which tends to be lost sight of, in the second it is the triplicity of the persons. Apart from Alexandria, fourth century Greek theology sees the unity of the three persons as coming from the Father; this represents a continuation of the general view of the New Testament. The Cappadocian Fathers attempted to explain the equality of the persons by the introduction of the concept of relation, which had first been adopted in Arian circles. In this view the words

"Father" and "Son" represent relations. The same concept was also applied to the Holy Spirit, when reflection came to be given to him. Augustine took up the idea of the persons as relations in his theology of the Trinity, though without using the term relation itself. In the systematic theology of the West, apart from some few exceptions which remained ineffectual, the Alexandrian-Augustinian conception of the Trinity prevailed. The result of this was that belief in the Trinity came to have little influence on the whole of theological thought. In the exercise of the faith, however, particularly in the Roman liturgy, the biblical-Greek conception remains operative, as can be seen from the formula "through Christ in the Holy Spirit to the Father."

Terminology presents a special difficulty here. It was a long time before words could be agreed upon that would express the reality in God that was characterized as one and that which was characterized as three. Plotinus named the highest form of divinity and its principal emanations "hypostases." The word *prosopon* increased in importance in the fourth century through the influence of the Modalists, the Cappadocians, and the Antiochenes, and also through the Council of Chalcedon; but in the sixth century it lost ground. Origen named the three divine persons "hypostases." According to him, they are united through the correspondence, in fact the identity, of the *ousia*. In Latin theology the expression "three hypostases" was translated into *tres substantiae* and also *tres personae*. The second, coined by Tertullian, prevailed. The general vagueness of the terminology is seen in the fact that the Arians speak of the second, or third, divine hypostases, in the sense of the Neoplatonic scheme of gradations (the "One"—the Nous—the pneuma, or the world-soul). For this reason the Council of Nicea condemned the concept of three hypostases. In God, it taught, there is only one hypostasis, i.e., one substance and one reality. The Council employed the expressions *hypostasis* and *ousia* in an identical sense. Somewhat more than a generation later, however, the expression *hypostasis* was taken up again, though without the Neoplatonic-Arian gradation and division in God. Like the word *prosopon,* it was now used to designate the three "persons" in the one divine nature. For the rest, the word *homoousios,* first used by Paul of Samosata, which at the Council of Nicea became the party-cry of orthodoxy, had previously been rejected as Sabellian at the Synod of Antioch in 268 A.D. Basil the Great proposed the formula, already in use, *mia ousia-treis hypostaseis* (one substance, three hypostases, not three *prosopa*), and this prevailed. Around 380 the formula three *hypostases,* or three *prosopa,* was agreed upon (DS 421). But it was Leontius of Byzantium who first brought clarity to the matter in the East. In Latin theology, Augustine, continuing in the footsteps of the linguistically creative Tertullian, wrestled for a long time with these terminological difficulties and finally said it was simply a matter of convention to speak of *una essentia-tres personae.* In the course of the further development of Latin theology, however, it became the universal custom to use the word *persona* to designate the three divine subjects, and the words *essentia,* or *substantia,* or *natura,* to designate the one God-nature. Of course, it is essential that the analogical character of such terms be not forgotten.

With his metaphysical-psychological explanations, Augustine enlarged forever the doctrine of the Trinity beyond the concentration on the one substance which otherwise characterizes his viewpoint, and which undoubtedly did not come into being without Neoplatonic influence. In the mental life of man—*mens, notitia, amor;* or *memoria, intelligentia, voluntas,* to name only the most important triads—he saw the reflections of the trinitarian divine life. He gives this conception such an interpretation that not only the formal aspect (the question of terminology or expression), be it statically or dynamically understood, but also and above all the material aspect, that is, the content of the approach, is seen to be of value. In the exposition of the analogy Augustine shows himself stimulated in large measure by Plotinus. However, the Neoplatonist Marius Victorinus with his triad, *esse, vivere, intelligere,* exercised practically no influence on him. According to Augustine the inner-divine processes of begetting and breathing are to be understood as spiritual processes of knowing and loving. This Augustinian view was never forgotten. In the Middle Ages it was adopted and developed, to a great extent by Thomas Aquinas, and in part by Bonaventure.

Augustine thoroughly established the procession of the Holy

Spirit from the Father and Son as from one principle. The difference of view in relation to the Greeks is more a matter of expression than content. In the Greek doctrine it is immediately evident in the scope of the total conception that the Son receives his activity of spiration from the Father. The unity of the principle of spiration remains veiled however. In the Augustinian conception this unity becomes evident, but the reception of the activity of spiration of the Son from the Father remains veiled, though it is affirmed by Augustine without diminution. It underlies his statement that the Holy Spirit proceeds from Father and Son, but *principaliter* from the Father. Essentially the coordinating and the subordinating formulae are in agreement.

For the understanding of Augustine's doctrine of the Trinity it must not be overlooked that he joins the metaphysical view very closely with the idea of salvation history. In his great work on the Trinity he struggles continually with the metaphysical influence of Neoplatonism, and the salvation-historical influence of Scripture. It may well be said that the salvation-history view includes the metaphysical in itself, but not vice versa. Augustine concedes to the Neoplatonists (Plotinus) that they have advanced to knowledge of the Logos and in a certain sense also to knowledge of the Holy Spirit, but reproaches them in that they have not acknowledged the incarnation, that is, the element of salvation history.

The Trinity was described by Boethius in a purely metaphysical manner, and without the help of the Augustinian metaphysic. In particular it was by means of his definition of person that Boethius influenced the Middle Ages. He developed this definition in connection with the problem of Christology, but it plays its role in the doctrine of the Trinity also. It reads: *persona est rationalis naturae individua substantia*. This definition, of course, could not suffice, since none of the component concepts used could be employed without revision. In the twelfth century Richard of St. Victor replaced the Boethian definition by the following: *intellectualis essentiae incommunicabilis existentia*. Boethius used the Aristotelian concept of relation in an essentially more systematic sense than did Augustine, and thus gave it a penetrating power which it has retained. In his concept of relation everything is at hand in embryo that Thomas Aquinas later developed in full: the interpretation of relation as a special type of accident. The "being-in," *inesse,* determines the character of a thing as an accident, the *adesse* determines what kind of accident it is. In the case of the persons of the Trinity, their "being-in" coincides with the divine nature, since there are no accidents in God. With regard to the *adesse,* the relation is distinct from the divine nature, and so can operate to form a person. The Augustinian and the Boethian doctrines of the Trinity stimulated the medieval theologians. In the twelfth century the separation of the doctrine of God from the doctrine of the Trinity, which prevailed in theology until quite recently, gradually grew out of the conception of Boethius.

Before the final systematization in the thirteenth century, a very original attempt became prominent in the twelfth century, which occasional observations in Augustine could be found to support. Its author was Richard of St. Victor. He understood Father and Son as *diligens* and *dilectus* and the Spirit as *condilectus* (as loving one, beloved, and as co-beloved). In the *condilectio* (co-love) he saw the surety for the selflessness of love. He also (with others) believed himself able to bring forward "necessary" arguments for the Trinity. But the "necessity" here must be understood as hypothetical: the arguments have an inner necessity, but for us are recognizable as such only on the presupposition of revelation. In particular it is the concept of *summum bonum* from which he attempts, led by Neoplatonic conceptual themes, to deduce the Trinity. Richard's doctrine of the Trinity developed a certain force in Franciscan theology of the thirteenth century, but after that was almost forgotten.

Gilbert de la Porrée's (died 1154) conception of the Trinity caused a sensation in the twelfth century. He was reproached for accepting a real distinction between God and divinity (*deus-deitas*), as well as between the divine persons and properties (*pater-paternitas*). The distinctions he made, however, are not based upon an exaggerated realism, but rather upon linguistic-logical considerations. In spite of accusations and investigation he was not condemned.

Joachim of Fiore (died 1202) distinguished in the tri-personal

life of God three eras of salvation (*aetates*): that of the Father
before Christ, i.e., the era of the Law and the flesh, of the mar-
ried and the laity; that of the Son, the Christian, the period of
the clergy; finally the third and last, the era of the Holy Spirit
and the monks. The Fourth Lateran Council (1215) charged him
with teaching, to a certain degree, a *unitas collectiva et similitu-
dinaria* in God (DS 803).

In the thirteenth century the doctrine of the Trinity handed
down was developed further—by the early Dominicans and the
Franciscans more under the influence of the so-called Greek conception and the Neoplatonic train of thought; by Thomas more
under the influence of Augustine and Aristotelian thought, but
also not without the influence of Neoplatonism. Thomas represents a synthesis of Augustine and Boethius. Boethius, however,
would seem to have the greater importance for the Thomistic doctrine of the Trinity. In the thirteenth century the discussion concentrated on the question concerning the basis of constitution of
the persons. Is it the origin of the one person from the others,
containing a relation in itself, or is it the relation itself called
forth by the origin? Bonaventure accepted the first, Thomas the
second. In the Middle Ages the procession of the Holy Spirit
from Father and Son as from one single principle was considered
definitely established in the West. Over against the thesis, advocated by the Eastern Church since the ninth century, that the
Holy Spirit proceeds from the Father alone, the Second General
Council of Lyons in 1274 pronounced the dogma of the procession of the Spirit from Father and Son (DS 850; cf. also 188,
527, 1300, 1330f., and especially 1800).

The following centuries have seen further refinements of the
metaphysical conceptualization of the Trinity developed in the
thirteenth century particularly by Thomas, often to a most extreme degree of subtlety. In this regard the immense work of
Diego Ruiz Montoja (1562–1632) must be named especially. A
purely metaphysical treatment prevails in it, without any aspect of
salvation history.

The interpretation of the Trinity originating with Augustine and
Boethius suffers from a religious difficulty. Since in this way of
thinking the one nature comes to the fore, but the persons recede,

the question is, towards whom is the religious act directed. The answer, towards the one nature, conforms with this conception of the Trinity. However, then the nature itself would have to be conceived in some sort of way as subsisting as a person. The Greek conception does not suffer from this religious difficulty. Instead, it has to struggle with the theological difficulty respecting the oneness of God. If the Latin conception signifies a gain in speculative compactness, it signifies also a loss for the religious accomplishment of faith. If the Greek conception is in conformity with the religious act of faith, still it does not attain the height of speculative insight that the Latin does.

## THE OFFICIAL TEACHING OF THE CHURCH

In virtue of the Scriptural witness and the post-Apostolic development of faith, the following teaching developed in the Church. Some things here are to be understood as strict dogma, others as expressions of faith having greater or lesser connection with it. The boundary between the dogmas proclaimed by the Church and the statements of faith not meant as dogma is not easy to draw; but this does not play an important role for the life of faith; for this it is not necessary to reckon up the elements of the Church's teaching in detail according to their safety-factor. Given the immense significance of the belief in the Trinity for Christianity, and of the difficulty which the human mind encounters here, it is understandable that the Church repeatedly bears witness to its faith in the triunely personal God, and contrasts this faith with misinterpretations of it. Above all, the following doctrinal statements need to be taken into consideration: The Apostles' Creed (DS 6–63); a doctrinal pronouncement of Pope Dionysius (DS 112); the Nicene Creed (325 A.D., DS 125); The Creed of Epiphanius of 374 (DS 44); the Nicene-Constantinopolitan Creed (DS 150); the Creed of the Eleventh Synod of Toledo (675 A.D., DS 926); the Fourth Lateran Council, 1215 (DS 800); the Second Council of Lyons (DS 852); the Council of Florence (DS 1337); the condemnation of the trinitarian errors of Sozzini (Socinus) in 1555 (DS 1880); the rejection by Pope Pius VI in 1794 of some misleading expressions (DS 2697); the repudiation of trinitarian misinterpretations of the Viennese Anton Günther in 1857 (DS 2828); the pronouncements of Pius XII on the unity of the divine activity and the indwelling of the Holy Spirit (DS 3814).

According to these and other doctrinal pronouncements, the essential and binding content of the Trinity-faith can be presented as follows: the one God exists and lives in three persons. These are really distinct from one another but are identical with the divine nature, the divine substance. The oneness of God is founded in the oneness of the divine nature. For the sake of this unity it can be said that the one God exists as Father, Son, and Holy Spirit. Thus a quaternity is decisively excluded. In order that the real difference of the persons can be maintained nevertheless, a virtual, or formal, distinction between the divine nature and the persons must be accepted. The Father is without origin. The Son is begotten by the Father from the divine substance. The Spirit is not begotten but rather "breathed out" or "spirated." He proceeds in one single breath from the Father and from the Son as from one principle. In virtue of the divine procreation there are relations in God which constitute the persons, as well as personal characteristics which are at the same time distinguishing signs of the persons. The structural relations are Fatherhood, Sonship, and passive spiration. The three persons are, because of their relation to one another, in one another in the most intimate manner. The principle holds true: in God everything is one, so far as there exists no antithesis of relations. Like the divine nature, so also each act of the three persons is common, so far as the procreation of one person by another is not brought into question. They are one effective principle in regard to their external activity (*ad extra*). However, a distinction must be made between the activity of God as *causa efficiens* and as *causa formalis*.

The Church's doctrine is a developed expression of what Scripture and the tradition which interprets it testify. The metaphysical triune personhood taught by the Church appears within the salvation history attested by Scripture not only, but still above all as a Trinity of salvation history, i.e., as God's threefold act of salvation. The Trinity in history, however, is nothing other than the revelation of the metaphysical Trinity. In the creeds of the Church then, the salvation history Trinity too is not overlooked, but steps to the forefront of the witness of faith. This follows particularly from the Apostles' Creed and the Nicene-Constantinopolitan Creed, which have been authoritative for the liturgy of the Church.

THEOLOGICAL EXPOSITION

In this section the following questions will be treated: the origin of one person from the other or others, the relation of the persons to one another, and their saving relation to the world ("mission" in this special sense).

*Processions*

Father, Son, and Spirit can be understood neither in a static manner as external articulations of one divine nature, nor as the results of a divine process of becoming (be this interpreted as a development from below to above or from above to below). It is precisely through this that God differs from the world he created, which represents one single great process of becoming, of which it can rightly be said that God makes it make itself. To understand the divine procreations and processions, two things need to be kept in mind: they do not take place in time, with a "before" and an "after," and they are in no sense passive; they are eternal acts which lack any "earlier" and "later," which are always taking place, yet which simultaneously have also always reached their outcome. The fact that one person comes forth from another is identical with the act itself by which he comes forth. And if the single persons are not external articulations of the divine nature, still it is the uncreated and unending plenitude of the nature that is the ground of the issuance of one person from the other. In Scholastic terminology the divine nature is designated for this reason as the *principium quo,* the persons as the *principium quo,* the persons as the *principium quod* of the processions. The issuance of the Son from the Father, that is, of the second person from the first, is designated "generation" in Scripture, but there is no specific expression there for the issuance of the third divine subject. Theology affirms the identity of each divine subject with the divine nature, so that it can be said of the Son, "nature from nature," "light from light," "wisdom from wisdom," "God from God," "true God from true God." According to Holy Scripture and the teaching of the Church, the first divine person is the original ground of the two others. He is called Father, because he generates the second divine person. In this act of generation the reality which the word "Father" signifies occurs in a consummate way. All earthly fatherhood is a reflection of the eternal fatherhood of God. In the Patristic period the first divine person was characterized by the name *agennetos*. This is an ambiguous expression. It can mean either uncreated or unbegotten. This gave rise to great difficulties. Finally the solution was agreed on that *agennetos* (two "n's") meant "unbegotten," and *agenetos* (one "n") meant "uncreated." The Greek fathers, in continuing an idea of Aristotle, see, in addition, in the *agennesis* of the Father, i.e., the fact that he is unbegotten, the ground for his act of generation. In Latin theology (Hilary of Poitiers) the Greek *agennetos* is translated *ingenitus*. Augustine understood this word as a denial of the origin of the Father from one of the others (negative concept of a relational kind). In medieval theology, particularly in several theologians of the twelfth century and in the Franciscan theologians of the thirteenth century, continuing the ideas of the Greek fathers, the Father's unbegottenness was again seen chiefly as the ground for his activity of begetting (*innascibilitas*). Bonaventure thus speaks readily of the "first-ness" (*primitas*) of the Father. This idea is suggested by the Neoplatonic formula *bonum est diffusivum sui* (the good diffuses itself: Pseudo-Dionysius the Areopagite) and the idea is transformed and strengthened through the Aristotelian principle that the first of a series is the original ground of the series (*principium quia primum*).

According to the teaching of the Church the Holy Spirit proceeds from Father and Son as from a single ground of spiration in a single process of spiration (*una spiratione*). This connection is sufficiently indicated in Holy Scripture. According to John 15:26, the Holy Spirit proceeds from the Father. However, he is also called "Spirit of Jesus" (Acts 16:7), "Spirit of Christ" (Rom. 8:9; Phil. 1:19). According to the teaching of the Gospel of John, the Holy Spirit stands in the same relation to the

Son as the Son does to the Father (Jn. 6:46; 7:16; 8:26,38; 12:49; 15:26; 16:3; 17:3f.; 18:37). The Son bears witness to the Father, the Holy Spirit to the Son. The Son speaks what he hears from the Father, the Holy Spirit what he hears from the Son. The Son is sent by the Father, the Holy Spirit by the Son (Jn. 16:13–15). When John 15:26 says that the Spirit proceeds from the Father, this is not to be understood in an exclusive sense, as the other passages of Scripture just cited show. It means, rather, that everything that the Son has is from the Father, thus the procession of the Spirit too.

In the pre-Nicene period the fathers did not explain the data of revelation concerning the Holy Spirit more closely, because they were totally engaged by the discussion concerning the Son. They were satisfied to repeat Scriptural texts which refer to the Spirit. Materially, if not also formally, we meet the doctrine of the procession of the Holy Spirit from the Son in Alexandrian theology. For example, Origen says that the Holy Spirit owes his existence to the Son. We find a similar formulation with Athanasius. He nowhere says expressly that the Spirit proceeds from the Son. He speaks, however, of the procession of the Spirit in such a way that what he says would remain unintelligible if he did not have the conviction of the procession of the Spirit also from the Son (cf. the 3rd Speech against the Arians, No. 24; likewise, the 3rd Letter to Serapion, No. 1). We find the same teaching in the Cappadocians. Basil says that the Spirit proceeds from the Father through the Son. He rejects the opinion of Eunomius (died between 392 and 395) that the Father is the sole source of the Holy Spirit. Rather, the Son has everything in common with the Father, and the Holy Spirit is called in Scripture not merely Spirit of the Father, but also Spirit of the Son (e.g., *Contra Eunomium* 2,34; 3,1; *De spiritu sancto* 18,45). Gregory of Nyssa thinks no differently (cf. Rouet de Journal, *Enchiridion Patristicum,* 1037f.). Like Basil, Gregory has the Holy Spirit proceed immediately from the Son and mediately from the Father. In his work *Ancoratus* Epiphanius used the formula that the Holy Spirit proceeds from the nature of the Father and the Son, or from Father and from Son. In Western theology Tertullian (*Adv. Praxean,* 4) attests that the Holy Spirit originated not from some other place, but from the Father through the Son. Hilary (*De trinitate,* 2,29) teaches that Father and Son are the ground of the Spirit's existence. With Augustine the Western doctrine becomes clearly developed. He says that the Holy Spirit proceeds from both (*ab utroque*). However, he does not use the term *filioque* expressly. This formula appears to have originated in Spain. With Augustine we find in a certain sense a synthesis of the Latin and the Greek conceptions, when he occasionally says that the Father *principaliter* breathes forth the Holy Spirit. In the Greek interpretation it comes more strongly to the fore than in the Latin that the Son has his whole personal being, which includes the spiration of the Holy Spirit in it, from the Father. In the Latin conception the idea is more prominent that Father and Son procreate the Holy Spirit in a single act, without it being denied, however, that in doing so the Son also owes his activity of spiration to the Father.

So far as the official teaching of the Church is concerned, the procession of the Spirit from Father and from Son was pronounced at the Second Council of Lyons (DS 850), as well as at the Council of Florence (DS 1300ff.). Pope Leo III explained that the procession of the Holy Spirit from the Son too must be preached, but that the insertion of the formula into the Creed is superfluous. However, the formula *filioque* was inserted into the Creed, probably by Pope Benedict VIII about the year 1013 at the request of the Emperor Henry II. The Greek patriarch Photius (died 1078) made the procession of the Holy Spirit from the Father alone a principal dogma of the Greek Church, and thus provided a dogmatic foundation for the separation of the Eastern Church from the Roman, which was taking place primarily for reasons of Church politics. It is noteworthy that Pope Benedict XIV, in the year 1742 (the Bull *Etsi pastoralis*), said, "If the Greeks are likewise obliged to believe in the procession of the Holy Spirit from the Son too, they are, however, not obliged to confess this in the Creed."

For a deeper understanding of the immanent divine life processes it is important to interpret them in a manner appropriate to absolute Being. As we have emphasized earlier, the highest form of being is spiritual Being, and, in particular, not in such a way that the spiritual would be added to Being as a specific quality of it. Rather, Being itself in its highest and most actual form is spiritual Being, which exhibits itself in the acts of knowing and willing. We have understood as the measure of Being the power a thing has of returning to itself. It is *reflexivum sui.* We could also say: self-possession, which is not a static state, but a constant taking hold of self.

With these considerations we come to the idea of the personal. The personal has its home not in Greek thought, but in sacred Scripture. In it man is brought into relief, over against nature. He has, in a certain sense, absolute worth. He is God's conversation partner. God wants him as a conversation partner in a way so unconditional that he himself becomes man though without ceasing to be God. Thus it is understandable that the problem of the person emerges in the early Christian reflections concerning the triunely personal life of God and the structure of Jesus Christ. Even though we have already said something about the concept of the personal, yet the problem must be brought still more closely into view, firstly because the matter itself requires it, but also because today great attention is being given to the personal in the anthropological, as well as in the existential view, but in particular in the type of thought called personalism. The definition of Boethius given earlier was constructed in the framework of Greek thought with its concern for things and for essences. It not only cannot be employed as it stands to explain the triune personhood of God; it contains the danger of three gods, i.e., three divine individuals. In the sense in which Boethius defines the term we cannot speak of three persons in God. However, the concept created by Boethius can be opened up in such a way that it is freed from this danger and is transposed from a static to a dynamic form. It contains a synthesis of two elements, on the one hand a universal spirituality, open to the world, and stretching towards the entirety of the world, and on the other hand the individual and irreplaceable actuality of this openness in a concrete subject. According to this exposition, the medieval explanations of the personal, especially those offered by Richard of St. Victor, Albert the Great, Thomas Aquinas, and the Franciscan theologians, particularly John Duns Scotus, would be less a correction than a continuation of Boethius. In fact, to be sure, the medieval theologians

believed that for the sake of theology they had to criticize
Boethius. Richard of St. Victor defined the person as the *intellectualis essentiae incommunicabilis existentia* (the incommuni-
cable mode of existence of spiritual nature). Person is, according
to him, *existens per se solum iuxta singularem quendam rationalis
existentiae modum*. He believes this definition is applicable not
only to man, but also to the angels and to God. In a similar
manner, Thomas Aquinas speaks of *incommunicabilis subsistentia*.
The concept of person, according to him, refers not *ad essentiam
sive naturam, sed ad subsistentiam essentiae*. The openness for the
whole of Being, for Thomas, combines with the *redire in se ipsum*
(the return to itself). Thus he can frankly say that the human
spirit is in a certain sense everything. This return to itself he
identified materially with the act of subsisting. In Scotus we find
brought out even more strikingly the directness of man's relationship to God and man's freedom in openness to decide for the
entirety of that which he takes into himself in knowledge.

The concept of person is thus a question of the way in which
a certain type of nature takes on a concrete and actual existence.
This existence consists in an act of self-possession. Thus the ontological and the psychological combine into a unity. It would,
however, be a constriction to identify the being of a person with
his consciousness of himself. In the eighteenth and nineteenth
centuries the concept of person passed through innumerable trans-
formations. In contemporary personalism an attempt is made at
least in part to win back again to a certain extent the old ontological conception. However, the greatest weight is placed on the idea
that the being of a person comes into existence in dialogue. Frequently personhood is identified with a relationality, with the ordering of the one to the other, thus with dialogue or the capacity for
dialogue. As important as the capacity for dialogue is for the understanding of the personal, still it is one-sided to allow the personal to be merged in the capacity for dialogue. It must be stressed
that man, or the person, stands in himself and in his own initiative
opens himself in relation to the other, in relation to the Thou. A
man can open himself to another only when he is deeply founded
in Being. To be sure, if he does not open himself in relation to the
other, i.e., if he does not go beyond himself and in this going be-

yond the self to the Thou again return to himself, then his personality remains undeveloped and unfulfilled. Through the act of reaching out towards what is concrete man himself becomes more and more concrete. Were the personal seen only in encounter, in relation, then it would evaporate into a mere conglomeration of acts. If, on the other hand, men turn towards each other as persons from their basis as individuals, then it is a matter of Being, not merely of having, i.e., then they develop themselves to their true Being. To be a person is a foundation-giving act of Being over against nature. The essential mystery rests in this, that with each person a new, initial, original disclosure of Being as a whole is begun (Guggenberger).

Since Augustine, the divine act of begetting has been considered as an act of knowledge, and the divine spiration as a movement of love using the analogy of the human mind and will, and taking the Johannine Logos doctrine as point of departure. In this connection it must be stressed that it is not a matter of voluntary acts of God, but of the actualization of His God-being. God is *actus purus,* i.e., he exists as eternal self-comprehension, as eternal Being-in-itself in eternal self-comprehension.

In the statements of the Old Testament concerning God and · man it can be recognized that Being in the fullest sense has a dialogical structure. To spiritual Being, i.e., to Being in the proper and highest, in the fullest sense, it belongs essentially to go beyond the self and to return to oneself in the going beyond the self. When man becomes open in relation to the totality of reality, in the act of returning to himself, that is, in reflection upon himself, then he becomes distinct from others, and through that achieves his consciousness of self and at the same time knowledge of the other, towards whom he reaches out in the act of going beyond himself. This process of going beyond the self and returning to oneself holds true also for that process in which the man wants expressly to know only himself. Here the I differentiates itself within itself. It transcends itself and in this transcendence turns back again to itself. The I enters into a relationship with itself. It must, so to speak, double itself, in that it forms an idea of itself in relation to itself. Difference, transcendence, and relation belong for this reason to the formal structure of Being in the full sense. The personal being achieves the depth of his self-realization not when he circles around in himself, but rather only when, in virtue of the openness peculiar to him, he reaches out above himself and goes beyond himself towards objective values, but above all, when he goes beyond himself towards another subjectivity, towards a human Thou. This going beyond oneself towards the human Thou is characteristic of the human spirit. Only in this encounter does it achieve the depth of its existence. The internal human encounter, the encounter of the human I with itself, is effected in a truly meaningful way only when it contains within itself the inter-human encounter. The internal human dialogue presupposes the dialogue between human beings. Its depth is conditioned by this.[3]

The same process, with a specific modification, manifests itself in the will also. While the human spirit in knowing takes back into itself, as an image, the object which is grasped by him in an act which is self-transcending, and thus himself becomes, so to speak, the thing known, in willing he achieves identity within the object. In the act of the will, man, in openness to the entire world, but especially to other subjects, reaches out in free initiative towards the Thou, in self-transcendence and in transcending himself towards the Thou makes himself present in him. Thus he affirms the Thou, and in this act of affirmation he affirms himself. Therefore in the affirmation of the Thou he turns back to himself and thereby accomplishes his own self-affirmation and his self-possession. Consequently, he achieves identity with himself not in himself, but rather in the Thou, in the "object."

From such considerations we reach an approach to the immanent divine life-movements of generation and "spiration." It must be emphasized once again that the dialogical structure of spirit can be perceived only in virtue of the picture which the Old Testament gives of man and of God himself. We are not simply beginning with human experience then, when we attempt to perceive a dialogical structure in God. Rather, we come from God to man, and only in virtue of that which revelation tells us about man can we achieve again, in a retrogressive movement, knowledge of God. Thus our understanding of man receives a theological foundation, and, inversely, our understanding of God has a background and point of departure which are anthropological.

As Thomas Aquinas emphasizes, God too turns himself in his knowing and in his life towards himself. God's turning towards himself takes place, however, differently from that of the creature, without any mediation. In that lies the difference between the finite and infinite being. In his self-knowledge God too sets himself in a certain sense in relation to himself as knowing subject and known subject. God therefore encounters himself in self-knowledge in a manner similar to the way man does. But now the decisive question arises, a question which can no longer be answered from the considerations undertaken up to now, namely, the question of in what manner God as knowing subject stands in relation to himself as the one known. How is this inner-divine relation to be understood? From the divine self-disclosure and only from it, we know that it is not, as with the creature, a merely formal, but rather a real antithesis. We can surmise why this inner-divine self-antithesis of God is real. It has its ground in the depth of the divine being, in absolute Being. While the creature comes to the depth of his being only by way of mediation, in the encounter of I and Thou, the self-antithesis of God within the divine life leads to a real diversity, because the divine nature, as a result of its absolute depth, is able to present itself only in this way. This reality of the inner-divine difference between God as the knowing subject and God as the known object, which became accessible to us through the divine self-disclosure, leads to additional decisive insights. God as known is not "object." In no way does a subject-object relationship rule in God. God as known is simultaneously subject, i.e., he turns himself again to God the knowing. The relationship of person to person, of Father and Son, develops. As a result of the returning movement to the Father, the Son himself does not beget an additional person. There is, therefore, the relationship of a real encounter. The first divine person includes in his own consciousness the consciousness and self-comprehension as God; further, the consciousness as procreating subject and the consciousness of the second divine subject set over against him, the Son. The first divine person cannot have a consciousness of himself without the consciousness of the other, the Son. In God there is no supra-consciousness in which the Father's (and the Son's) consciousness is comprised as a partial form, but only a single divine consciousness of self and a single divine self-comprehension which is effected in the mode of consciousness as Father and Son. In this the divine essence, absolute Being cannot be understood as a background out of which grows the personal consciousness. There is in God absolutely no a-personal Being. The divine essence exists as Father and as Son. The divine essence is necessarily personal and, specifically, as we have seen before, in the form of double personhood.

In this a further idea is of great importance. In that the Father accomplishes the self-knowledge of God, he also knows the possibilities of emptying himself into non-divine reality. In the procreation of the Son through dialogical self-antithesis, he shares this knowledge of the world with the Son. Augustine stated, under the influence of Neoplatonism, that the world-ideas of God are expressed in the Son. Christian "exemplarism" has its foundation in this. With utilization of the concept of the Logos Augustine gave to the fruitful divine knowing the turn that the Father, in his penetrating and comprehensive self-knowledge, utters both himself and the world in a Word which is personal. The act of generation is a "speaking." The Son is "Word." By virtue of his return to the Father he is at the same time "answer" in German (*Wort* and *Antwort*).

In the turning back of the Son, brought forth in the act of knowledge of the Father, to the Father, the unity of Father and Son is effected. It carries the seal of love. This love is called in Scripture the Holy Spirit. This characterization, accepted today by almost all theologians, began with Augustine, after a prelude in Greek theology, perhaps with Basil and with Epiphanius. As a result of his function in effecting the unity of Father and Son, the Holy Spirit can be called the divine "we" (H. Muhlen, *Der Heilige Geist als Person,* Münster, 1963). In the exposition of his thought here, Augustine is again influenced by Neoplatonism. He himself refers to those passages of Scripture in which the Holy Spirit is brought into relation with love. Our considerations have shown that with the "psychological" processes it is a matter of metaphysical aspects and implications of absolute Being. These considerations originated with Augustine, but experienced various modifications in medieval and modern theology. Of course, the processes in God can in no way be understood as a true becoming. We can speak of God only in human ways. What we can express by words which mean "becoming" is to be understood in God as an eternal, absolute consummate Being. This consummation, however, is not a rigid block of essence. It is the deepest and highest vitality. But in order to be able to express this, we must make use of anthropomorphic expressions.

A final word should be said concerning the procession of the Holy Spirit. Love is, so to speak, the heavenly climate, the life sphere of God. As a result of this, all true love in the earthly realm can be understood as an epiphany of God. In the Johannine writings God himself is called love (1 Jn. 4:8). According to our earlier explanations, the word "God" in that passage designates the first divine person. From this aspect we can characterize from the outset the process of knowledge in which God sets himself over against himself in the inner-divine realm and thus procreates the Son as a knowledge born out of love. In this view it becomes yet more profoundly understandable that the Son, procreated by the Father, devotes himself again to the Father in love. The Holy Spirit appears then as expression, sign, or guarantee of the connection of Father and Son. The dialogue in the inner-divine realm thus shows itself as a dialogue of love.

Regarding the dilemma that we do not have a similarly characteristic designation for the third divine person, as for the first and second, Augustine explained somewhat artificially that as the Father and the Son's love he is common to both and thus deserves that designation, namely the designation "holy" and the designation "spirit," which belongs to each of the two. The designation of the Spirit as "gift," occurring in Scripture and frequently treated by the Greek as well as the Latin Fathers, has a connection with the characterization of the Spirit as the love of the Father for the Son and of the Son for the Father, thus as the self-affirmation of the Son in the affirmation of the Father and the self-affirmation of the Father in the affirmation of the Son. According to Augustine, the Spirit is called "gift" precisely because he is love. The first gift of love is indeed love itself. The Holy Spirit is, according to Augustine, God's gift to men. In this view it is likely that the Holy Spirit will be seen less in his inner-

divine-metaphysical than in his functional salvation-historical significance (see Jn. 7:38f.; 4:7–14; Acts 2:38; 8:29; 10:45).
However, the expression has a deeper meaning insofar as the risen
and glorified Christ promised and sent the Holy Spirit to his own.
All those who believe in Christ and are baptized in his name are
bearers of the Holy Spirit. Augustine seeks to meet the objection
that the characterization of the Spirit as gift endangers his eternity
by pointing out that though the Spirit is not a gift from eternity, he
is capable from eternity of being given (*donabile*); but precisely in
this way the relationship of the Spirit to creation is a constitutive
element of his personhood.

## Relations

In the exposition so far the divine relations have often been spoken
of, without the phrase having been more closely explained. To understand the Church's belief in the Trinity a more precise interpretation of that which we call inner-divine relations is indispensa-
ble. This conception, derived from the concept of relation created
by Aristotle, was employed in the Trinity theology of the Fathers
of the fourth and fifth centuries with various shadings, although
they were not aware of its precise origin. For the interpretation
of the inner-divine life it acquired a decisive significance. The
concept attained such importance that in a statement of faith of
the Council of Florence (DS 703) it was emphasized that there
are real relations in God.

By a "relation" is understood the ordering of one thing to another. A distinction can be made between the bearer of the relation, the goal or term of the relation, and the ground or basis of
the relation. If we apply these elements to God, then we come to
the conclusion that the divine persons stand in relation to one
another in virtue of this origin. The bearers of relation are Father,
Son, and Spirit. The divine processions are the foundations of the
relations. The Father, Son, and Spirit differ from one another only
through these relations. The Father is, therefore, distinguished from
the Son through a relation based on the procreation of the Son.
The Son is distinguished from the Father through the relation based
on the proceeding of the Son from the Father. Father and Son are

in turn distinguished from the Holy Spirit through the relation which is based on the spiration of the Spirit. The Spirit is distinguished from Father and Son through the relation which is founded in his procession from Father and Son.

We must go a step further. As a result of God's Oneness, ruling throughout the whole of absolute Being and which we must maintain with all vigor in spite of the dialogical character, the relation of the one to the other is always identical with the activity of bringing forth or of going. forth. Since the individual divine persons are distinguished from one another only through the processions and the relations identical with these, we come to the astonishing outcome that the persons, under the aspect of their mutual diversity, must be designated as relations. Here the metaphysical character of the inner-trinitarian divine life is raised to its highest point. However, one would err if one wanted to maintain that the persons are nothing other than relations. They are different from one another through the character of the relations which belong to them respectively. As Thomas Aquinas says, they are subsisting relations. This signifies that each of the relations is identical with the divine nature itself. The divine nature subsists in three relations. The divine persons are constituted in their diversity through the relations. They are, however, constituted as persons through the twofold element of nature and of relation, in connection with which it must be observed that the relation is identical in each case with the nature itself.

Here follows a scarcely soluble difficulty. It lies in this, that on the one side the relations are identical with the divine nature, but that on the other side the relations, or rather the relations founding the diversity, are three in number. Thus it appears that an identity and a non-identity of relation and nature is to be admitted, if the triplicity is not to be lost in the oneness. As indicated, Thomas Aquinas attempts to solve this difficulty through a very subtle distinction in the concept of relation. It appears, however, that through such an attempt at solution the incomprehensible mystery is more emphasized than illuminated. The formal distinction made by John Duns Scotus, under the influence of statements by Augustine and Bonaventure, and strictly carried out by him through the whole of his theology would seem to lead further. According to Scotus, each nature is that which is expressed through its definition. In its nature expressed by its definition, no thing can be identical with another nature that is expressed by another definition. It is and must be different from it. That in God it does not, as in the creature, come to real differences of the essences expressed through their respective definitions is founded in the fact that through the radical eternity of God all attributes or modes of relation, expressible through differing definitions, are held together in unity. According to Scotus, it cannot, however, be denied that by the word "nature" we mean something other than by the word "relation"; that by the word "righteousness" we mean something other than by the word "love." Were we, according to him, to admit a real identity, then our statements concerning God would no longer be significant. They can retain their sense only when that which we mean by our statements also remains preserved in God according to its formal content. Thus, according to Scotus, a formal distinction exists between the nature of God and the relations, a distinction which, however, does not further develop to a real one. In virtue of this formal distinction, there can, according to him, be three relations, even though there is only one single divine nature.

How far the Scriptural statements in this realm were further developed by the doctrine of the Church is clear from the statement of the Council of Florence (February 4, 1441) laying down the principle in God everything is one where there is no opposition of relations (DS 703). This formula has a long previous history, beginning with Gregory of Nazianzus, according to whom there is full identity among the three divine persons, with the exception of the relations of origin. But Augustine too played a significant role in the adoption of this formula. He says: God is absolutely simple, because he is what he has, with the exception of that which each person is with regard to the others. The development of the sentence "God is love" leads to the sentence "God is a dialogue of love."

At the close of this consideration there is one further characteristic distinction between the so-called Greek and Latin conceptions of the Trinity that should be mentioned. The Greek Fathers understand the divine relations as media for the mutual life-exchange of the persons founded in their distinctness through the relations. The Father, identical with the divine nature, communicates himself in begetting, i.e., in the fruitful knowledge of himself, continually to the Son, so that an eternal movement from Father to Son takes place. Something similar must also be said of the Son and the Holy Spirit in the appropriate manner. Here, of course, the Greek and the Franciscan theology of the Middle Ages, which adopted the former, have to struggle with a difficult problem, the question, namely, of how the Father as procreating subject can become active, if he is constituted in his personhood only through the relation to the Son which consists in the activity of begetting. In the Patristic period there was no reflection upon this. In the medieval theology of the Franciscans a distinction was made between the initial personhood and the full personhood of the Father. In any case, the Greek Fathers defend their doctrine of relation in a more dynamic than static manner. Augustine, on the contrary, cultivates a static conception. He takes the existence of the divine persons into view, rather than their origin. He starts from the oneness and seeks to explain how the oneness presupposed by him is not endangered by the tri-personhood. To this he answers: because the three persons are of a relative character. While the Greeks emphasize more the mutual interpretation of the divine persons, the Latin conception expresses the inseparable togetherness of the persons. It will be found that these distinctions have important consequences for the understanding of the incarnation.

*The Three Divine Persons as One Efficient Cause*
*in External Activity*

The activity of the three divine persons by way of efficient causality in regard to the world constitutes one single and simple act. This means that they do not join together in a kind of working community. Scripture indicates this unity of action both in regard to the act of creation and also to that of salvation. For example, John has Jesus say, "In very truth I tell you, the Son can do nothing by himself; he does only what he sees the Father doing: what the Father does, the Son does, for the Father loves the Son and shows him all his works, and will show greater yet, to fill you with wonder. As the Father raises the dead and gives them life, so the

Son gives life to man, as he determines. And again the Father does not judge anyone, but has given full jurisdiction to the Son" (5:19ff.). Scripture ascribes one and the same act at one time to the Father, at another to the Son, and at another to the Holy Spirit.

In official declarations of the Church this unity of the divine efficient causality is presented as an expression of the uniqueness of God. It is a logical consequence of monotheism (cf. DS 531, 851, 1331). It was stated clearly by Pope Pius XII in his encyclical *On the Mystical Body* (1943; DS 3814f.).

It does not contradict this view to see, as it were, certain inner stages in this single activity of God, for example, to follow the Greek conception of the Trinity and view the Father as the beginningless beginning of every divine act and the Son and Holy Spirit as receivers. In this view the one ground of all divine activity is the Father. In Latin theology it is the one divine nature. If the trinitarian God approaches man only as one active subject, then man can turn in faith or prayer only to this one active subject. But in this case we encounter the great difficulty of trying to decide what would constitute one active subject. For example, should we pray to the divine nature? The tendency of a view like this is to remove the Trinity from the life of faith.

As a result of this situation it has become customary in theology to ascribe particular qualities or activities to particular persons of the Trinity without understanding these qualities or activities as peculiar to that one person: appropriations, but not *propria*.

### "Missions"

While the unity of God's action in the world is a matter of efficient causality, the divine missions are a matter of formal causality. They function therefore in a different realm. We have already seen that the idea is common in the New Testament of one divine person "sending" another. Typically, it is never said of the Father that he is sent. The Son is sent by the Father. The Holy Spirit is also sent, sometimes by the Father, sometimes by the Son, sometimes by the Father through the Son.

These "sendings" or "missions" represent the ways in which

God communicates himself to his creation. Here we must anticipate some considerations that would normally come later. God exists as Father by the fact that he generates a Son in an act of knowledge and communicates himself to him; and he brings forth the Holy Spirit in an act of love with the Son, and again gives himself to him with the Son. Likewise the personhood of the word is identical with the fact of his being generated by the Father. When the Father sends the Son to the man Jesus and in this way communicates himself to Jesus, Jesus' personhood becomes identical with that of the Eternal Word. Thus the Father of the Eternal Word is at the same time the Father of the man Jesus. Despite its immanent character, therefore, God's eternal fatherhood is directed towards historical fatherhood.

This situation does not contradict the principle previously established that God's acts of efficient causality in the world are always the unified act of the three divine persons, because this is not a case of efficient causality but of formal causality.

If it is true that the Father is in this way the ultimate principle of Jesus then we must say that the Father's sending of the Son reaches its culmination only in the risen Christ. It is only in the transformation that accompanies the resurrection that the sending of the Son, the Word, reaches its goal.

However, we cannot isolate Jesus from the rest of mankind, and this leads to the sending of the Holy Spirit. On the basis of Jesus' transformation the Holy Spirit is sent to mankind, both to the community of the Church, and through the Church, to the rest of mankind. It is he who leads men to unity with one another, since he is the love which unites Father and Son. Because of him Jesus and mankind form a "We."

The personhood of the Holy Spirit consists in the fact of his going forth from the Father and the Son. Those who live in his influence, therefore, are brought, if only in an analogous way, into the relationship of the Spirit to the man Jesus, whose spirit is one of total devotion to the Father.

The idea of "mission" then represents the movement of salvation from God through the risen Christ in the Holy Spirit to men, and then a return movement of the men thus gripped by the Spirit, through the Son, to the Father. It works much better with

# 168

168 *The Christ Event*

the Greek conception of the Trinity than with the Latin. Correspondingly, the missions have an eschatological character. The movement of the world towards its consummation represents a continuation externally of the inner life of God. They have as their goal the absolute future, of which Paul says that then God will be all in all (1 Cor. 15:23).

*Notes*

[1] See Mt. 15:24; Lk. 1:43; 7:3; 9:52; 14:32; 19:14; 19:32; 20:20; 22:8; Jn. 3:17; 3:34; 5:36; 6:29, 57; 7:29; 8:22; 10:36; 11:42; 14:16f.; 14:25f.; 15:26f.; 16:5–11; 17:3, 8, 21, 23, 25; 20:21; Acts 3:20; 3:26; 10:36; 1 Jn. 4:9; 4:14; 1 Pet. 1:12.

[2] Cf. R. Schnackenburg, *Das Johannes-evangelium*, Part 1 (Freiburg, 1965), pp. 169–257.

[3] Cf. H. Kringa, *Transcendentale Logik* (Munich, 1964); see also B. Welte, *Auf den Spuren des Ewigen* (Freiburg, 1965).

# ◄II

# The Person and Nature of Jesus

# ‹7

# *The Testimony of Scripture*

In presenting the evidence of the New Testament the early Christian beliefs about the historical Jesus which appear in the Acts of the Apostles should be set down first. After that the three Synoptic Gospels will be considered, then the image of Christ in the Pauline epistles, in the Letter to the Hebrews, John's writings, and finally a supplement from the remaining epistles of the New Testament. Attention must be given to the difference between the Jesus who preached and the Christ who was preached. But this difference will not provide the basis of division for the following presentation. Important as it is, it is not as fundamentally important to dogmatic theology as it is to biblical studies: the theologian can simply proceed from the conviction that the whole of Scripture is inspired.

## ACTS

In Acts we find old traditions, specifically those of the early community of Jerusalem. In the speeches of Peter and Paul, especially, our attention is called again and again to the fact that it is the Old Testament God of the Covenant who sent Jesus and worked through him. It was he who led him to his death and raised him from the dead, who completed his plan of salvation, and through whom he addressed his final words of salvation to men. Therefore final salvation is attached to the eschatological savior-personality of Jesus of Nazareth. The Old Testament God of the Covenant who continues to lead the destiny of his people, whether in judgment or mercy, is behind all the events in Jesus' life: through him God has decisively entered into history. Jesus accomplished only what God gave him to do, and what he did constitutes the fulfillment of the well-known promises of the Old Testament. Even though this fulfillment did not occur in the way that had been expected, the believer could recognize that Jesus had fulfilled the prophecies about the Redeemer. Whoever is against Jesus is against the living God himself; whoever affirms the self-revelation of God must also affirm Jesus, and this will bring him salvation. Considering the significance of these testimonies of faith, it is appropriate to quote two somewhat lengthy passages from Acts, in which we find the essential belief of the early Church. These are Acts 2: 22–36 and 3:13–26. The first is Peter's Pentecost sermon, the second the sermon he gave on the occasion of the healing of the man born lame:

Men of Israel, listen to me: I speak of Jesus of Nazareth, a man singled out by God and made known to you through miracles, portents, and signs, which God worked among you through him, as you well know. When he had been given up to you, by the deliberate will and plan of God, you used heathen men to crucify and kill him. But God raised him to life again, setting him free from the pangs of death, because it could not be that death should keep him in its grip.
For David says of him:

I foresaw that the presence of the Lord would be with me always,
For he is at my right hand so that I may not be shaken;
Therefore my heart was glad and my tongue spoke my joy;
Moreover my flesh shall dwell in hope,
For thou wilt not abandon my soul to Hades,
Nor let thy loyal servant suffer corruption.
Thou hast shown me the ways of life,
Thou wilt fill me with gladness by thy presence.

Let me tell you plainly, my friends, that the patriarch David died and was buried, and his tomb is here to this very day. It is clear therefore that he spoke as a prophet who knew that God had sworn to him that one of his own direct descendants should sit on his throne; and when he said he was not abandoned to Hades, and his flesh never suffered corruption, he spoke with foreknowledge of the resurrection of the Messiah. The Jesus we speak of has been raised by God, as we can all bear witness. Exalted thus with God's right hand, he received the Holy Spirit from the Father, as was promised, and all you now see and hear flows from him. For it was not David who went up to heaven; his own words are: The Lord said to my Lord, "Sit at my right hand until I make your enemies your footstool." Let all Israel then accept as certain that God has made this Jesus, whom you crucified, both Lord and Messiah.

The God of Abraham, Isaac, and Jacob, the God of our fathers, has given the highest honor to his servant Jesus, whom you committed for trial and repudiated in Pilate's court—repudiated the one who was holy and righteous when Pilate had decided to release him. You begged as a favor the release of a murderer, and killed him who has led the way to life. But God raised him from the dead; of that we are witnesses. And the name of Jesus, by awakening faith, has strengthened this man, whom you see and know, and this faith has made him completely well, as you can all see for yourselves.

And now, my friends, I know quite well that you acted in ignorance, and so did your rulers; but this is how God fulfilled what he had foretold in the utterances of all the prophets: that his Messiah should suffer. Repent then and turn to God, so that your sins may be wiped out. The Lord may grant you a time of recovery and send you the Messiah he has already appointed, that is, Jesus. He must be received into heaven until the time of universal restoration comes, of which God spoke by his holy prophets. Moses said, The Lord God will raise up a prophet for you from among yourselves as he raised me; you shall listen to everything he says to you, and anyone who refuses to listen to that prophet must be extirpated from Israel. And so said all the prophets from Samuel onwards; with one voice they all predicted this present time.

You are the heirs of the prophets; you are within the covenant which God made with your fathers, when he said to Abraham, "And in your offspring all the families on earth shall find blessing." When God raised up his Servant, he sent him to you first, to bring you blessing by turning every one of you from your wicked ways.

According to both these passages Jesus of Nazareth was raised to the right hand of God: God made him Lord and Messiah. In his redemptive work Jesus showed himself to be the servant of God, which was what God had chosen him to be, but these formulations require a more exact explanation. The more the people of Israel were governed by foreigners, the more they expected another

David, an ideal king, embraced by and filled with the spirit of God, who would free them from foreign rule, unite them as a sacred people on earth and rule with justice. Naturally, in Jesus' time it was from Roman rule that they expected liberation. These sermons, handed down in the Acts of the Apostles, use the familiar predicates of high position for the Savior sent by God, but at the same time these are interpreted in a completely new way, a radical transformation from national-political to spiritual-religious perception. Peter explains that Jesus is David's successor, indeed his lineal descendant, but he sees his work as liberation from sin and the establishment of peace with God. It is in this sense that he has been exalted by God to the position of the anointed one, the Messiah, the Christ, the Savior. The term Messiah (Christ), in this connection, is not yet thought of as a proper name, but as an indication of function. David himself spoke of the raising from the dead of the Anointed One, and of kings and princes conspiring against the Anointed One of the Lord (Acts 4:26). But it is in the light of their own experience that the twelve announce the message of salvation about Jesus as the Christ, the Savior sent by God. Salvation consists in the fact that Jesus the leader has been raised from the dead (Acts 3:15), because he led a life from and with God (Acts 5:30f.). At the end of history he will be sent again by God to bring the time of new life. Because of the divine command he will judge the living and the dead (Acts 10:42). His function as savior and his special relationship to God are also presented in Peter's sermons, where Jesus is called "the Holy One of God" and "the Just One." The expression "the Holy One of God" means that Jesus is the conveyor of the Spirit, armed with full power and might to destroy the power of evil (cf. Is. 42:1; 61:1). Jesus was chosen by God for a special task and was equipped by God to do it (R. Asting, *Die Heiligkeit im Urchristentum*). The term "the Just One" is also a designation for the promised Messiah. Jesus' life and nature corresponded, in a unique sense, to the will of God (Acts 22:14). In the prayer of the community (Acts 4:24–30) as well as in Peter's speech in the temple, it is evident that the appellations "the Just One," "the Holy One," and the "Messiah" have the same meaning as the term "the servant of God," a term which was an expression of humility as well as a title of honor for pious Israelites and for the whole people. In the Old Testament and in late Judaism it was applied to men such as Abraham, Moses, and David, who were chosen by God for special tasks. In non-canonical and post-canonical writing the Savior to come is occasionally addressed by Yahweh as "my servant," but in Jesus' time this term was not an independent title of honor signifying without further paraphrasing or elaboration a special kind of savior; hence when it is used the meaning of the term must be understood from its context. Like David, Jesus his descendant is also a servant of God, the holy servant of God, whom God himself has anointed (Acts 4:26). Through this servant of God, signs and miracles were to occur (Acts 4:30), so the title does not point to suffering, but to rule and power. The Old Testament background for this is not Isaiah 53, but Isaiah 42:1 and 61:1: "The spirit of the Lord is upon me, because the Lord has anointed me." Ultimately "servant of God" means nothing other than Messiah. Perhaps this predicate represents the oldest explanation of the mystery of the person and work of Jesus. It is almost a sacred phrase.

Only once do we encounter the term "son of man" in Acts. In the Synoptic Gospels it is used exclusively as a self-designation of Jesus; in Acts we find it only in Stephen's speech—he cries out: "Behold, I see the heaven opened and the son of Man standing at the right hand of God" (Acts 7:56). Here it is used, in contrast to its use in the Synoptic Gospels, as a designation for the risen Lord. But it never appears again in Acts.

In Acts the proclamation of Jesus reaches its climax with the designation *Kyrios,* Lord. Here Jesus is given the name of the Old Testament God of the Covenant. This became an especially popular title for him in Hellenistic Christianity. Of the first Christians it was said that "they praised God and enjoyed the favor of the whole people. And day by day the Lord added to their number those whom he was saving" (Acts 2:47). The Apostles gave testimony to the resurrection of the Lord Jesus (Acts 4:33). Baptism was conferred in the name of the Lord Jesus (Acts 8:16), and faith in God took the form of faith in him (Acts 5:14).

All these terms record the idea of the closeness of the one Jesus, in both his earthly and glorified condition. The relationship between these two modes of existence is, however, not clearly defined. The most advanced understanding of Jesus is shown by the Hellenistic deacon, Stephen, at his death; his last words represent a parallel to Jesus' words from the cross: " 'Lord Jesus, receive my spirit,' then he fell to his knees and cried aloud: 'Lord, do not hold this sin against them' " (Acts 7:59–60). As F. R. Geiselmann rightly says: "Here the purely salvation-historical significance of Kyrios Jesus is surpassed and the path to Kyrios-Theos begins. This is understandable: for Stephen, who thinks and feels as a Hellenist, it was natural to attribute the ministry of God to Kyrios-Jesus. Kyrios is a common predicate for God in the Septuagint. The Hellenists who were dispersed after Stephen's death carried with them their belief in the Kyrios, and it became the central predicate for Jesus in the proclamation to the heathen. Thus, the proclamation of the Gospel of the Messiah Jesus became the proclamation of the good news of the Lord Jesus (Acts 11:20). It is probably not coincidental that Paul preached in the name of Jesus to a group of Hellenists in Damascus, but in the name of the Lord in Jerusalem (Acts 9:27–29). Faith in Jesus came to be seen as a conversion, a turning of oneself to the Kyrios (Acts 11:21), a state of being caught up by his teaching of the Kyrios (Acts 13:12), and faith in the Kyrios (Acts 14:23).[1]

## THE SYNOPTICS

### The Prophet

With the historical figure of Jesus as seen in the Synoptic Gospels we come up against boundaries where human explanations fail us: the mystery really begins here.[2] It is proof that Jesus cannot have been invented by men. We will pursue the main categories described in the three Synoptic Gospels: Jesus as the prophet; the Messiah and the servant of God, the King; and finally the son of man and the son of God.

A return of the phenomenon of prophecy, which had long since disappeared, was expected to herald the final time of salvation promised by God (Mk. 6:15; Jn. 1:21; Mal. 3:1; Mt. 3:1–3; Dt. 18:15ff.). Hence John the Baptist, with his penitential preaching, was understood as a prophet of a new era (Mk. 11:32; Mt. 14:5). Even the so-called apocalyptics who appeared from the end of the second to the end of the first century B.C., with their claim to be able to explain the Mosaic law in an especially profound way, and to understand God's plan of salvation, had a far-reaching and impressive effect. In those days then, abounding in prophetic expectations, Jesus was naturally interpreted as being a prophet. Great numbers of people believed that in him Elias had returned, or Jeremiah, or one of the other prophets (Mk. 6:15ff.; 8:28; Mt. 16:14; Lk. 9:19). Even Moses was expected to come again (cf. Dt. 18:15ff.). It was expected that a new miracle worker would repeat and even surpass the saving miracles of Moses. Even though Jesus never specifically applied the title of prophet to himself (see Mk. 6:4; Lk. 13:33ff.; Mt. 23:24,37), he carried out all the functions characteristic of prophets. He saw into the hearts of men (Lk. 7:39); he was consumed with zeal for God; he announced the final and ultimate time of salvation which would bring judgment upon those who were not converted. In proclaiming his own death, he was anticipating a prophet's usual destiny (Lk. 13:33f.). Lastly he proclaimed the destruction of the Temple, the end of the world and of human history.

We are dealing here with Jesus' own words, even though certain additions may have been made to them. It was precisely because of his own prophecies of his Passion—even though these are reported in a somewhat stylized fashion—that the early Church believed that his path had been marked out by God himself to lead him from degradation to exaltation, just as the Old Testament had foretold.

But Jesus is more than a prophet. The prophets were often chosen by God against their will or after a long period of resistance, and they had to prove their legitimacy through special works of God. Nowhere do we hear that Christ received a special call from God for the work he was to do. (The story of the baptism does not represent such a call: Mk. 1:9–11.) Neither is he an apocalyptic figure; there are no withdrawals from the world, trips to heaven, visions or other marvels recorded of him, as there were of late Jewish apocalyptics, or even the visionary of John's Apocalypse. Rather he is a prophet by his very nature, and

therefore more than a prophet (Mt. 12:41f.; Lk. 11:32). He appears with a sovereign autonomy: he does not have to prove his
legitimacy; he rejects the demand for such a proof.

Nevertheless, he accomplishes works by which his contemporaries can see that a new prophet has come; indeed that he is
greater than all the other prophets, even Moses, and this is why
his contemporaries were guilty when they did not believe his
words. All the prophets of the past had introduced their message
with the words "Thus speaks Yahweh," but Christ speaks on his
own authority. His "I" takes the place of "Yahweh says." This
is a sign that his own person occupies the position or role of the
God of the Old Testament. What he says flows from a unique
relationship with God and from his exclusive awareness of being
the Son. Even as a twelve-year-old he had this awareness, as the
scene in the Temple shows: "Did you not know that I must be in
that which belongs to my father?" (Lk. 2:41–50). These words
do not fit into any of the patterns of speech handed down in the
Old Testament. The introductory terminology of his parables and
appeals is also characteristic: "Amen" or "Amen, Amen"; "Verily"
or "Verily, verily, I say to you." His statements have an immense
force: contrasting himself with the Old Testament prophets he can
say: "Something greater than Jonas is here—yes, even greater than
Solomon" (Mt. 12:41–42).

Certainly his hearers were bound to ask what it was that was
"greater." Above all it is of immeasurable importance that Jesus
places himself above the authority of Moses. This means that
since his coming the unqualified criterion set down by Moses no
longer holds—he not only rejects pedantic interpretations of the
Torah, he puts himself above the Torah itself. The lowliest person
in the new time of salvation is greater, he says, than the greatest
of the old period (Lk. 7:28). He attacks the narrow interpretations of the law and the purely ritualistic piety of the influential
party of the Pharisees. Instead of this, in the Sermon on the
Mount, he proclaims a radically new moral-religious order which
is to prevail in the period of salvation which has just begun. This
represents an interiorization and simplification (Mt. 5:1ff.; Mk.
7:2–15). Further, he declares that truth must be told without
equivocation (Mt. 5:33–37).

In order to draw attention to the serious intent of his struggle against all alienation and untruth he almost seems to provoke the Pharisees deliberately, as, for example when he heals the man with the withered hand on the Sabbath (see Mk. 3:1–6; Lk. 13:10–17; 14:1–10). It could be said that this was not an attack on the Sabbath law in itself, but on the sophistical casuistry of the Pharisees. It would then be seen as an appeal to a true inner piety. But Jesus goes beyond this when he says: "The Sabbath was made for man, not man for the Sabbath" (Mk. 2:27f.). Such words must have seemed outrageous. But Jesus always speaks from the position of one superior to the law: he even claims to be Lord of the Sabbath (Mk. 2:27f.). All others are subordinate to Moses, but Moses is subordinate to Jesus, whose authority is the greater. This is shown again in his attitude to the Mosaic divorce law, when, in contradiction to it, he proclaims the indissolubility of marriage (Mk. 10:9–12).

Jesus' claim to preeminent authority is again evident when he differentiates himself from the rabbis (teachers of the will of God). He behaves like a rabbi, especially in instructional and controversial dialogues, and he goes to the synagogue to explain the law, but he does not limit himself to this. Unlike the rabbis of his time he travels through the countryside teaching in the villages, in the streets, on the seashore, from a boat, or on a mountainside. He calls to him people who were condemned by the Pharisees—publicans and sinners—and there are women and children among his followers. That Jesus proclaimed salvation for all, particularly for the poor and lowly, was felt as an intolerable provocation. It was a "shaking of the foundations," a dissolution of the accepted bonds of religion and the status of the pious. By abandoning the categories of achievement and reward, he proclaimed the incomprehensible love of God, which embraces all sinners and forgives all who repent (Lk. 15:1–35). He even claimed to be able to forgive sins: the Pharisees were right when they said that God alone could do this, but Jesus justified his claim by a miracle of healing, in which the saving power of God was shown: his words of forgiveness proclaimed the merciful forgiveness of God (Lk. 7:49; Mk. 2:1–12).

By challenging people to follow him personally, Jesus goes

further than the prophets of old or the rabbis of his time. He calls people away from their professions, and not just for a short time or until they have understood his teaching; they become his companions for good. Behind this call to discipleship and initiation is the decisive fact that Jesus proclaimed a radically new message—the message that the ultimate reign of God begins with him. This reign of God, until then only promised, is now beginning to be realized in Jesus, though its final form is still in the future; he announces the Kingdom of God which is to come, but in contrast to earlier promises, God's rule begins to be realized in him.

It is precisely this sovereign calling of individuals to a community of life and destiny with Jesus which is a sign of the present rule and power of God (R. Schnackenburg). It is because the kingdom of God, the time of salvation, is beginning once and for all, and Jesus' demands are so urgent and unconditional, that his listeners are terrified. They are outraged by his teachings (Mk. 1:22); they are astounded (Mk. 2:12, 5:42, 6:51, 9:15; Lk. 4:22, 8:56, 9:43). Jesus' relatives try to stop him from teaching; they want to take him home. But with unrelenting intensity Jesus demands love for God and that love of neighbor which is grounded in it and expresses it; this love alone, he teaches, is the norm for the observance of all the other commandments. He is unlike the teacher of righteousness in Qumran in his radical demands for conversion. The righteousness of the Qumran consists in interpretation of the Mosaic law, in the conjunction of ethical and ritual purity. It is characterized, moreover, in contrast to Jesus' teaching, by love only of one's fellow-believers and hatred of all others. Jesus' unqualified appeal for the love of God and neighbor is expressed in warnings to those who let the hour of conversion pass, and so are in danger from the eschatological judgment (Mt. 11:21ff.; Lk. 10:13ff.; Mt. 18:7ff.; Lk. 17:1; Mt. 23:13–to end, 24:44; Lk. 11:42–52; Mk. 14:21).

In the light of this claim to a preeminent authority transcending all the religious ideas of the Old Testament, the responsible leaders of the people, the elders as well as the scholars, besides large numbers of ordinary people and even his own disciples and closest relatives, were forced to ask themselves: "Who is this man? What sort of doctrine is this?" (Mk. 1:22,27; Lk. 7:49, 8:25). It was precisely responsible people who felt they had to address these questions to him, since his teaching attacked the previously valid order of faith—an order which stemmed from Moses, and through Moses from God himself (Mt. 21:23; Mk. 11:28; Lk. 20:2). This questioning of his authority did not stem from a culpable ignorance or from ill-intentioned stubbornness, but from a profound sense of responsibility. It became culpable only when these responsible people could not persuade themselves to believe that Jesus was indeed the promised messenger of God. He knew himself to be the promised savior and so proclaimed himself (see, for example, Mt. 13:24–30, 21:33–44; 22:1–14; Lk. 14:15–24, 20:9–19; Mk. 12:1–12). Jesus is so closely connected to God and his rulership that a rejection of his person is a rejection of God and therefore of the religion previously established by God. He knows himself to belong completely to God, indeed to be God's Son in a unique sense, and it is because of this that he knows himself to have absolute authority. But no one can grasp what Christ is without first ridding himself of all his sense of the certitude and sufficiency of his own convictions. He must be ready to listen for the approach of God and his message, ever coming anew. One cannot put one's faith in the present or the past: he alone is able to accept Jesus who is always open to what is new—and this will always prove to be a further fulfillment of what has been promised in the Old Testament, the supreme realization of what God himself has planned.

Jesus' claim to authority and the new era beginning with him are expressed in one decisive statement. It is recorded by Matthew, and is undoubtedly in Jesus' own words:

At that time Jesus spoke these words: "I thank thee, Father, Lord of heaven and earth, for hiding these things from the learned and wise, and revealing them to the simple. Yes, Father, such was thy choice. Everything is entrusted to me by my Father; and no one knows the Son but the Father, and no one knows the Father but the Son and those to whom the Son may choose to reveal him.

"Come to me, all whose work is hard, whose load is heavy; and I will give you relief. Bend your necks to my yoke, and learn from me, for I am gentle and humble-hearted; and your souls will find relief. For my yoke is good to bear, my load is light" (Mt. 11:25–30).

Therefore blessed are those who see and hear and comprehend the meaning of this hour; and the words and deeds of salvation which Jesus says and does. In typically Semitic fashion he cries out: "Happy the eyes that see what you are seeing! I tell you, many prophets and kings wished to see what you now see, yet never saw it; to hear what you hear, yet never heard it" (Lk. 10:23–24; Mt. 13:16f.).

## The Messiah and the Servant of God

In the Old Testament the king and the high priest were often referred to as anointed ones, or the anointed of God (Messiah or Christ). The word is not often used as a title for the anointed redeemer who is to bring final salvation. For him the designation "king" is usual (see, however, Ps. 2,2; Dan. 9:25). Not until the Apocalyptic psalms of Solomon, which date from the first century B.C., is the coming savior-king called Messiah. According to Psalm 2 this messianic king has the task of conquering the tribes rebelling against God and securing his royal claims over the peoples of Israel and the world in a just and peaceful reign. This long-awaited king was visualized as another David, but at the same time he was expected to surpass David: he is to be grasped by the spirit of God in a special way (Is. 7:14, 9:1–7, 11:1–5; Mic. 5:1ff.). In later Jewish writings (Zech. 3 and 4, 6:9–14) and especially in the Qumran literature, a second Messiah appears beside him: a priestly Messiah.

Jesus had great reservations about using this title himself: it is really surprising that "Christ" should have come to be used as his proper name. But that the designation Messiah is used *of* him throughout the New Testament and applied to him in his sufferings shows that it must represent something in the core of his own preaching and cannot be a backward projection from the belief in the resurrection and ascension. We can see that Jesus could not have simply said "I am the Messiah" unless he had wanted to raise political hopes to the point of danger, or at least arouse political unrest. That a Messiah was universally expected at this time made the danger all the greater. John's penitential preaching had produced a state of tension; indeed people were wondering if John himself might not be the Messiah (Lk. 3:15), and Simeon the Just was awaiting the Anointed of the Lord promised by God (Lk. 2:25f.). Jesus evaded every attempt of the men of this time to force him into a political role.

On the other hand, since his mission was to reveal himself as Savior, he could not simply conceal the secret that he was the Messiah entirely, and this is why he led his disciples on to realize and announce it.

On their way to the towns of Galilee he asked them, "Who do people think I am?" They answered, "John the Baptist, or Elias, Jeremiah or one of the other prophets." Apparently everyone was convinced that there was a mystery about him. He asked again, this time of the disciples themselves, "Who do you think I am?" This implies that he expected more understanding from them. It was Peter, speaking for them all, who answered: "You are the Messiah" (Mt. 16:13–16). It is significant that Mark adds that he charged them to tell no one (Mk. 8:27–30).

It is clear from this incident that Jesus did not wish to dissuade his followers from believing him to be the Messiah: he accepted Peter's answer and so indirectly admitted its truth. But because of the dangers arising from the general situation he demanded silence (see also Mk. 1:24,34,44; 3:11f.; 5:43; 7:35f.; 8:29f.; 9:9; and parallel passages). He did not want to encourage false hopes of a political Messiah either among his own disciples or the general public. This is why he told them that the Son of Man will suffer much, be condemned and killed by the elders, high priests, and scribes, but will rise from the dead after three days (Mk. 8:31).

Here Jesus clearly connects his function as Messiah with that of the servant of God prophesied in Deutero-Isaiah. The difficulty the disciples had in accepting the unpolitical character of Jesus' Messiahship and particularly his connection with the figure of Ebed-Yahweh is evident in Peter's reaction. He reproaches Jesus for the prophecy of suffering, and for this he receives an unexpectedly sharp reprimand: "Away with you, Satan! You think as men think, not as God thinks" (Mk. 8:33). The statement of his sufferings had been made in bitter earnest; it is inseparably connected with his role as Messiah. This is also the point of the words Jesus used when preaching to the people: "Anyone who wishes to be a follower of mine must leave self behind; he must take up his cross, and come with me. Whoever cares for his own safety is lost; but if a man will let himself be lost for my sake and for the Gospel, that man is safe" (Mk. 8:34f.). Jesus saw his violent death as part of his function as Messiah, and to it he ascribed a saving power; he saw his approaching death as a divine imperative (Lk. 15:20, 13:33f.), and he saw the significance of his death in its representative function for the many as an act required in the redemptive plan of God (see Is. 53:4–12). He was expressing this conviction when, according to the oldest available tradition of his words at the Last Supper he says: "This is my blood of the Covenant, which is poured out for many" (Mk. 14:24). It can hardly be denied that he is referring here to Isaiah.

So Jesus the Messiah fulfills the Old Testament promises, but in a completely unexpected way. He will certainly save his people, but the salvation will be from sin (Mt. 1:21). Thus his Messiahship is not directly tangible or visible, and we can easily understand how John the Baptist, filled with profound longing for the Savior, and hearing in prison of his works, but of no change in the general condition of things, could ask, "Are you he who is to come or shall we look for another?" In his reply, Jesus, taking account of the political situation, did not give a direct answer. Instead, he pointed to the signs foretold by Isaiah: "Go and tell John what you hear and see: the blind receive their sight, and the lame walk, lepers are cleansed and the deaf hear, the dead are raised up and the poor have the good news preached to them" (cf. Is. 35:5f., 61:1). "And blessed is he who takes no offense at me" (Mt. 11:4–6). This last can undoubtedly be understood as a warning to John to free himself from political hopes and remember that the Messiah is to be characterized by the signs of which Jesus speaks.

In Luke's account, Jesus speaks even more clearly. It is after he has returned from the desert where he was tempted by Satan, when his reputation had begun to spread through the surrounding country:

So he came to Nazareth, where he had been brought up, and went to synagogue on the Sabbath day as he regularly did. He stood up to read the lesson and was handed the scroll of the prophet Isaiah. He opened the scroll and found the passage which says,
 "The spirit of the Lord is upon me because he has anointed me;
 He has sent me to announce good news to the poor,
 To proclaim release for prisoners and recovery of sight for the blind;
 To let the broken victims go free,
 To proclaim the year of the Lord's favor."
He rolled up the scroll, gave it back to the attendant, and sat down; and all eyes in the synagogue were fixed on him.
 He began to speak: "Today," he said, "in your very hearing this text has come true" (Lk. 4:16–21).

And because of this it is a time for rejoicing, like a wedding (Mk. 2:18f.). Hellenistic influence in Luke's Gospel gives most testimony to Jesus as a merciful helper (Lk. 7:13), as the savior of sinners and defender of the poor (Lk. 6:20f., 7:36–50, 14:12f., 18:9–14, 19:2–10, 23:43), and as the redeemer (Lk. 2:11). If they had understood the signs of the times, his contemporaries could recognize by Jesus' deeds of power that the messianic kingdom was beginning. These deeds of power include healing the sick, expelling demons, raising the dead, and miracles of nature— the calming of the storm at sea, the great catch of fish, multiplication of the loaves and fishes, walking on the water. The meaning and purpose of these miracles is not primarily the compassionate solution of immediate problems, still less are they meant to attract attention or satisfy the curious (see Mt. 6:5, 13:53–58, etc.). Rather, they are God's seal of approval on Jesus' proclamation concerning himself, and even more they are signs of the approaching reign of God. They herald the dawn of the definitive future and are therefore to be understood as eschatological in significance, revelations of the present and future glory of God, and so God's testimony to the words of Christ (Mt. 11:2–5, Mk. 2:1–12). The report of the healing of the paralytic

(Mk. 2:1–12), which has already been mentioned, is especially illuminating. It was sensational, and also disturbing. No doubt it had cost the sick man and his friends something to get to Jesus, and they must have been confused and puzzled when the Lord promised what they had not asked for, the forgiveness of the sick man's sins, and yet did not at first grant the cure they sought. The paralytic must have felt both disappointed and embarrassed when Jesus spoke openly of his sins, even though at the same time he assured him of forgiveness. But it was a healing disappointment: Christ uncovered the man's underlying distress, which he himself had not recognized, and consequently had not asked to be cured of. But all our troubles are symptoms of the same thing. When the condition of the sick man's soul was brought to light all present realized their own condition. They heard Jesus claim the power to do what no other human being can do: cure the fundamental and original problem of all mankind, separation from God. There were three ways in which they might have taken such a claim: they could laugh at it, or sympathize with it as a sign of madness, or condemn it as blasphemy. If they did not recognize Christ as sent by God and enabled by him to perform miracles, they could only condemn him. Apparently Christ made such an impression of nobility, dignity, and greatness that the first two reactions did not occur to them. So they could only repudiate Christ for behaving as if he were equal to God—unless, of course, they could bring themselves to believe in him as indeed empowered by God Almighty.

Even the manner in which Jesus enters Jerusalem a few days before his Passion illuminates his awareness of being the Messiah (Mk. 11:1–10). The Jews saw him as a king intending to take possession of his kingdom (Mk. 11:10; Lk. 19:38). Jesus first openly confesses his claim to be the Messiah before the Court of the High Council. When Caiphas asks whether he is the Messiah, the son of the Blessed One, he answers openly, "I am" (Mk. 14:61f.); "You have said so" (Mt. 26:64); "You say that I am" (Lk. 22:70). Jesus is accused of inciting the people and is brought before Pontius Pilate, the representative of the Roman occupying power. Pilate asks him if he, as his countrymen say, is really the King of the Jews, and Jesus answers, "The words are yours" (Mk. 15:2; Mt. 27:11; Lk. 23:3); "You say that I am a king" (Jn. 18:38). It would be wrong to assume from these texts that Jesus attributed the opinion that he was the Messiah to Pontius Pilate or the High Priest, while taking no position on the matter himself. He had been accused before he was questioned, and his answer concedes the accusation against him. Hence the cross bears the inscription of his admission of guilt: King of the Jews (Mt. 27:37; Lk. 23:38). At the same time he announces that he will come again on the clouds of heaven to judge all mankind, including his present judges. The expression "on the clouds of heaven" means only that he will come again in power, from his seat at the right hand of God Almighty.

### The Son of Man

The phrase "Son of Man" appears in the Synoptic Gospels some seventy times, and it is invariably used by Jesus of himself. A fully satisfying and generally accepted explanation of the origin and meaning of the phrase has not yet been found. It is the Gospel of Mark especially that uses the idea to point to the messianic secret of Jesus. In late Judaism the phrase was by no means a common designation of the awaited Messiah. However Jesus' reference to himself as the Son of Man has a background in late Judaism. Daniel sees in a vision four world empires symbolized by four animals which, by their arrogance and inhumanity, draw down upon themselves the judgment of God. A new reign can then begin. Daniel sees someone with the appearance of a man coming on the clouds of heaven: he goes up to the Ancient of Days and from him receives power, glory, and the kingdom, for all eternity.

The phrase Son of Man in this account refers primarily to the Jewish people (Dan. 7:27), that is, it has a collective significance. But already in verse 13 of chapter 7 it has moved over into the sphere of the individual and personal. In the rabbinic tradition and the Old Testament apocrypha (4 Esd. 13:1ff.; En. 36–72, especially 46) the term Son of Man comes to mean the Messiah. In the Book of Enoch it is very definitely a title of authority. The Hellenistic deacon Stephen also used the term in this

way (Acts 7:56). There can be no doubt that Jesus used the
term Son of Man himself. We can also be quite certain that he
used it to mean that he would come again (parousia) and that
he would then judge the world (Mk. 8:38; Lk. 12:8; 17:24–26).
When, confronting death, he proclaimed clearly that he would
come again to judge the world (Mk. 14:62) he was referring to
Daniel 7:13f. The theology of the Son of Man must therefore
include that of his exaltation or glorification. He is endowed
with a glory not of this earth, and with power over the whole
world (Mk. 13:26, 14:62, 8:38; Mt. 13:41, 16:27–28). But the
term does not refer to the future alone, it also holds good in the
historical present, for with his claim to be the Son of Man he
joins the claim to possess the authority to forgive sins (Mk.
2:10) and to be Lord of the Sabbath (Mk. 2:28). This is why
he cures those who confess that he is the Son of Man. He is the
redeemer and savior (Lk. 19:9; Mt. 21:42, 10:32), but the man
who is scandalized by his humble appearance and rejects him is
lost (Lk. 12:9).

Like the concept of the Messiah, that of the Son of Man is
connected with the idea of lowliness. The Son of Man did not
come to be served, but to serve (Mk. 10:45); he is the Lord
of Creation and of history, yet he is poorer than the animals. He
does not even have a bed to sleep on (Mt. 8:20). He is not
looking for the world's great and influential men, but for the
lowly and the lost (Lk. 19:10). But it is when he walks the way
of the cross that the Son of Man will take on himself most completely the lowliness of the servant, for he will be delivered into
the hands of men (Lk. 9:44); he will suffer mockery and violence
and they will spit on him, scourge, and kill him (Lk. 18:31f.;
Mk. 14:21; Mt. 16:21, 17:12). In all this lies what is new and
original in Jesus' designation of himself as the Son of Man—he
allies the authoritative figure of the Son of Man, who is to judge
the world, with the humble figure of the suffering Messiah who
sacrifices himself.

## The Son of God

For a clear understanding of the problems found in this title we
must distinguish between "Son of God" and the simple use of

the term "Son" by itself. Different explanations have been found for the use of the title "Son of God." The "history of religions" school is of the opinion that it is of Hellenistic origin. The idea was prevalent in Hellenistic culture of sons of God or divine human beings and was, they believe, carried over to Jesus (W. Bousett). Others see in it a counterpart to the Judaic idea of the Son of Man (S. Schulz). For Bultmann and his school of thought, Jesus of Nazareth is a charismatic, talented man of God, an eschatological prophet, whose self-awareness we know nothing about.

It was not until the experience of Easter that his disciples created the title "Son of God" and other titles of authority and applied them to Jesus. The expressions "Son" (pais) and "Son of God" were already to be found in the Old Testament. But we must ask whether the term "son" already has that metaphysical depth which is expressed in the Pauline and Johannine writings as well as in later ecclesiastical doctrine about Jesus. The word "son" can be understood merely as implying a special moral relationship to God. Thus the king is called the Son of God in the ancient Oriental world, biblical and non-biblical. Priests also were occasionally designated by this term, and in the Old Testament the Messiah-King who is to come is proclaimed as the Son of God in this moral or adoptionist sense (Ps. 2:7). But because of its absolutely monotheistic faith a metaphysical sonship of God was foreign to Old Testament thought and a long struggle was necessary before this faith-conviction could be established— namely, that God has a son, co-equal with him in nature, without thereby ceasing to be one God. Even in the New Testament the passages where the Son of God is mentioned do not by any means all imply a direct metaphysical sense. Thus, the peacemakers and those who love their enemies are called sons of God (Mt. 5:45), and divine sonship is promised by Jesus as an eschatological gift: those who wish to become sons of God must strive for perfection according to his example (Mt. 5:45,48; 11:29).

Leaving aside the question of the way in which the words "Son of God" may be used, according to the Synoptics Jesus never expressly and formally used this title to refer to himself. But in three passages in the Synoptic Gospels he does refer to himself as the "Son" in an absolute sense (Mt. 11:27, 21:37, 24:36, and parallel passages). Whether these sayings are to be directly attributed to Jesus is, of course, open to question. But the arguments so far brought forward against their authenticity are more of an ideological than a scientific-philological character. We find the oldest usage of the title "Son of God" in Romans 1:3ff. and in one of Paul's speeches in Acts (13:33). In the first it is used in reference to 2 Samuel 7:14,16, with the descendant of David who is mentioned there understood in a Christian sense. In the second we find an explicit reference to Psalm 2:7, and here the resurrection of Jesus and his installation at the right hand of God are seen as the fulfillment of the Old Testament promises, as part of the history of salvation, and Jesus is therefore called the Son of God in a functional or soteriological sense (see Acts 2:4ff.; Ps. 110:1).

We must ask whether the following passages are not to be interpreted in the same sense: Lk. 1:31–35, 3:22 (Ps. 2:7; Is. 42:1); Lk. 22:70; Mt. 2:15 (Hos. 11:1); Mt. 14:33, 16:16. The first of these texts describes the annunciation to Mary. One could only imagine that the term Son of God had a metaphysical meaning here if Mary had received a special revelation about the relationship between God and the descendant of David who was to be conceived and borne by her, and such a revelation would have been contrary to ideas about the Son of God which necessarily came from the Old Testament religion. Nevertheless, it is precisely this statement that her son would be given the throne of David his father and that he would rule eternally over the house of David that makes it clear that the term as it is used here concerns the history of salvation. In the second passage (Lk. 3:22): "Thou art my Son, my Beloved, on thee my favor rests," "son" must certainly be understood as "servant of God," endowed with his spirit, one having a difficult and important task to do. In Luke 22:70 the term "Son of God" would have solely a messianic significance for a Jewish audience. But these last passages bring a Christian depth to the Old Testament meaning to this extent, that Jesus as the Son of God has a task to fulfill as Savior.

It would be wrong to impose a rigid "either-or" on these texts: "either" moral "or" metaphysical. Even to the adoptionists, moral sonship, familiar to the first witnesses to Christ from the Old Testament, has different levels. The words heard from heaven at Jesus' baptism were developed further in a messianic sense. This may be seen in the story of the temptations (Mt. 4:3–10; Lk. 4:2–12), and particularly in the account of Jesus' transfiguration (Mk. 9:7, compare Mt. 17:1–13; Lk. 9:28–35). This text clearly points to Deuteronomy 18:15: "The Lord your God will raise up for you a prophet like me from among you, from your brethren—him you shall heed." The interpretation of the concept "Son of God" does not really enter the metaphysical dimension before the writings of Paul, the Letter to the Hebrews and the Gospel of John. We must now consider this dimension.

There are two reasons why the problem of metaphysical sonship has not been solved or even illuminated by our considerations so far. As we have already said, Jesus calls himself "son" three times in the Synoptic Gospels and this in a completely exclusive way. Beyond that, his claim to supreme authority reveals his unique awareness of belonging to God, an awareness well expressed in the word "Son." This absolute use of the word son can only be explained in terms of Jesus' direct awareness of his unique relationship to God. His claim to authority flows from his awareness of being the Son. Thus, even if the term itself did not give an absolutely plain explanation of Jesus' ultimate relationship to the one God of the Old Testament, nevertheless it paved the way for the Church's later preaching of Jesus as the Son of God in a metaphysical sense. This was done by the manner in which his sonship is described by himself and by his listeners and by the way in which he himself claims it. He claims to have a power which belongs to God alone and he speaks of God as his Father in a way which no one else had ever done (Jn. 17:20ff.). He says: "Not everyone who calls me 'Lord, Lord' will enter the kingdom of Heaven, but only those who do the will of my heavenly Father" (Mt. 7:21). He knows his Father's will as no one else knows it: he reveals and represents it. Because he knows the will of the Father he has power even over the laws of the Old Testament—even the law of the Sabbath (Mk. 2:28, 7:1–23, 10:1–12; Mt. 5:21–48, 12:1–6, 12:10ff.). Because with him the distance between the eschatologically acting

God and the Savior sent by God is removed, a man's fate is decided by his attitude to Jesus. So he can say, "Whoever will acknowledge me before men, I will acknowledge him before my Father in heaven" (Mt. 10:32f.; Mk. 8:38; Lk. 9:26, 12:8ff.).

Jesus constantly distinguishes his sonship from that of others. To them he speaks of "your father" or "your heavenly father" (Mk. 11:25; Lk. 12:32, etc.). He is God's only beloved Son (Mk. 12:6), "the" son (Mk. 13:32). He is therefore greater than the Temple (Mt. 12:6). Because he is "the" son, he can forgive sins, that is to say, he can bring order into man's relationship to God (Mk. 2:5). He sends his disciples to preach with divine authority (Mt. 10:16; Lk. 10:1–16). He can promise that he will always be with them (Mt. 28: 18–20) and they can depend on this promise. His words have eternal validity (Mk. 13:31); because he is the Son all his promises, decisions, and warnings are valid. All matters to do with salvation appertain to him: he is the center which divides all paths and times, all minds and destinies; around him all those who love God gather. He is the one against whom Satan will struggle until the end; for his sake good is sought and done, for him men live and die (Lk. 18:22; 21:12; Mk. 13:13; Mt. 18:5). The intensity of his awareness of being the Son explains why the early Church could use only the term "Son of God" to express perfectly clearly their belief in Jesus (Mk. 1:1–11, 9:7, 14, 61; Lk. 1:35, 22:70; Mt. 2:15, 14:33, 16:16, 27:43).

If this conceptualization is not found as fully developed in the testimony of the early Church as we find it at the Council of Nicea, it is still quite clear that Jesus testified to being entirely on the side of God, even though he was a complete human being. Matthew 11:27 expresses this most clearly, and this text, far from representing a gnostic revelation-expression, has strongly accentuated Old Testament-Judaic features. That knowledge is central in this text could give the impression that salvation through self-knowledge and contemplation is to be preached (R. Bultmann), but what is basic here is the idea of God's power in history. An all-inclusive right is attributed to God to reveal himself as he pleases, by his own perfectly free decision. The knowledge of the Father, which the Son claims, can be understood as an element of this encompassing authority given to him by the Father. This authority includes the Son's power to reveal: he knows that it is the Father who establishes the decree of salvation. He knows the Father and the Father knows him in such a way that the knowledge which the Father has is required in order to know the Son. And conversely, only with the Son's knowledge is it possible to know the Father. Finally we can say that this text sufficiently assures us of Jesus' awareness of being God's son in an absolute and exclusive way. One cannot expect mathematical certainty; this is impossible from the nature of the case. But Jesus' awareness of himself as Son of the Father formed a sure basis for the early Church's Christological doctrine of the Son of God.

This title was probably used at first because of messianic, specifically Old Testament ideas which were seen as applicable to Jesus and a fitting expression of his entry into glory (Ps. 2:7f.). Perhaps Isaiah 7:14 was also influential. Because of Jesus' awareness of himself as the Son, passages about the Son of God could be reflected on more profoundly and be used as interpretations of Jesus' awareness. These reflections tended towards metaphysical understanding, but this was only achieved in Paul and John's theology and that of the Letter to the Hebrews and did not attain full linguistic formulation until after the apostolic era.

Even though no one knows the Father but the Son, Jesus' knowledge as man has limitations: he does not know the hour of the parousia, this is known only to the Father (Mk. 13:32), and the Father alone has made ready the kingdom for the chosen (Mt. 25:34,41). The Son's greatness lies in the fact that he sits at the right hand of God, which means that he participates in the reign of God (Mk. 14:62, 12:36). The Father's kingdom, bringing consummation, will be the Son's also (Lk. 22:29), but we know from the fifteenth chapter of the first Letter to the Corinthians that that hour will come in a great movement in the history of salvation when the Son submits everything to the Father, so that the Father will be "all in all."

## THE EPISTLES OF PAUL

Paul experienced the power of Christ in his vision on the road to Damascus, and the experience brought him into Christ's service.[3] Thenceforward he could—and must—bear witness to Jesus as the Lord whose power and glory he had been shown. He was introduced to the Christianity of the early Church first by Ananias in Damascus and then by the Christians in Jerusalem. This is recorded in his speeches in Acts as well as in his own epistles—at the beginning of the Epistle to the Romans, in the fifteenth chapter of the first Epistle to the Corinthians, and in the hymn to Christ in the Letter to the Philippians. He is a witness to the tradition as well as to the theology developing from it.

Although he did not know Jesus during his earthly life, he testifies that the Son of God was born of a woman (Gal. 4:4), further that he is human, a Jew, and was born under the law. Jesus' crucifixion and his cross are essential points in Paul's preaching (Gal. 1:3f., 1 Cor. 2:2). According to 1 Corinthians 15:3–5, Jesus' death and burial are contained in the tradition as well as the risen Christ's appearance to Peter, his disciples, and many others. This agrees with what Paul says in the sermon in the thirteenth chapter of Acts.

Like all his sermons, this shows a definite plan. It is in three parts: (1) the Passion and Death of Jesus according to Scripture; (2) his burial and resurrection, again according to Scripture; and (3) the appearances of the risen Christ to his disciples. It is also part of this tradition that Jesus, on the night before he was betrayed, celebrated the Last Supper and established this to be a commemoration of himself (1 Cor. 11:23ff.). Although Paul says that he does not wish to know anything but Christ crucified, this Christ is for him simultaneously the risen Christ. He begins his Letter to the Romans with a passage which reflects the earliest Christian beliefs, as they were handed on to him in a standard formula:

From Paul, servant of Christ Jesus, apostle by God's call, set apart for the service of the Gospel. This Gospel God announced beforehand in sacred scriptures through his prophets. It is about his Son: on the human level he was born of David's stock, but on the level of the spirit—the Holy Spirit—he was declared Son of God by a mighty act in that he rose from the dead: it is about Jesus Christ our Lord (Rom. 1:1–4).

His hymn to Christ in the second chapter of the letter to the Philippians goes beyond even the functional or salvation-history conception of Jesus derived from the Old Testament theology of promise. It represents a tradition which Paul took over, but to which he added the idea of humiliation unto death on the cross. This hymn contains the idea of pre-existence, which does not appear explicitly either in the Gospels or in Acts, though it is hinted at in pre-Pauline theology when Jesus is called the Son of God in a metaphysically oriented sense.

Let your bearing towards one another arise out of your life in Christ Jesus. For the divine nature was his from the first; yet he did not think to snatch at equality with God, but made himself nothing, assuming the nature of a slave. Bearing the human likeness, revealed in human shape, he humbled himself, and in obedience accepted even death— death on a cross. Therefore God raised him to the heights and bestowed on him the name above all names, that at the name of Jesus every knee should bow—in heaven, on earth, and in the depths—and every tongue confess, "Jesus Christ is Lord," to the glory of God the Father (Phil. 2:5–11).

It is easily seen that the basic intention of this text is not to present the doctrine of Christ's pre-existence, but the kind of behavior which should characterize those who believe in Christ, which consists in the following of Christ. But as the ground which would make this following of Christ possible, Paul offers a picture not of Jesus' being, but of his destiny, his fate. This destiny is consummated in three stages: his pre-existence, his humiliation, and his exaltation. The exaltation itself also includes three stages: the exaltation itself, the proclamation of it, and the worship of Jesus which results. In a certain sense Christ is enthroned as the Father's partner.

The Judeo-Hellenistic wisdom doctrine probably had an influence on the formulation of the concept of Christ's pre-existence. In this doctrine wisdom was understood as a pre-historical reality already active in the work of creation (Job 28:20–28; Prov. 8; 22–31; Sirach 1:4,8; 24:1–21; Wis. 7:25f., 9:9f.). There are also a number of Pauline texts which speak of Jesus having a role in the act of creation (1 Cor. 8:6; Col. 1:15ff.; cf. Heb.

1:2f.; Jn. 1:10f.). The concept of humiliation, inserted by Paul into the pre-Pauline hymn of Philippians 2, goes back to Deutero-Isaiah (Is. 45:23, as well as 53:3–12; 55:11). Through his glorification Jesus became the lord (Kyrios) and so has a right to worship. The word "Kyrios" was taken from the Greek translation of the Old Testament, the Septuagint, where it is regularly used to translate the Hebrew name for God, Yahweh. The New Testament term *Kyrios,* therefore, is derived not from the Hellenistic world but from the Old Testament, and in the New Testament it signifies that Jesus shares the throne of God and by his authority is ruler of the universe. It is only in the Holy Spirit, however, in the power and light of God Himself, that it is possible to say, Christ is the Lord (1 Cor. 12:3; 2 Cor. 4:4f.). He who is not illuminated by God sees Christ simply in the flesh, as the human being he appears to be.

By speaking of Christ as Kyrios Paul states in effect that the risen Lord is still active for man's salvation, that he occupies a position of supreme authority in the universe, and that therefore the Christian faith stands in opposition to the Hellenistic mystery cults. A Christian is someone bound to Christ the Lord, taken into the realm where his death and resurrection are efficacious. He is one who allows Christ to be his Lord and submits himself to him (Rom. 6:3–11; Col. 2:12). The Christian communities are the work of Christ, and those who believe in him are called to share in his glory (2 Thess. 2:14). Until the day comes when this glory will be revealed (1 Thess. 2:19; 1 Tim. 1:12) the Christian must walk worthy of his Lord (1 Cor. 11:27; Rom. 12:11; 16:17f.; 1 Cor. 12:5; Col. 2:12; 3:24; Eph. 1:15; 6:13). The proclamation that Jesus is the risen Lord frequently leads to the moral injunction to live as befits one taken into the death and resurrection of Christ (cf. 1 Cor. 6:12–20; 12:7ff.). In this way Christ becomes the savior of those who believe in him. Paul uses the term savior (Soter) frequently. But he also says that Jesus will come again as judge, and then he will speak, on each man and on the whole of creation, the last decisive word for salvation or loss (1 Cor. 4:4). The believer looks forward to this in trust and confidence (1 Cor. 1:8); more than that, he longs for the return of the Lord (2 Tim. 4:8) It is his own Lord who comes to judge, the Lord who in immense mercy has called him to holiness and righteousness. The Christian then can glory in his Lord, who was crucified, but in no other (Gal. 6:14). No doubt there are other gods and lords in heaven and on earth as Paul says with Hellenistic religion in mind, but we have only one God, the Father from whom everything comes and for whom we exist, and only one Lord, Jesus Christ, through whom everything including ourselves was created (1 Cor. 8:6); to him alone praise is due for all eternity (2 Tim. 4:18).

By saying that Christ as Lord is also savior, Paul adopted a common expression of the times in order to express Jesus' function and nature (cf. Acts 13:13: Paul's speech at Antioch in Pisidia). We await the savior from heaven, the Lord Christ (Phil. 3:20). According to the Epistle to the Ephesians (5:23) Christ is the savior of his body, the church. The frequency with which Paul speaks of Christ as savior seems to betray a polemic undertone: in contrast to the multiplicity of savior figures Jesus is the one and only true savior (cf. also Titus 1:4; 2:13; 3:6; 2 Tim. 1:10). When Paul says that Christ has become Lord through his resurrection and enthronement in glory he begins his function as judge and savior.

Paul's statements about Christ reach their climax in his use of the term "Son of God." The phrase has different levels of meaning for him. Sometimes he uses it to designate Jesus' function, as do many passages of the Synoptics. But sometimes it is also a statement about Jesus' nature. The term unites Jesus' task and being, and Paul uses it in reference to all stages of salvation history: pre-existence, earthly life, especially the death on the cross, and resurrection. Paul proclaims Christ as "Son of God" become man, given to death, glorified, and one day to return (Rom. 5:10; 1:16; 8:32; 1 Cor. 1:9; 1 Thess. 1:10). In Paul the Son of God concept is not drawn, at least not directly, from the Hellenistic world which was replete with sons of God and divine men; it represents his development of the idea of Christ which he had received from the Christian tradition. He sees in Christ the Son of God sent by the father in the form of man (Rom. 1:3f.; 8:3; 2 Cor. 1:19; Gal. 4:4; Phil. 2:5–11). The proclamation that Jesus is Lord is identical in meaning with the statement that the father has sent his son into the world, and it is he who is the fulfillment of all the promises of God (2 Cor. 1:19f.). The apostle is to preach him to the Gentiles (Gal. 1:16), that it is through him, through his death and resurrection, that God has reconciled us to himself, when we were still sinners (Rom. 5:6–11; Eph. 1:6), that we are called to community with the Son of God (1 Cor. 1:9), our Lord Jesus Christ, that through him we have access to the Father (Eph. 2:18), that God has taken us into the kingdom of his beloved son (Col. 1:13). He is *the* Son and has no equal (1 Cor. 15:28).

The judge whose coming the Christian awaits, for whom he longs in the stress of the times, is the Lord who was raised from the dead, and he is none other than the Son of God himself (1 Thess. 1:3–10; 2:19; 1 Tim. 6:14). He is able to give us to share in the life of God because the fullness of God dwells in him (Col. 2:9f.). In the future resurrection of the dead we will become like him (Rom. 8:29; 1 Cor. 15:49).

The question has been discussed at length whether the Epistle to the Romans (9:5) explicitly terms Christ God or not. The passage runs: "Theirs are the patriarchs, and from them, in natural descent, sprang the messiah, God, Supreme above all, blessed forever! Amen." The question is whether the final phrase "God, supreme above all [be] blessed forever" is a description of the Messiah or a doxology added simply at the end and not referring to the Messiah. Both interpretations are possible, though the first seems grammatically more likely (cf. K. H. Schelkle, *Paulus der Lehrer der Vater,* Düsseldorf, 1956, pp. 331–344). In any event it is a fact that Paul prays to Christ, so that it is not impossible that he should use the words "theos" of him (O. Cullmann, *Christology of the New Testament*). However, the principal evidence that Paul considered Jesus divine is his repeated use of the term Kyrios.

The text of Colossians 2:2 is uncertain. The form of the text which has the better witnesses, however, does not directly state that Jesus is God. The New English Bible translates the passage thus: "I want them to continue in good heart and in the unity of love, and to come to the full wealth of conviction which understanding brings, and grasp God's secret. That secret is Christ himself." However, in the text adopted by Nestle the words "secret," "God," and "Christ" are all in the genitive case and it would be possible to understand "Christ" as in apposition to "God." On the other hand the Epistle to Titus, though not written by Paul, does contain an explicit identification of Christ with God (2:13): ". . . looking forward to the happy fulfillment of our hopes when the splendor of our great God and Savior Christ Jesus will appear."

## THE EPISTLE TO THE HEBREWS

The Epistle to the Hebrews occupies a special place in the course of the early Church's reflection on the activity and nature of Jesus Christ. Its thinking is advanced, it is written in the spirit of Paul but still in a very independent fashion, and it belongs to the world of Hellenistic Judaism. Within the apostolic era it is surpassed in depth of thought only by the Johannine writings. The author interprets the activity of being of Jesus as the fulfillment of the sacrificial worship of the Old Testament so that the figure of the High Priest occupies the central point of his interpretation of Christ. The letter has taken up a great heritage, drawing deeply on the tradition of the early Church, and has developed it further. Like Paul and John it stresses the absolute significance of Jesus for the creation and redemption of the world. Jesus comes from heaven to be the leader who brings many sons to glory (2:10). Because of his close bond with his brothers (2:11f.,17) he was able to be the mediator of a new covenant for them through his sacrifice on the cross offered once for all time and valid forever (7:17; 8:6; 9:15; 9:23–28; 12:24). He continues to intercede for them in heaven (7:25; 9:14). He is the son, the reflection of God's glory, "the effulgence of God's splendor and the stamp of God's very being, and sustains the universe by his word of power" (1:3). He is raised above the angels who must adore him (1:4–8). He has sat down at the right hand of the majesty on high (1:13; 3:1–6; 4:14f.; 8:1; 12:2). He is raised even above Moses. He is the same yesterday, today, and forever (13:8). A Jew who took this last passage literally would almost automatically take it to refer to Yahweh (T. Bornhauser, *Emp-*

*fänger und Verfasser des Briefes an die Hebräer,* Gütersloh, 1932, p. 39).

As Son, Jesus is also lord (2:3; 7:14; 13:20). On the one hand he is pictured as one who is faithful to his creator, who is like us in everything, and so can consider us his brothers. On the other hand, passages from the Old Testament which refer there directly to God (for example, Ps. 45:7–8; Ps. 2:26–28) are here applied without any reservation to Jesus, and he is explicitly called God (1:8–9). Jesus is clothed with glory and has the place of honor at the side of God. Yet this is not the final stage in the glory allotted to him. The world to come has already been made subject to him and God has made him the heir of all creation. However his rulership is not yet apparent and it must be made so. He will come again, for all those who look to him for their salvation (1:2; 2:8; 9:27f.; cf. O. Kuss, *Der Brief an die Hebräer,* Regensburg, 1966, pp. 143–152).

## JOHN

### Prefatory Note

The Johannine writings represent the high-water mark of the early Church's reflection on the Jesus of history, up to and including his resurrection. In the light of the most recent researches it is no longer possible to maintain that the Gospel of John is basically a gnostic document or represents simply an attempt to come to grips with gnosticism, although that is clearly part of it. The Gospel takes up traditions of the early Church and develops them further. It takes the synoptic tradition as its basis but goes much further in its theological interpretation of Jesus; although it must be said that the decisive step had already been taken by the Synoptics. It cannot be said without qualification that the Gospel has taken even its terminology from gnosticism; it is taken principally from the Old Testament, more accurately from late Jewish writings, although on the other hand it is clear that the author has taken account of widespread gnostic conceptions and formulations. The Gospel is an answer to the central questions of gnosticism. Contrasts which characterize gnostic thinking, such as that between the above and the below, between spirit and matter, also characterize the thought of the Gospel. The central point of all gnostic conceptions is the pre-existence of the essential core of the human soul (not its totality), which has sunk down into matter and remains unredeemed there. However, man can regain his true self and achieve salvation through reflection on this pre-existent core of his being. That is to say, through such reflection and meditation man can come to return again to his heavenly home. This view is expressed in many mythical formulations, and in these it is invariably the vertical dimension of life which predominates. On the other hand the Johannine writings, like the Old Testament, emphasized the horizontal dimension of life, through the union and contrast of present and future. The vertical dimension is certainly not absent from Johannine thought, but its significance is different from that in gnosticism. In the Johannine writings the opposition or contrast which counts is that between the holiness of God and the sinfulness of men; that is, it is a question of the relationship between God and human history. Even the vertical dimension here takes on the character of a horizontal one, since the opposition between God and the power of sin is overcome in the course of human history.

Quite a number of christological conceptions from the synoptic tradition have been adopted in the Gospel of John, and are fused there in such a way that it is difficult to distinguish them from one another. Following Schnackenburg's researches we can say that these titles for Jesus stand out especially in the first chapter of the Gospel: Logos, God, Life and Light, the Only Begotten, the Son, the Lamb of God, the Son of God, the Chosen One of God, the Messiah, the King of Israel, the Son of Man. Not many new titles occur in the subsequent course of the Gospel and those that do do not add a great deal. They include: the Savior of the World (Jn. 4:42) and the Holy One of God (Jn. 6:69); however, the title that especially characterizes Jesus throughout the entire Gospel is that of "Son." Because he is the Son he is the Bread of Life, the Light of the World, the Good Shepherd, the Vine, the Way, the Resurrection and the Life, the Truth.

*The Pre-existence of Jesus*

Like the Synoptics, John reports that Jesus is taken for a prophet (6:14; 7:40,52). The title rabbi (master, teacher) is also given to him (1:38,49; 3:2; 4:31; 6:25; 9:2; 11:8). This title is sometimes used interchangeably with Kyrios (6:34,68; 13:6,9,13). But whereas the word Kyrios has an exceptional significance in the Pauline writings, since there it stands for "Yahweh," in John this is not the case and the term has no special significance.

Similarly, John speaks often of Jesus as Messiah (Jn. 1:19–51). John the Baptist undertakes the task of introducing him as the promised Messiah to the people of Israel (Jn. 1:30f.). He does this because he sees Jesus as one who possesses and can bestow the spirit of God with special power, and for this reason can baptize men with the spirit (Jn. 1:31f.; cf. 1:42,49). The arguments about Jesus' Messiahship reported in chapters 7 and 9 of the Gospel are, of course, relevant here also.

A special characteristic of the Gospel is its insistence on the pre-existence of Jesus. If John emphasizes the historicality of Jesus (the Word was made Flesh, 1:14), he stresses the pre-existence of Jesus with no less intensity, and, in fact, takes it as a matter of course (1:1,30; 6:62; 8:58; 17:5,24; cf. 6:33f., 50f, 58; 7:28f.; 8:14,23,26,42; 16:26ff.).

To the concept of pre-existence John unites that of Jesus' descent from heaven and his return there, the idea that he was sent by the Father and that he will come again. Such formulations are also to be found in gnostic mythology, especially in the myth of the Primal Man. However, it seems likely that the descent-ascent theme in John is not a borrowing from gnosticism but the further development of a tradition already found in the Synoptics and in the Old Testament. We find the idea already in a hymn to Christ that antedates Paul (Phil. 2:6–11). When Jesus says (Jn. 8:58f.): "Before Abraham was, I am," he claims to be the savior foretold in the Old Testament. This statement goes far beyond Jewish ideas, and in a fashion that must have been scandalous to them, although only in the form in which Jesus makes it.

The idea of Jesus' pre-existence is also implied in those passages of Scripture which speak of the Messiah having a role in the act of

creation (1 Cor. 8:6; Gal. 4:4). The wisdom doctrine of the Old
Testament certainly played a role in the formulation of these statements (Heb. 1:3; cf. Wis. 7:25f.), as in the pre-Pauline hymn of
Colossians 1:15ff. The essential difference between the pre-existence of the Logos, as maintained by John, and the pre-existence
of Wisdom in the Wisdom literature consists in the fact that John
ascribes personality to the Logos. However, the author's principal
concern is the exaltation or glorification of Jesus. In contrast to
the Synoptics he sees this already in Jesus' death on the cross
(Jn. 3:14). In contrast with Luke he views the glorification of
Jesus not in the two stages of resurrection and ascension but as
one single event which begins, however, with the crucifixion.

Unlike the hymn in Philippians 2, John does not speak explicitly
of Jesus' being exalted above everything else. Paul does: with his
glorification Christ begins to exercise a kingly and salvific rule
over mankind which he did not do before he entered this world.
In point of fact, however, the difference between the two is not
essential: after the Son's glorification, which is simply his return
to the glory which he had before he came into the world, he is to
glorify his father, by the fact that he gives eternal life to those
who believe in him. It is only in this way that he makes full use
of his authority over all flesh and actually exercises his kingship
(cf. Jn. 17:1f.).

John's basic interest centers on the idea of salvation. "There
were indeed many other signs that Jesus performed in the presence
of his disciples, which are not recorded in this book. Those here
written have been recorded in order that you may hold the faith
that Jesus is the Christ, the Son of God, and that through this
faith you may possess eternal life by his name" (Jn. 20:30f.). The
issue at stake is this salvific activity of Christ. "God loved the
world so much that he gave his only Son, that everyone who has
faith in him may not die but have eternal life" (3:16). By the
fact that the Son returns into glory he makes it possible for those
who believe in him to follow him there (Jn. 14:3f.; 17:24). He is
able to prepare a dwelling place for them with his Father. Here
the contrast to gnostic mythology becomes especially clear. It is
not by reflection on the nature of man, on his origin and goal, on
the inner core of his being, that salvation is achieved but through

community of life with God which is bestowed on him who believes in Jesus Christ, the Son of God. This is probably the reason
why the historical reality of Jesus is so strongly emphasized in the
first epistle of John (1 Jn. 1:1–4), when John says, polemically
and also parenetically: "Do not trust any and every spirit, my
friends; test the spirits, to see whether they are from God, for
among those who have gone out into the world there are many
prophets falsely inspired. This is how we may recognize the spirit
of God; every spirit which acknowledges that Jesus Christ has
come in the flesh is from God" (1 Jn. 4:1–2). On the one hand
this emphasizes the historical reality of Jesus and at the same time
illustrates the radical difference between the gnostic and Christian
ideas of salvation.

### The Logos

If we keep this in mind we will see in a new light John's emphasis
on the pre-existence of the Logos. The purpose of it is to provide
the basis of the salvific power of the Christian redeemer. Because
he comes from on high he can lead men back there. This is probably the chief reason that John prefaces his Gospel with the
Logos hymn. Rudolf Schnackenburg sees a confirmation of this in
the long speech of chapter 6, where the theme of Jesus' descent
from heaven and his return there is most fully developed. It is
stated with great emphasis here that the bread of God is he who
has come down from heaven and gives life to the world (Jn. 6:33;
cf. verses 41, 42, 50, 51, and 58). Until then it is clear that the
true divine life, lasting and indestructible, had not yet been given
to men. For this to happen he must come who had been truly in
heaven, who has come down from heaven, and who, therefore,
precisely as such stands above all that is of this world (3:13–14);
he alone possesses unlimited authority from God (3:35), the fullness of the Spirit (3:34), and so he alone can give to man the
spirit and life of God, although this will take place in fullness only
when he has returned again to his father (7:39). Because Jesus
is conscious that he has come from God (13:3), and not from
himself (3:31f.; 7:28; 8:42), he knows that it is his Father's work
that he is doing (4:34; 9:4), and this is the salvation of the world.

The words he speaks are the Father's words, for God has given him his Spirit (3:34; 12:49; 14:24). It is the Father then who is acting in Christ, and who through him achieves the salvation of the world (6:38ff.). Because he comes from the Father he will one day hold judgment over the world, and his judgment will be true because it will be in agreement with his Father's (8:16). For those who believe in him, however, he is the way, light, truth, the resurrection and the life (11:25; 14:66,35ff.).

## The Son of Man

The relationship between the synoptic tradition and the Gospel of John shows itself rather clearly in the conception of the "Son of Man." In John the idea is linked with the theme of descent and ascent. There are thirteen distinct passages where the formula occurs, and in a large group of these reference is made to the exaltation of the Son of Man (3:13; 6:27; 3:14; 8:28; 12:2ff.; 13:13; 13:31). In other passages the people ask whether he is the Son of Man, and what this Son of Man is (9:35; 12:34). In the Prologue the phrase is used to express the constant union of the Logos with God (1:51). In 5:27 the Son of Man is linked with the idea of judgment. Both the Synoptics and John state that it is the Son of Man who will hold the judgment to come. Although 5:27 is not an addition made by the early Church to the text, as maintained by those who see in John only a realized eschatology, still the reference to the future judgment is made largely because of its significance for the present: the Son of Man both gives life and judges here and now. Both John and the Synoptics state that the Son of Man must suffer much (3:14). Behind this stands the figure of the suffering servant of God of Isaiah 53.

But in John the events of the cross and glorification are seen as a unity (3:14; 8:28; 12:32–34). Some of the statements that most characterize the idea of the Son of Man in the Synoptics are missing in John: that he has the power here and now to forgive sins (Mk. 2:10), that he is lord of the Sabbath (Mk. 2:28), that he has no place to lay his head (Lk. 9:58). John's conception of the role of the Son of Man in the present then differs from that of

the Synoptics. Their agreement in attributing future glory and
power to him stands out all the more as a result of this. It is necessary that the Son of Man be lifted up, namely to the death of the
cross (12:34), before he can come again in glory to judge, though
his listeners cannot grasp this. His death will itself be his glorification (13:31). And then, the descent of the Son of Man from
heaven is already the beginning of the path that leads to his death,
but also with it to his original glory and power (3:13f.), by which
he becomes the sovereign savior of mankind (Jn. 8:28).

## The Son

We come to the final title of significance, the simple one of "Son."
Here we must distinguish the statements of Jesus about himself
from the statements of John and his contemporaries, so far as
that is possible. The expression "Son" or "Son of God" is the principal title of Jesus in John. Jesus speaks of himself as the Son, indeed as the only Son of God (3:18). He is the Son in a unique
sense, which he shares with no one else. God shows his love for
men precisely by the fact that it is his son, whom he loves, that
he has sent into the world (3:35), not in order to judge the world,
but to save it (3:16). He who believes in the Son can have eternal
life, he who does not believe in the Son remains in death (3:36).
It is their attitude towards the Son that decides the fate of men.
On the other hand, it does not lie in the power of man ultimately
to decide whether he wishes to live or to remain in death: it is the
Son who decides with free and sovereign authority to whom he
will give life. He has the power to give life because he himself
possesses it in fullness and is "alive" (5:26). The same honor is
due to the Son as to the Father (5:23), and if the Son is dishonored, by that fact the Father is dishonored (5:23). God is the
Father of Christ in a way in which he is not the Father of anyone
else (2:16; 5:17–43; 6:32; 19:48–54, etc.): "I am ascending to
my Father and your Father, my God and your God" (Jn. 20:17).
He is from eternity (17:5; 8:58); he is one with the Father both
in being and in action (5:17; 10:30).

It is particularly in the numerous "I" statements that Jesus expresses his close relationship to the Father, and even puts himself

in the place which the Old Testament reserved for Yahweh. In his farewell speeches to his disciples he asks them to believe in him and in the Father; he places himself together with the Father in a single "we," and he desires to bring his disciples into this bond too.

As a result of this, the early Church recognized Christ as the Son of God. However, it should not be overlooked that John places words in the mouths of his contemporaries, such as John the Baptist, which would have been possible only after the experience of Easter (cf. Jn. 1:20–35).

The Gospel of John bears in a special way the character of a testimony of faith given in the light of the Easter experience. The evangelist considers Jesus as the Logos who existed in the beginning, who was with God, and who in fact was identical with God (Jn. 1:1f.). This cannot be taken simply as the designation of a function: it is an ontological statement. The Prologue speaks of the Logos as God. There is no further reflection on how this divinity of the Logos is related to the one God of the Old Testament. In any case, however, the Logos belongs to the life-sphere of the one God. Martha, the sister of Lazarus, says, even before her brother is raised from the dead, "I believe that you are the Messiah, the Son of God who was to come into the world" (Jn. 11:27). The apostle Thomas, confronted with the risen Lord, confesses, "My Lord and my God" (Jn. 20:28).

Not only his friends, but also his enemies heard and understood Jesus' claim to a unique sonship. They persecuted him not only because he broke the Sabbath, but because he called God his own Father and made himself God (Jn. 5:18; 10:33). In the light of the monotheism of the Old Testament that was an immense blasphemy, deserving death (Jn. 10:39). The Jews expected a Messiah whose origins would be shrouded in mystery (Jn. 7:27), but not one who would break through the barrier between creator and creature, between transcendence and immanence. From their monotheistic viewpoint it is understandable that they would say, "We have a law, and by that law he ought to die, because he has claimed to be Son of God" (Jn. 19:7).

*The Signs*

Jesus' statements about himself are confirmed in John by the deeds of power which he works as the Son, or which the Father works through him. Usually seven of these are distinguished:

the changing of the water into wine at Cana (2:1–22),
the healing at a distance of the official's son in Capharnaum (4:46–54),
the healing of the cripple at the pool of Bethesda (5:1–9),
the feeding of the five thousand (6:1–12),
the walking on the water (6:16–21),
the healing of the man born blind (9:1–41),
and the raising of Lazarus from the dead (11:1–44).

These events are reported by John as "signs" of the glory of Jesus. (In the case of the walking on the water, the event lacks public character, and perhaps should not be counted among the "signs.") John also uses another word in speaking of Jesus' deeds of power, namely "works." The works bear testimony to Jesus and are intended to bear witness that he is sent from God. They are testimonies of the Father in behalf of the Son. They are works of the Father through the Son. The idea around which the "works" center is that of Jesus' "being sent," and so they function in John primarily as a summons to faith. The "signs" however presume the presence of faith in the onlooker. To him who truly believes they show the glory of Jesus. But for those who do not believe the "signs" are simply astonishing events. In either case what is at stake, what is being shown forth in them, is not only the glory of Jesus, but also the glory of God (2:11; 11:4; 11:40). This notion is not to be explained in terms of Platonic philosophy, in which a picture or sign is the appearance of an actual reality, making it present; it derives from the miracles reported in the book of Exodus accompanying the liberation of the Hebrew people from slavery in Egypt, and from the wonders worked by the prophets to support their warnings and promises. The deeds of power which the Synoptics report are largely identical with those in John, and are also to be understood as signs. However there is a certain difference in their function. In the Synoptics they are signs of the reign of God; that is, their significance is soteriological rather than Christological. In John however they are the epiphany of God in Jesus, they reveal the nature of Jesus himself: in Jesus salvation is already present. The healing of the official's son at Capharnaum, and of the cripple at the pool of Bethesda, and the raising of Lazarus are signs that the Life has already appeared among men. The Life which Jesus restores by these acts is a symbol and pledge of eternal life. For John this eternal life is not only something future, however, it is also something present here and now, and is given by Jesus to those who believe in him. The signs which show Jesus as the Resurrection and the Life then are revelatory in character. While the signs worked by the Old Testament prophets are to be understood as a creative anticipation of the future to come, that is, as a revelation of events which God intends to happen in the future and so are simply a heightened form of prophetic utterance, the signs worked by Jesus are not revelations of his future glory, but of the glory already present in him.

The first Epistle of John speaks of Jesus as the eternal Son of God who has appeared in history and is the mediator of man's salvation: "We know that the Son of God has come and given us understanding to know him who is real; indeed we are in him who is real, since we are in his Son Jesus Christ. He is the true God, he is eternal life" (1 Jn. 5:20).

## The Book of Revelation

In the Book of Revelation the figure of Jesus is presented to us by means of visions, acclamations, and titles of authority. The central idea of the book is summed up in the image of the "Lamb of God" who is wounded unto death, but still lives and reigns, who opens the seals of the book of life which contains the meaning of human history, who brings to nothing the enemies of God, holds judgment, and unites himself with those who believe in him in a love portrayed as that of a bride and groom. But even here Jesus is not the end but the way. The goal is the Father, God, who makes his dwelling among his people. The book has a radically eschatological character in that it proclaims an absolute future.

*Notes*

[1] F. R. Geiselmann, "Jesus Christ," in H. Fries, *Handbuch theologischer Grundbegriffe*, vol. 1, p. 759.

[2] G. Bornkamm, *Jesus of Nazareth* (New York: Harper & Row, 1960), p. 51.

[3] See Th. Seidenstücker, *Paulus, der verfolgte Apostel Jesu Christi* (Stuttgart, 1965).

# ◂ 8

# *Theological Development After the Apostolic Era*

## THE PROBLEM

With their confession "Jesus is the Christ," "Jesus is the Lord," the primitive Christian community took leave of the Old Testament faith-community, even though the first Christians still exercised the traditional Old Testament forms of worship for a while. On the one hand this confession of Christ can only be made "in the Holy Spirit." On the other hand, however, it only had meaning in the light of the Old Testament belief in the one God. It is he who made Jesus Christ and Lord. God alone can be the savior of man, and yet he gives man salvation through Jesus whom he sends into the world, and this salvation can be appropriated only through the activity of the Holy Spirit. It would appear then that there are three different bearers of salvation to man, who yet in some fashion or other are united. Are there two, or three Gods? If not, how are these three related?

Some reflection on this problem had already begun during the apostolic age, but no clear conclusions were reached. The principal concern of the New Testament writers was not for Jesus' metaphysical relationship to God (ontological Christology), but for what he did, his salvific significance (functional Christology). A number of passages, in the Synoptics, somewhat more in Paul, and especially in Hebrews and the Gospel of John, lead off in a metaphysical direction, but without actually confronting the problem.

The proclamation of the three bringers of salvation and the problem of their relationship to the God of the Old Testament posed a task which was to strain some of the best of minds for centuries. Again, the basic interest was not speculative, a matter of abstract information for the sake of abstract information, but practical or existential, the process of man's salvation. The primary purpose was not to discover what Jesus was in himself, but his exact significance for us. However, this leads necessarily to the question what he was in himself, since it is on this that the value of his activity for us depends.

The question of Jesus, that is, of the relationship of Jesus and the Spirit to the one God, raises the question of our understanding of God himself. So the efforts to arrive at a satisfactory Christology run largely parallel to the attempt to formulate a satisfactory conception of the tri-personal God. That is, the question of the process of man's salvation becomes a strictly "theological" question: *oikonomia* becomes *theologia*. However this theological problem, the problem of God, was only a part of the Christological problem. However Jesus' relationship to God was to be understood, his relationship to the rest of mankind also had to be explained. This then raised the question of his human nature.

So there are three problems: the relationship of Jesus to God, his human nature, and the mutual relationship of the divine and the human in him. The chief lines of development of the first problem have already been sketched in our treatment of the trinity above, but may be briefly recalled here. In the centuries which followed the apostolic era the expressions "Son" and "Logos" played a decisive role, the problem of the Holy Spirit remained for a long time in the background, which is not surprising since Jesus had been a historical figure and had stood directly before the gaze of men. Furthermore, there would be no insurmountable difficulties in relating the Holy Spirit to God if it once proved possible to understand Jesus as divine within the framework of continued belief in the one God of the Old Testament.

The struggle of the first four centuries in this matter was many sided, sometimes extremely subtle and complex, and carried on with great bitterness. Much human weakness, self-righteousness and vanity, desire for power and even the use of violence, and plain stupidity came to the surface. On the other hand the question at stake was a matter of immense importance, the salvation of man. One result of the struggles was a set of official Church dogmas, which will be treated in a separate section. These can be understood only in the light of the long years of argument which preceded them. On the other hand they themselves do not represent any final solution: they pose new questions, and stand under the law that all our thought and talk is piecework (1 Cor. 13:9).

A just judgment of the theological discussions must take into account the various types of mentality involved. There is a type of mentality that we can characterize as Eastern or Oriental and which stands in contrast to another type usually thought of as Western. This latter type is more concerned with clarity of conception and formulation, while the former type is content with an effective description and tends to consider emphasis on clarity as a restriction or hindrance to a true appreciation of reality. If we are to judge properly the formulations arrived at by the Church councils, we must attempt to follow not only the development of the theological discussion itself but also the mental climate, the type of thinking which is being expressed. In almost every case the discussion led to a dogmatic formulation which appears to have the clarity of Roman or Western thought, and yet the principal protagonists were from the eastern part of the Mediterranean. We must ask ourselves whether the resulting statements are so closely connected with a particular mentality, for example, Roman thought forms, that they cannot be expressed in another form such as the Eastern; in fact the question is whether we are not obliged to do this if they are to be genuinely intelligible to a large portion of mankind.

Passages such as Gal. 4:4; 1 Cor. 2:8; Phil. 2:5-11; Col. 2:9; Heb. 1:3; Rom. 1:3; 10:3,9; and Jn. 1:14 were taken as the point of departure for the subsequent discussion. The basis accepted by all participants was the monotheism inherited from the Old Testament: although the interpretations of Jesus go in almost every conceivable direction. The theological movement which led even-

tually to the councils of Nicea (325) and Chalcedon (451) began with Ignatius of Antioch who tried to derive from functional
Christology an ontological one, that is, the relationship of the Son
to the Father. Irenaeus, in his doctrine of the *anakephalaiosis,*
understood, as Hippolytus did, the world and history as Christocentric, and so developed a theology on a cosmic scale, which,
however, does not seem to leave sufficient room for the incalcu-
lable elements in history.

The big question is whether it is possible to maintain a strict
monotheism and still admit differentiation within the life of God.
For Jewish-Christian thought this was impossible, yet the Council of Nicea arrived at the conviction that the two were not necessarily incompatible. For people who based their thought on the
Old Testament there could be only one God and Lord, and so the
view put forward in the post-apostolic era that Jesus was to be
understood simply as a savior, with no intrinsic relationship to
God, was termed monarchianism. This view appeared in two
forms, the dynamic and the modalist. The oldest form of dynamic
monarchianism was the view of the Ebionites (the "Poor"), that
Jesus was nothing other than a man adopted by God and equipped
with special power *(dynamis)*. This conception fits in particularly
well with Isaiah's idea of the Messiah as the "servant of God." To
complicate things a little further, the Ebionite view itself developed
in two forms, one of which attributed the miraculous birth of Jesus
from the Virgin Mary to the Holy Spirit, while the other denied
this. This Christology, coming from the East, found its way to
Rome through Theodotus the Tanner, and his disciple, also called
Theodotus, the Money-Changer, and Asklepiodotus. According to
Theodotus the Tanner Jesus, a mere man, was filled with the Holy
Spirit and with divine power at his baptism, and became the Son
of God. We find such ideas later with Paul of Samosata and
Lucian of Antioch and his disciples. It was from this school that
Arius came. Ebionitism itself survived only briefly, but modalistic
monarchianism assumed greater proportions. While dynamic mo-
narchianism emphasized the transcendence of God, the modalistic
form of it, otherwise known as patripassianism (implying that the
Father suffered) or Sabellianism (after one representative of this
view), stressed also the immanence of God in the world. Novatian

drew the lines clearly in his work on the Trinity: "They who say that Jesus Christ is the Father argue as follows: If God is one, and Christ is God, Christ is the Father, since God is one. If Christ be not the Father, because Christ is God the Son, there appear to be two Gods introduced, contrary to the Scriptures. And they who contend that Christ is man only conclude on the other hand thus: If the Father is one, and the Son another, but the Father is God and Christ is God, then there is not one God, but two Gods are at once introduced, the Father and the Son; and if God is one, by consequence Christ must be a man, so that rightly the Father may be one God. Thus the Lord is, as it were, crucified between two thieves" (chapter 33). By identifying Christ with the Father both the divine monarchy and the divinity of Jesus are maintained. By appearing in history in the form of Jesus the Father took on the function of being Revealer, Word, Logos. The word Logos then signifies the Father insofar as he exercises a revelatory function in Jesus. If this thesis is to be properly understood, it must be remembered that the Old Testament speaks of angels of God or of the Wisdom of God and means by this God himself acting in human history. However, such Old Testament conceptions probably have little influence on the development of modalistic monarchianism; it is rather the product of the Stoic Logos doctrine, according to which the one God, who is immanent in the world, can be called by various names according as He makes himself known. According to Hippolytus, monarchianism is the opinion that that which is called Father and Son is one and the same being, given different names according to the different times of his appearance. Modalistic monarchianism itself developed in different forms in the theologies of Praxeas and Sabellius. The interpretation which the Christian Church adopted officially goes beyond both the modalist identification of the divine element in Jesus with the Father, and the Ebionite view of Jesus as simply a man with heavenly power.

The basis for the official Christian interpretation was laid by the Apologists of the second and third centuries. These writers made use of a variety of conceptions to cope with the problem, their first step being to interpret the generation of Jesus Christ from God not only as a matter of what we would call salvation history, but as a process within the Godhead. They were helped in this by the Johannine Logos doctrine and the Old Testament personification of Wisdom. Seen in this light, the "generation" of the Son was a spiritual act in some way or other. They were also influenced by the great figure of the Alexandrian Jew Philo, who spoke of the Son of God as Logos, and distinguished a *Logos endiathetos* and a *Logos ekdiathetos*. As a result of Philo's theology the Christian writers of the second and third centuries considered the Logos as the eternal reason of the Father, but as having at first no distinct existence from eternity; he received this only when the Father generated him from within his own being and sent him to create and rule over the world. The act of generation then was not considered as an eternal and necessary life-act remaining within God, but as one which was free, and had a beginning in time, which meant that the Son was not equal to the Father, but subordinate to him. Irenaeus, Justin, Hippolytus, and Methodius of Olympus share this view, called Subordinationism, with the great Origen. It took a long time and much effort before the function of the Logos in the creation and redemption of the world could be clearly distinguished from his role within the Godhead, a distinction which was eventually made by the Council of Nicea.

## JESUS AS TRUE MAN

The most important material concerning this has already been considered in the treatment of the identity of the risen Christ with the historical Jesus. Neither Paul nor the Epistle to the Hebrews intends to express more than this identity. Even the Gospels provide us with no biography of Jesus; they do not even make it possible for us to reconstruct his journeys. However they do give us some details of Jesus' life in the course of carrying out their primary aim, which is to give testimony of their faith in him. Matthew and Luke give some information about his childhood. According to Mt. 2:1 and Lk. 1:53, and the story of Mt. 2 attached to the name of Herod, Jesus was born during Herod's reign, that is, probably in the year 4 "B.C." Although he was born in Bethlehem, his actual home is in Nazareth in Galilee. Whether it was originally Jesus or Joseph who was called a carpenter in Mk. 6:3

cannot be discovered with certainty. The Gospels give only one explicit date for the activity of the Baptist (Lk. 3:1ff.), almost certainly between October of the year 27 and September of 29 A.D., and in the light of this it seems most likely that Jesus' public activity lasted somewhat more than two years.

We find an account of the inner and outward development of the growing Jesus, and his attitude towards the world around him, in Luke 2:14–52. As a public teacher he is not dependent on Hellenistic thinking or on ideas developed by contemporary Jewish piety (apocalypticism, Qumran, the Essenes, the baptism movement), but the presence of these developments during his time does enable us to understand better both the content of his teaching and the method he used to convey it. The historicality of Jesus is especially emphasized by the introduction of names which do not belong to salvation history: the Roman emperor Tiberius who ordered a census of the population, the Roman governor of Syria, Quirinius (Lk. 2:1f.), the Roman procurator Pontius Pilate, King Herod (Lk. 2:4; 3:1ff.), and these provide us with some definite dates. After initial enthusiasm the great mass of the people withdrew from him when it became plain that he was not going to fulfill their hopes for a radical change of their political and social situation. The leading circles become increasingly hostile to him, eventually he is arrested in Jerusalem by the Sanhedrin, delivered up to the Roman procurator, condemned to death, and executed on Friday the fourteenth (John) or fifteenth (synoptics) of Nisan. Although he certainly died, and was given honorable burial, the history of Jesus does not end there. On the contrary it begins anew, on a different level, by the fact that his disciples, who had held his cause for lost, and knew him to be dead, experienced him as alive in numerous appearances, and interpreted their experience in this manner, that God had raised Jesus from the dead.

What is most striking and enlightening is the strong emphasis on the historicality of Jesus in the Johannine writings. "The Word became flesh and dwelt among us, and we have seen his glory, glory as of the only-begotten of the Father, full of grace and of truth" (Jn. 1:14). One clothed with the dignity of God, of whom it is said that he was with God, in fact that he was God himself, has entered the world of men. He had in fact always been present in spirit (1:9), but now he has "set up his tent" among men, as a man. The Logos is not changed into flesh, but neither is his humanity a mere appearance. The Logos is man. This event has taken place in order to open up to men the way to divine life. It is the turning point of human history.

It is worthy of note that John does not simply say "the Logos became a man." The word "flesh" signifies something bound to the earth, something weak and transient, that is, the typical character of human existence in contrast to heavenly existence, although without an implication here of sinfulness. The whole passage is directed against a form of "docetism." This word is used to designate a group of very various interpretations of Jesus, and we find one form of it already prominent at the end of the first century. In its various forms docetism taught that God is absolutely transcendent, and so cannot enter directly into relationship with the world; in order to do this he makes use of intermediate beings. Cerinthus concluded that Jesus could not be God, but was simply a man. Other forms of docetism maintained that Jesus' body was a mere appearance, and so his death was not a real death, but only an apparent one, just as his birth and earthly life were only appearances; or that the man Jesus was not identical with the divine Logos; or that redemption was not carried out by a concrete man of flesh and blood, and that this was not necessary, since salvation could be obtained through reflection and meditation. Such ideas were already on the scene during the apostolic age, and needed to be refuted (cf. 1 Jn. 3:22; 4:2f.; 5:1,5f.). The sharp statement that the Word became "flesh," like the strong statements of the Johannine epistles, is a protest against docetic types of thinking, not one of the innumerable forms of gnosticism. This is not the language of mythology. Jesus is spoken of in a totally antignostic, antimythical way, as a human and historical figure. It also seems likely that such ideas are being fought again in the Epistle to the Colossians and in the pastoral epistles.

Shortly after the apostolic period docetism was attacked with great severity by Ignatius of Antioch and by Irenaeus. Ignatius emphasizes that the birth, life, death, and resurrection of Jesus were actual events, because only in this way does he see salvation guaranteed, and the meaning of his own martyrdom. Irenaeus rejects the opinion that Jesus' body was a mere appearance, especially the idea that the virgin birth of Jesus was possible because his body, being heavenly, could simply pass through Mary's flesh, and that Jesus gave only the appearance of suffering.

It is of immense importance for Christianity that Jesus be understood as truly man, and so it is understandable that the Church should have made a number of official statements to that effect (cf. the Councils of Lyons, DS 462, and Vienne, DS 480). However, official condemnation of docetism has not by any means eliminated the dangers which it presents, for there are subtle forms of it which can go unnoticed yet greatly influence one's conception of Christianity. Docetism is present wherever the full humanity of Jesus is undervalued, or its significance insufficiently realized: for example, if we imagine that Jesus did not possess true human spontaneity and freedom, a genuine power to make his own decisions and an authentic sense of responsibility. This creates a mental attitude in which the formula of the liturgy, "through Christ to the Father," has lost its earnestness and meaning.

The seed of future troubles lay, for example, in Origen's thesis of the pre-existence of all souls, including that of Jesus. Origen himself emphasized very strongly the truly human nature of Jesus. His motive was soteriological, and it was he who worked out the principle which was subsequently adopted almost universally: *Quod non est assumptum, non est redemptum:* whatever was not assumed (i.e., taken into union with the personality of the Logos) was not redeemed. But the relationship of the soul to the body remained unclear. Two hundred years later this theology led to a crisis, the development of the so-called Logos-Sarx Christology. The thesis was put forward that in Jesus the place of the human soul was taken by the Logos, which was united directly to Jesus' body. The thesis arose in Arian circles, though not all Arians supported it: some simply did not speak of Jesus' soul, without denying its existence. According to Athanasius (*Contra Apollinarem*), Arius himself confessed only to the flesh as the sheath of the Godhead. In the case of Jesus the Logos took the place of our "interior man," that is, the Logos was the principle of all psychic and spiritual life. The decisive element in human nature, the spiritual principle, was denied to Jesus as a man. Apollinaris of Laodicea and his disciples continued this theology.

How great the temptation to such a theology was, we can see

from the fact that even so orthodox a theologian as Athanasius of Alexandria does not really know what to make of the soul of Jesus. He did not deny its existence, but he did not consider it particularly important either. The school of Antioch, on the other hand, were very clear on the matter; they had a strong appreciation of the full humanity of Jesus, which was expressed in their "Logos-Anthropos" theology. However, they contributed to the confusion in another way, by too radical a separation of the divine from the human in Jesus. It was only at the Council of Chalcedon (451) that a balance between these conflicting views was achieved.

## THE RELATIONSHIP OF THE DIVINE AND THE HUMAN IN JESUS

We turn to the third problem, the mutual relationship between the divine and the human elements in Jesus. The concepts which proved decisive for the discussion of this question were formulated by the African theologian Tertullian, and it was he who set up the framework within which the discussion took place. In his book against Praxeas (chapter 27; cf. *De carne Christi,* Nr. 13):

We see in Christ a twofold state, which is not confounded but conjoined in one person, Jesus, God and man. The property of each nature is so wholly preserved that the Spirit on the one hand did all things in Jesus suitable to Itself, such as miracles and mighty deeds and wonders; and the flesh, on the other hand, exhibited the affections which belong to it. It was hungry under the devil's temptation, thirsty with the Samaritan woman, wept over Lazarus, was troubled even unto death, and at last actually died.[1]

The Council of Nicea, giving the first official definition on a matter of faith made by the Church as a whole, declared that our Lord Jesus Christ is the true Son of God, that he is generated from the being of the Father, not by his will, and is therefore of one nature (*homoousios*) with the Father. Taken literally, the word *homoousios* means only that the nature of the Son is not different from the nature of the Father. But since the Creed which the Council adopted declares at the beginning that there exists only one God, namely the Father, and that the nature of the Son is the same as that of the Father, it follows that Father and Son are numerically one, even if this is not explicitly stated. The God-head of the Son is based on the Godhead of the Father. But it is worth noting that the Council does not use the word "God" of the Son, but only of the Father, although it says that the Son is of the same nature as the Father. In the Council's formulation, the Son is precisely the Son *of God*. It is also a matter of interest that the Council speaks of the one God as the *pantokrator,* that is, the one who rules all, rather than as "almighty," that is, it uses a dynamic word rather than a static one. Of this God it is said that he is the creator of what is visible and of what is invisible, while Jesus is called Lord, and the Son of this God. Although the Council ex-presses the biblical statements about the relationship of the Son to the Father in metaphysical language, it maintains a certain ele-ment of salvation history insofar as the structure of the Creed which it drew up follows a historical sequence.

In any event, the course of subsequent theological discussion followed along the lines begun by this Council. Tertullian had al-ready transferred over to Christology the most important concepts developed in the theology of the Trinity, such as "person" and "substance," and the terminological bridge between the two branches of theology was built up further by Novatian. For Am-brose the mystery of Jesus Christ is the supreme reality in the world of faith, and he states that Jesus is an individual both divine and human, not two individuals: *utrumque unus, non alter et alter.* Pope Damasus made an important contribution to the develop-ment of the doctrine of the two natures in Christ by a compre-hensive view summed up straightforwardly in the phrase *verbum-homo.* Augustine's achievements in this field were manifold: it was as a result of his efforts that Tertullian's Christology was fully adopted in the West. Although he uses the relationship of body and soul as an analogy for the relationship between the divinity and the humanity of Jesus, he does not even come near to falling victim to an Apollinarian truncation of the human element in Jesus. He makes use of the common formula *homo assumptus,* but while in the school of Antioch this denoted a separation of the divinity and humanity, for Augustine it indicates simply that Jesus possesses a fully human nature, without any suggestion that he was not one person.

Greek theology took the Council of Nicea as its point of departure in general. However, the previous custom continued of making statements about the humanity of Jesus and statements about his divinity statically alongside one another without any connection, and so there was a continued tendency to speak as if there were two subjects. But it was now done with the Nicean decision in mind. Rather than look for conceptual clarity, there was a tendency to treat the problem in terms of images or similes: the human nature, for example, was penetrated by the divinity like a glowing iron by fire. An effective formula for speaking about Jesus was developed through the theory of the "communication of idioms," according to which it is possible to predicate divine qualities of the man Jesus and human qualities of the divine Jesus (e.g., Jesus knows all things, God died). This theory, however, was rejected by the school of Antioch. These theologians emphasized very strongly the full humanity of Jesus, in accordance with Nicea, against Arius and Apollinaris, and to this extent they stand in the mainstream of Christian tradition, which was carried on by Didymus, Epiphanius, the two Gregorys, and the synods of Antioch (379), Constantinople (381), and Rome (377, 381, and 382) under Pope Damasus. But the theologians of Antioch went their own way when it came to the question of the relationship of the divine and the human in Jesus (Eustathius, Diodorus of Tarsus, Eusebius of Emesa, and Theodoret of Cyr). The most prominent of this group was Nestorius and after him the Christology of Antioch was known only insofar as it was condemned. Nestorius brought the situation to a crisis when, towards the end of the year 428, he condemned the use of the word "Theotokos" of Mary. This title, "God-bearer," was a product of Alexandrian theology, and was used frequently by Christian writers of the third and fourth centuries. It represents almost an extreme case of the communication of idioms. Nestorius's rejection of it provoked forceful opposition in Alexandria, especially from the bishop, Cyril. We only know Nestorius's views from Cyril's account of them, and recent research has shown that his is considerably biased; he gives them in a form that is exaggerated and one-sided. According to Cyril, Nestorius maintained that Jesus' humanity and divinity were two separate entities, bound together only by the bond of love. The ultimate subject of both divine and human attributes was not the Word, but Christ, the *prosopon* resulting from the union of the two. Mary then should be called "Christ-bearer," because she gave birth not to God, but to Christ united with God. An examination of Nestorius's views shows that in actual fact his principal concern was to preserve the full humanity of Jesus against attempts to reduce it, and he considered that Alexandrian theology implied such a reduction. If this attitude is to be intelligible, we must give a brief account of Cyril's theology. While Nestorius, in the interest of man's salvation, laid the greatest stress on the humanity of Jesus, Cyril, out of the same concern, stressed the unity of the humanity with the divinity: only if the man Jesus was most closely connected to God could he have opened the path to God for us. Cyril was carrying on the theology of Athanasius, but he expressed the unity of Jesus by the phrase: "the one nature (physis, hypostasis) made flesh," or "the one nature of the Logos made flesh," and he also speaks of one being *in* two natures, though without intending to remove the distinction between the divinity and the humanity (cf. Letters 40, 46). It cannot be denied that these formulas have a monophysite ring, so that the protest out of Antioch is understandable. The Archimandrite Eutyches, who represents monophysitism in its developed form, will say later that Jesus had only one nature, because the human element in him was absorbed by the divine. However Cyril cannot justly be accused of monophysitism, because he understood the word *physis,* or nature, in the sense of a concrete individual entity with its own activity and he emphasized the unity of the incarnate Logos in this concrete existence. Nestorius, on the other hand, in Antioch understood the word "nature" in the Aristotelian sense of abstract essence. In this sense Cyril's formula could only be understood as a mixture (*krasis*) of the divine and the human, destroying both. Nestorius was concerned to preserve the integrity of each of the natures in Christ. He declared himself ready to accept only the doctrine put forward by Pope Leo I in his letter against monophysitism (June 449). Also he did not reject the term "Godbearer" of Mary in every sense: he stated rather that the Logos as Logos could not be subject to an earthly event and therefore Mary must have given birth to a man indissolubly united to the Godhead; but this man, because of such a union with God, must himself be called God. However we cannot remove all blame from Nestorius. If he states that both natures are united in one *prosopon*, still he does not explain this key concept in his theology, and most of his formulations are somewhat ambiguous. On the other hand, much the same thing is true of Cyril whose terminology was quite uncertain and could be easily understood in a monophysite sense against his intention.

The term *theotokos* was officially confirmed by the Council of Ephesus in 431 in agreement with Cyril's second letter to Nestorius. But the real reconciliation between the theologians of Antioch and Alexandria came only after long and weary negotiations in 433. Bishop John of Antioch composed a statement of faith which served as the basis of a creed which even Cyril of Alexandria could accept. This creed states that it had no other intention than to confirm what was declared by the Council of Nicea:

We confess therefore our Lord Jesus Christ, the only-begotten Son of God, perfect God and perfect man consisting of a body and a rational soul, begotten of the Father before all ages according to his divinity, but in these last days, for us and for our salvation, [born] of the Virgin Mary according to his humanity, consubstantial with the Father according to his divinity and consubstantial with us according to his humanity. For a unity of the two natures has been made; wherefore we confess one Christ, one Son and one Lord. According to this unity which cannot undergo confusion we confess that the holy virgin is the mother of God, because God the Word has become flesh and man, and from the time of his conception united to himself the temple which he assumed from her (DS 272).

The last statement especially shows that we have here a compromise formula intended to include both the Alexandrian concern for Christ's unity and the Antiochian concern that the fullness of Jesus' humanity be preserved. Arianism and Apollinarism were condemned again (the latter had already been rejected by the Council of Constantinople, 381). The creed is not drawn up in exact language but it is interesting that in contrast to Cyril's theology it speaks not of one *physis,* but of the union of two natures. This is balanced by an emphatic statement that it is one and the same (*ton auton*) who is of the same nature as we in his humanity, and of the same nature as the Father in his divinity.

The significance of the Council of Ephesus lies in the fact that it emphasized the unity of the subject in Jesus, although it did not succeed in producing either a conceptual or a linguistic solution to the problem.

In an exaggerated and unnecessary battle against Nestorianism Cyril's successor, Dioscuros, came to view the divinity and humanity of Christ not only as a unity in the person but declared that Christ possessed only one nature, both divine and human. Eutyches joined with Dioscuros in Constantinople and the two succeeded in calling a synod (the so-called "Robber Synod" of Ephesus, 449). At this point Pope Leo the Great entered into the argument, with a letter to the Patriarch of Constantinople, Flavian, in which he takes up a position against monophysitism. The letter contained the clearest theological formulation of the question so far. The resulting arguments led to the Council of Chalcedon in 459, which, with the Council of Nicea, represents the most important decision on a matter of faith in the first thousand years of the Church. Just as Nicea proclaimed the dogma of the trinity in a way which became decisive for the future faith of the Church, Chalcedon did the same for Christology. The decree runs as follows:

Following the holy Fathers, therefore, we all with one accord teach the profession of faith in the one identical Son, our Lord Jesus Christ. We declare that he is perfect both in his divinity and in his humanity, truly God and truly man composed of body and rational soul; that he is consubstantial with the Father in his divinity, consubstantial with us in his humanity, like us in every respect except for sin. We declare that in his divinity he was begotten of the Father before time, and in his humanity he was begotten in this last age of Mary the Virgin, the mother of God, for us and for our salvation. We declare that the one selfsame Christ, only-begotten Son and Lord, must be acknowledged in two natures without any commingling or change or division or separation; that the distinction between the natures is in no way removed by their union but rather that the specific character of each nature is preserved and they are united in one person and one hypostasis. We declare that he is not split or divided into two persons, but that there is one selfsame only-begotten Son, God the Word, the

Lord Jesus Christ. This the prophets have taught about him from the beginning; this Jesus Christ himself taught us; this the creed of the Fathers has handed down to us. As these truths therefore have been formulated with all possible accuracy and care, the holy, ecumenical council has ordained that no one may bring forward or put into writing or devise or entertain or teach to others any other faith (DS 301f.).[2]

The Council intended to give expression to Christian tradition, and it can justly be said that it actually did this. We find in it the theology of Ignatius of Antioch and Irenaeus of Lyons and especially the statements of faith of Nicea and Constantinople. It is especially significant that to a large extent it adopted the Antiochian creed of 433, but it is also clear that the concerns of Cyril of Alexandria and of Pope Leo have been fully taken into account. The formula of Chalcedon is a particular interpretation, resulting from new arguments of the Christological formula of the Nicene creed which speaks of the only-begotten Son of God the Father. The emphatic statement that it is one and the same who in one sense was born from all eternity and in another sense was born in time takes full account of the Alexandrian concern for the unity of Jesus. But this concern is no longer expressed by speaking of one nature, as Cyril had wished; there is an equal emphasis on the true and undiminished humanity of Jesus which incorporates the essential views of the school of Antioch. This attention to the Antiochene concern becomes quite apparent since the expression "truly man, truly God" is a phrase of Theodoret of Cyr (Letter 151). Another statement of the Council seems to be taken from Theodoret's commentary on 1 Cor. 11:3: with regard to his humanity he is of the same nature as us, and with regard to his divinity he is of the same nature as the Father.

But Chalcedon went beyond previous formulations in a decisive way. Its task was to explain how Christ could be at the same time one and two. We must admit that it did not give an entirely satisfactory answer. But we must also add that such a thing is probably impossible. This question is the innermost mystery of the hypostatic union; different aspects of it may be clarified from time to time, but it is not open to total explanation. In spite of this limitation it must be said also that Chalcedon represents a climax in the Christological interpretation of the New Testament, especially such passages as Jn. 1:14.

With regard to its technical terms, the Council decided to use *physis* as a key word, following Alexandrian theology. However, it used the word to designate the elements that make for duality in Christ, not for unity, and in doing so it unconsciously altered the meaning of the word. Cyril of Alexandria had used it to designate the single, concrete being of Jesus; the Council however used it in the Aristotelian sense of an abstract essence. In contrast with this it used the words *prosopon* and *hypostasis* to designate the unity of the two natures in the one "person" of the Logos.

But it used these terms more in a popular sense than with philosophical exactitude. It failed to explain the relationship of the concept of *hypostasis* or *prosopon* to the concept of *physis*. That is, the Council did not reflect on the question of how the human nature of Jesus could subsist in the *prosopon* of the God-Logos. The central question, how the human nature could maintain its own reality if it did not possess its own personality, remained unanswered.

Still, it was a significant step forward that the expressions *physis* and *hypostasis* were used definitively for the realities we call nature and person: in Jesus there are two *physis* and only one *prosopon* or *hypostasis*. With this, terminology which had long been used of the Trinity was transposed over to Christology.

The statements of Chalcedon should not be looked at as primarily metaphysical utterances. The matter at stake was the possibility of man's salvation. This can be seen clearly from the fact that the Council took up a position explicitly against those who dissolved the historical figure of Christ, and so denied the *oikonomia,* the divine plan for man's salvation. It is true that Chalcedon's definition does not, like the statement of Nicea, have a structure which follows the course of salvation history. It takes one element of this out, but precisely in order to emphasize its importance from the view of salvation history.

After the Council an argument began about the meaning of its statement. The result was a compromise theology which intended to hold on to the content of the Council, but at the same time to give more emphasis to the position of Cyril than it had done, and this led in turn to the councils of Constantinople in 553 and the Lateran in 649. A distinction is usually made then between strict Chalcedonianism and Neo-chalcedonianism, although the actual difference was not great.

In one respect the terminology of Chalcedon remained behind that of Cyril, namely in the fact that it overlooked the dynamic or active element in his conception of the Incarnation. It creates a picture of Christ in which divinity and humanity exist alongside one another in a static fashion, even if, on the other hand, it is not impossible to fit the dynamic qualities of the living Jesus into the picture. The achievement of Chalcedon was such that future exploration of the Christological problem would be possible only on the basis that it laid.

After Chalcedon theology faced the task of clarifying the ideas of *hypostasis, prosopon,* and *ousia.* Both Greek and Latin theologians participated in this work. Leontius of Byzantium understood *hypostasis* (which we usually translate as "person") as existence-for-oneself. The deacon Rusticus considered it as the act of remaining in oneself. Of decisive significance was the definition given by Boethius, in which personhood is constituted by substantiality, intelligence, and individuality. Rufinus invented the word *subsistentia* as a Latin rendering of the Greek *hypostasis. Ousia* was translated into Latin as *substantia* or *essentia.*

At the present time Christology is in a period of new stimulation, and faces a number of exceptionally interesting tasks, deriving from the increased sense of the personal, from a new conception of the relation between God and the world, from the idea of salvation history, and a widespread desire to recover the full dimensions of the humanity of Jesus.

## THEOLOGICAL REFLECTIONS ON THE HYPOSTATIC UNION

The Christian understanding of Christ, which has taken shape as a result of the work done by the theologians and councils described above, can be put as follows. There is only one God. This is the basic truth arrived at by the revelation of the Old Testament. But the historical Jesus of Nazareth, the son of Mary, of the family of David, crucified in Jerusalem, and raised from the dead on the third day, is truly the Son of this one, living God, he is the Son of Yahweh. In fact, he is himself truly God. This Son of Yahweh, at a time chosen by God, became man, not by the conversion of his nature into that of a creature, so that he ceased to be God, but by taking a creature up into his own divine and eternal existence. In the course of this he remains the same person, Jesus Christ. So it must be said: Jesus is fully God like Yahweh his Father, and as fully man as we. Yet he is one as a person. Because of this unity of the personal the man Jesus is truly the Son of God, and conversely the Son of God is truly man. This means that he lived a truly human life, like us in everything except sin, a life of truly human activity in freedom and human consciousness. The one divine person of the Logos acts both through the divine nature, which is identical with himself, and through the human nature which he has adopted. The one person of the Logos possesses two natures, one divine and the other human, though he possesses them in different ways. His human nature is not diminished or lessened, but concrete, individual, and entire.

All this raises a number of very difficult questions. The first and most obvious is: How can the human nature of Jesus remain a fully human nature when it does not exist in its own personality, but in the personality of God? A second question is: how are we to understand the relationship of this human nature living in the personality of the Logos to the divine nature identical with the Logos? Many other questions arise along with these. Could any one of the divine persons become the ground of subsistence of a human nature in this way or is it possible only for the person of the divine Logos? What is the relationship between the structure of the man Jesus and the Christocentric character of the cosmos and especially of human history? What is the significance of the structure of Jesus for our understanding of the Church, of grace, for the problems of eschatology?

As regards the first question we must recall what was said earlier about the concept of the personal. According to the usual definition personhood implies self-possession, self-determination, and responsibility. These three elements were supplemented in the philosophy of the nineteenth century by psychological considerations: they are possible only in the dimension of conscious life. This is a valuable addition to the purely ontic conception of personhood, and leads us from the realm of the ontic to that of the ontological. However, it would amount to a destruction of the concept of person to overlook the ontic structure, which forms the foundation of the psychological.

Even within the field of the ontic, however, it would be a mistake to remain within the purely static conception of personality which is expressed in the three elements mentioned. It was mentioned earlier that, according to Thomas Aquinas, man possesses himself in the fact that he continually returns to himself. Self-possession, therefore, is a dynamic act: to possess oneself is to take possession of oneself.

Man determines himself and exercises responsibility insofar as he reaches out beyond himself, transcends himself, both towards the material world and especially towards his fellow men. He comes to consciousness of himself only in encounter with what is not himself, and especially in the encounter with his fellow man: it is here that he becomes aware of his own ability to say "I." This necessarily includes the awareness of the "Thou." Whenever we say "I," a "Thou" is implicit in our statement. An essential element of the personal, therefore, is the relatedness of the "I" to the "Thou," that is to say, dialogue. However, if we identify personhood with the capacity for dialogue, the ontic basis of the relationship would disappear. There is both an ontic and ontological foundation which is the presupposition of the capacity for dialogue essential for personal existence. This foundation in its turn does not reach the heights of the personal if it does not express itself in dialogue. It is only in dialogue that personhood expresses itself in a recognizable and credible way.

When we say that man possesses himself by the act of taking possession of himself, this should not be understood in the sense of an exaggerated actualism as if man constituted himself as a person from moment to moment by passing from one act of self-possession to another. Personhood is a persistent quality which cannot be interrupted and then regained. But it is of the greatest importance for our understanding of personhood that it comes to appearance in the act of reflection by which man takes possession of himself. For this means that he can stand over against himself, he can be related to himself. Man can stand over against himself not only as subject but also as object, and in this case he is related to himself as person to nature. Insofar as man is the object of his own act of self-possession, he is nature. Thus we see that an analysis of the concept of person leads to the element of nature.

In point of fact there is nothing in man's environment that he cannot make the object of his knowledge and activity, including his fellow man. Up to a certain point he even must treat his fellow man as an object, that is, as nature. But, of course, if he only treats him as an object, then he will not do justice to the decisive element, the personal. If he wishes to arrive at a genuine understanding of his fellow man, he must encounter him in another way than he encounters the world of things. The world of things is nature alone, it is exclusively object and cannot give rise to true and genuine encounter.

As a result of man's identity with himself, despite his ability to be related to himself, it is possible to say that personhood consists in the subsistence of the human being. The necessary precondition of this, to come back to the definition of Boethius, is the spiritual character of the being of man, or more exactly, the spirituality in the decisive layer of the being of man. We would be doing an injustice to matter if we considered that only matter belonged to the realm of nature, and not also the spirit. It is precisely the unity of the spiritual and the material that can be called the nature of man, insofar as it is the object of man's act of self-possession. It is through and in this nature that man acts as "I," and he acts through both his bodily and his spiritual nature, that is, through his nature as such. If it is personhood by which man transcends himself, it is nature which makes this act of transcendence possible. If we apply these reflections to the humanity of Jesus, we arrive at the following results (in the course of this it must be remembered the divine persons themselves can only be understood as relations, though as relations which are identical with the divine essence: they are not persons in the usual sense that each possesses his own individual mind and will). According to the New Testament and the reflections of theologians in subsequent centuries, the God of the Old Testament is Father (that is, first person) by the fact that in reflection on himself he gives expression to himself, he utters himself, and in this way brings forth a Word, real and standing over against himself. This means that both the Father uttering himself and the Word uttered are identical with the being of God, although in order to stand over against one another, they must be either virtually (Thomas Aquinas) or most probably formally (Duns Scotus) distinct. In the Holy Spirit, the love uniting Father and Son proves to be a "We," precisely in the person of the Holy Spirit. The Holy Spirit can only exist as the expression and sign of this We of the Father and the Son. He owes his difference to relation, but his personality, that is, his subsistence, to his identity with the divine being. So it is possible to say in a certain sense that the three divine persons are three forms of the one divine nature or being. God exists as three divine persons who are three forms of the one divine nature or being.

This thesis holds even if the Greek conception of the Trinity is accepted, that it is the God of the Old Testament who is the originless origin of the Son and of the Holy Spirit. Without the richness and fertility of the divine being, the one God, who constitutes himself as First Person or Father by the act of bringing forth, could not carry out this act of bringing forth. If we take the one God of the Old Testament as point of departure, which suggests itself from the viewpoint of salvation history, then we must make some sort of distinction between personhood and being in God, while still preserving their identity. God is real, he is the absolute God in no other way than in threefold personality. Absolute Being by its very nature then is trinitarian. Both the oneness of God and his threefold personhood are essential for an understanding of the hypostatic union, the unity because it is the basis of the fact that the three persons act as one in their dealings with the non-divine. All the external works of the tri-personal God (*ad extra*) are wrought by him as by a single efficient cause. This thesis is not only theological speculation, but the official teaching of the Church.

It is not incompatible with this, in fact it follows necessarily, that each of the three divine persons acts according to his own character. What is done is done by the three persons on the basis of the divine nature. The divine nature decides the manner of the activity. However it is the three persons themselves who determine the act itself.

It follows from this basic thesis that each man is created by a tri-personal God. How this is to be understood, we have tried to explain above. But if this is true of every man, it is also true of the man Jesus Christ. He was created by a tri-personal God. But his human nature, created in a single act by the three persons, is meant from the beginning for the Logos alone, not for either of the other persons; that is, it is meant to be taken up into the personhood of the Logos. Augustine expresses this as follows: it is not as if the human nature were first created and then taken up into union with the Logos; rather it was created by the fact that it was taken up into union with the Logos. Since the act of adoption can only be an act of the Logos, but the creation is an act of the three persons together, it is not easy to give logical sense to this statement of Augustine's. It would be necessary to assume that in the act of creation itself there is already an activity proper to the Logos, that of adoption. This idea of the adoption of Jesus' human nature was very widespread in the first centuries, as we pointed out earlier, but it carries the danger of making the human side of Jesus an independent entity apart from the Logos himself. The purpose of Augustine's statement is to avoid that danger. When, having said that the Son, the Logos, is the goal for whom the human nature is created by the three persons, we then say that he adopted the human nature, we are no longer dealing with efficient causality, to which alone the rule given above applies, but with formal causality.

A common example of formal causality is the role played by spirit or soul in the human being. The material cause of a thing is the matter out of which it is fashioned. The formal cause on the other hand is that principle in the thing by which the matter takes on a certain form. The Council of Vienne (1311) defined that the soul is the *forma corporis*, that is, the factor by which the human body is the type of thing that it is, namely a living human body rather than a lump of clay. In a human being matter is formed, is fashioned, and stamped by a spiritual principle without losing its own character as matter. One result of this is that spirit shows itself or becomes visible in the body.

If we apply these categories to the Logos and his human nature, then we conclude that it is the person of the Logos which determines the manner of subsistence of Jesus' human nature, though without depriving it of any element that belongs to human nature. The human nature of Jesus is fully human: as a man Jesus has human spontaneity, human freedom, human responsibility, and human capacity for growth not only in the physical realm but also in the mental and spiritual. What is altered is not the quality of Jesus' humanity, but the manner in which it subsists: it subsists in virtue of the Logos. This is the essential mystery of the man Jesus, that he is fully a man, with all those qualities which go with being human, but that his humanity does not carry within it, as ours does, the ground of its own subsistence: the Logos of God is the ground of his subsistence.

If we look at this from the point of view of the divine activity involved in it, we see that the relationship of the divine and the human in Jesus is not static, but dynamic. It is not as if the Logos took to himself this human nature in a single event: he possesses himself, including his human nature, in a continuous act. If this is true of persons in general, it is all the more true of God who is himself pure act. The divine Logos has taken up the human nature of Jesus in the fullness of human life, with all the joys and with all the limitations and frustrations of life, to suffering and death; only, he was without sin. The act by which he does this is not something done once and for all; it is a constant dynamic act without interruption. Furthermore, just as there was never a moment when the human nature of Jesus was not penetrated by the Logos, so it has been a constant part of the Christian tradition that this relationship will never come to an end.

The question can be raised whether it is still possible to speak of a true human nature if it does not exercise its own act of existence. The question is thoroughly legitimate, since the only human natures we know are ones which exist in themselves. As we saw earlier, the problem of being has been handled in various ways, especially during the Middle Ages. Sometimes being and existence were denied to God (Dionysius) because that would represent a limitation in the only meaning we could give to the terms. Sometimes true being and existence were denied to creatures, because there is a sense in which God alone truly is. Thomas Aquinas seemed to have found a solution in his distinction between being and existence, or being and esse. But in the light of Meister Eckhardt's mystical theology this became questionable. Whatever view one comes to, it is essential that the full human reality of Jesus be not diminished or reduced through its relationship with the divine.

Perhaps the following reflections can shed some light on the mystery of the Incarnation, though it would be futile to attempt to explain completely so close a union of the human and the divine. Man exists only in relationship to his fellow man. All human existence is essentially coexistence. This expresses itself for example in speech especially. If a man exists with his fellow man in friendship and love, then to that extent he transcends himself, he goes beyond himself to the "thou" of the other, who has it in his power to open himself up and receive him, or to close himself up. The ego is thus fashioned and formed by its relationship to the "thou" of the other. Our actions, our thoughts, our desires, our judgments, our growth receive their direction and their form from our relationship to our fellow man. That is, the "I" lives from the "thou." What happens to all of us in friendship and love happened in a unique way, with an ultimate and incomparable force, when God became man. Now there is a man for whom the divine Logos is the personal power giving subsistence to his "I." Paul's statement holds good in a unique sense: "Not I live, but Christ lives in me" (Col. 2:20). His human "I" was fashioned by Christ, so much so that Paul could speak of the death of his old "I" fashioned by the world, and of the resurrection of a new "I." In the Incarnation the self-communication of the Logos to the human "thou" took on such power that the human nature was, as it were, drawn out of its own center, and in its place came another center, that of the divine Logos. The "I" is no longer the one immanent in the man, but the transcendent "I" of the Logos. But this transcendent "I" enters so powerfully into the man Jesus that despite its own transcendence and without losing its transcendence, it becomes the "I" of this man.

Bernard Welte puts forward a thesis that carries these considerations further. He points out that according to Thomas Aquinas a constitutive element of immaterial being is openness to that which is not itself, to the "other," an openness which shows itself in knowledge and love. The principal "other" is God. But this relationship to the "other" implies an "oppositeness." If this is so then we must posit in Jesus such an oppositeness to God. Such an "oppositeness" cannot be explained simply in terms of the Trinity, as the relationship of the Son to the Father, nor simply from the point of view of the human nature of Jesus, since it is precisely a question of the relationship of Jesus himself to God. Furthermore, it would be natural, for such an oppositeness, as a state of dynamic tension, to undergo a historical development in the life of Jesus.

Another way of approaching the matter is as follows. The human word is a force; it has the power to move the heart and mind of others, depending on its own intensity. The word of God is the most powerful of words. It "is alive and active. It cuts more keenly than any two-edged sword, piercing as far as the place where life and spirit, joints and marrow, divide" (Heb. 4:12). God has spoken many words, but into the human nature of Jesus the Father spoke his personal Word, that in which he gives expression to himself eternally. Such a word has the power to fashion a human nature so that it exists no longer by its own power of subsistence but by the power of this Word; it becomes the "I" of Jesus' human nature.

The idea of the transcendence of God can lead us perhaps still further. The human nature of Jesus was created by the tri-personal God, in an act identical with adoption by the Logos so that the Logos alone constitutes the person of Jesus. But creation is an act of self-communication by God; in creating, God gives himself and expresses himself. On the other hand his creative act is identical with himself and remains in himself. This means that there is a very close relation between God and what he creates. God's gift of himself in creating is different from that which we call grace but it is still self-communication. It does not reduce the human element in man, but precisely creates it, so that an intensification of this self-communication brings an intensification of humanity, and vice versa, an intensification of humanity only takes place through an intensification of God's self-communication. But because God transcends man this means that man becomes himself more fully only by transcending himself. This self-transcendence can be viewed from an evolutionary perspective as a movement towards a new future, but it also can and must be seen as a vertical movement either towards the depth of his own being or towards its height. It is a basic theory in the thought of Teilhard de Chardin, and in fact in every evolutionary theory, that it is through self-transcendence that an increase of being takes place.

Since God expresses himself analogously and realizes himself analogously in every creative act, it is not meaningless to say that every man is an incarnation of God, an idea characteristic of Far Eastern religions. God becomes incarnate countless times. There is, of course, an essential difference between these incarnations of God and the unique incarnation which took place in Jesus, but there is no need to overlook the similarity between them in order to stress their difference.

We find another especially interesting conception of the incarnation of God in Hegel's theology of history, which views God as the Absolute or the Idea, which unfolds itself in the fullness of the world, especially in man where it attains self-consciousness. The incarnation of God takes place then in a great historical process. In this historical process God becomes himself. Although the biblical conception of the incarnation of God is very different from that of the Far Eastern religions and of Hegel insofar as these are pantheistic, they still provide us with a means of access to it. In the light of these conceptions the biblical notion does not have the appearance of being completely extraordinary: it belongs within a great framework. The history of religions shows that the idea of the incarnation of God or of the divine is widespread. The incarnation which took place in Jesus must be viewed as the climax of something that is worldwide, as the fulfillment of a great human dream.

This interpretation of the man Jesus would lead to serious misunderstandings, and in fact become mythical, if it were taken to imply that the infinite were transformed into the finite. God's gift of himself to the man Jesus does not remove the distinction between God and man but emphasizes it. Unity with God and distinction from him grow together.

The eternal Son exists only in relationship to the Father; he is in fact nothing other than this subsistent relationship to the Father, and so Jesus' human nature is taken up into this relationship to the Father. The man Jesus then is the son of the heavenly Father in a real and true sense like the eternal Logos. From eternity the Father engendered his Son, the Logos, as one who was to take on human nature. Thus the incarnation is the continuation, in fact the goal, of the trinitarian event. The fatherhood of God is directed towards Jesus, and in and through Jesus, towards the whole of creation.

In the patristic period the close relationship between the divine and the human in Jesus, based in the unity of his person, was termed the *perichoresis* of the two natures, an expression which stems from Gregory of Nazianzus. Maximus the Confessor compares the relationship between the two natures with the way body and soul, or a word and its meaning, exist in one another. The human nature in Jesus cannot act without the divine, because of the unity of his person. The word *perichoresis* is used for the first time in a strict sense by John Damascene in regard both to the relations between the persons in the Trinity and especially the natures in Christ: he uses it to stress the unity of Jesus in opposition to Arianism and the duality of his nature in contrast to Nestorianism. John speaks of each being in the other, not of each moving in the other: for the Trinity the basis of the *perichoresis* is the one nature, and for the hypostatic union, the one person. In the Middle Ages the expression *circumincessio* was used for this, by Albert the Great, and also the Franciscan theologians, Duns Scotus and Petrus Aureoli, with reference to the Trinity; whereas, later, Gerson used it of Christ, but the Christological usage later lapsed. In both cases, the relationship—between the persons in God or between the natures in Christ—can be viewed either statically or dynamically. In the latter instance the relationship is viewed as an act of mutually relating to each other rather than as a state or condition

## JESUS' SELF-AWARENESS AS AN ELEMENT
## OF THE HYPOSTATIC UNION

The adoption of the man Jesus by the Logos takes place first of all in the ontic dimension. The question has been raised whether the man Jesus was aware that he possessed not a human but a divine subsistence. Did Jesus know that he was God and to what extent he was God? It would be strange if he were not aware of the decisive element in his personality. In his human self-awareness, then, we must conclude that Jesus made the unutterable discovery that he was the only Son of the heavenly Father. His entire inner life must have been stamped by this awareness, a religious experience given to no other man. As a result of it he was able to say that no one knows the Father except the Son and no one knows the Son except the Father (Mt. 11:27). Because of this unique experience of God he was able to give a revelation about God that possessed an absolute character. Jesus could not be humanly aware of himself without knowing that God was his Father, both in the way that God is the loving Father of all men and also as the first divine person.

The question of the "I" awareness of the man Jesus has been much discussed in recent theology. Must we say that he possessed only a divine "I" awareness or can we say that he also had a human "I" awareness? And that he has human knowledge of this divine "I" only by the fact that he sees the Logos united to it and so in a certain sense sees the trinitarian God?

This question raises a problem not only of fact but also of terminology. It cannot be denied that Jesus has a human center of activity. If we agree to call this a human "I" awareness then there is no difficulty in saying that Jesus possesses this. But this "I" awareness does not have the character of a subsistence awareness. It will be simply a comprehensive awareness of his human spontaneity and freedom. This would make it necessary to distinguish different levels in the concept of person, especially to distinguish the psychological element from the ontological and consider them separable. It does not seem psychologically impossible to hold to such a separation, that is, to attribute to the man Jesus a human "I" awareness without human subsistence.

However, it seems to correspond better to the personal unity
of Jesus to say that the ontological element and, in fact, the subsistence of the divine Logos enters into the "I" awareness of the
man Jesus so that this includes both the human center of activity
and the divine subsistence. This would be to maintain a number
of levels in the "I" awareness of Jesus, though without destroying
its unity. Jesus' self-awareness is both composite and unified, containing both the consciousness of being a true man and that of
subsisting by virtue of the subsistence of the divine Logos. Such
a view would not go against the Council of Chalcedon's statement
that Jesus' two natures are both unseparated and yet unmixed. As
man, the man Jesus cannot experience himself as God, and on
the other hand he also cannot, without self-deception, consider
himself a human person. Whatever view is adopted must give full
weight to Jesus' awareness of being truly a man. We must say
that his awareness of being the Son of God does not weaken but
heightens his consciousness of being truly and fully a man, living
in history with death awaiting him.

The question has also been raised whether Jesus was always
fully aware of being the Son of God. Is it possible to hold that
this divine self-awareness was what the scholastics called a "hab-
itus," which could be actualized but was not always actual?

Karl Rahner has put forward the following approach:

The fact that Christ's humanity is substantially united to the Logos,
insofar as this is a determination ("act") of the human nature itself,
cannot be simply "subconscious." For as something ontically higher,
this determination is something real which cannot be simply unconscious at least in the case where its subject has attained that grade of
actuality in being which involves a presence to itself (*Bei-sich-selbst-
sein*) of this entity. At least in the case where this presupposition
is satisfied, it is metaphysically impossible that this actuality of the
subject should be simply unconscious, when we remember that this
actuality is entitatively higher in comparison with the level of actuality proper to the subject, and that this subject is present to itself; it is
impossible that the immediate subject of the human presence-to-itself
should not also be present to itself precisely insofar as it is wholly
and substantially made over to the Logos. Here we must be careful to
note that this "presence to itself" is not to be confused with a "knowl-

edge of an object." Presence-to-itself is the inner being-illuminated of actual being for itself; more precisely, for the subject which possesses this being in its own self. From this it follows that it is opposed to the true teaching of the scholastic metaphysics of knowledge to say that Christ's human soul knows of the *unio hypostatica* only in the way in which an object is known (and so through the "visio immediata" as the vision of an object). Inasmuch as the *unio hypostatica* implies or involves an entitative determination, namely the being-united (*Vereintsein*) of the human reality with the Logos, as an ontological determination of this human reality, Christ's human soul is "with the Logos" in an immediately ontic and conscious way. The "visio immediata" is (if we may be allowed to make our point in this way for the sake of clarity) the consequence and not the presupposition of the conscious being-with-the-Logos of Christ's soul. It is not (in the last resort) a *donum,* conferred as a moral "title" on the human soul on account of its being united hypostatically to the Logos, for reasons of *convenientia* or *decentia;* it is the hypostatic union itself, insofar as this is necessarily an "intelligible actu" in the *intelligens actu* of Christ's human soul. Once again, in the measure and manner in which the *unio hypostatica* is (or includes) a real ontological determination of the human nature, and indeed its ontologically highest determination; further, in the measure in which this human nature is by itself "present to itself": the union must also be a datum of the self-consciousness of this human nature of its very self, and cannot simply be part of the content of its object-knowledge given "from without."[3]


## INCARNATION OF THE SON ALONE?

In medieval theology the question was asked whether another person than the Logos could have become man. The question presupposes a purely abstract concept of God which overlooks the biblical view of salvation history. It calls to mind the late scholastic notion of the *potentia* or *potestas Dei absoluta,* the thesis that God in his absolute power could have done anything whatever, without regard to contradiction. Thomas Aquinas has no such notion, although he raises the question mentioned above and answers that it would have been possible for another person than the Logos to become man. From the biblical viewpoint of salvation history, both the question itself and especially a positive answer to it are impossible. On the contrary, it would seem to contradict the meaning of the tri-personal life of God to maintain such a possibility. As we have seen, the incarnation means God's communication of himself to his creation, in that the Father gives himself to the Son and that this act of giving is, as it were, prolonged into creation.

But if the Father gives himself directly to his creation, then his Son and his Spirit are left, as it were, outside of the process. This would mean that the Father expresses himself adequately in the Son, within the Trinity, and then expresses himself inadequately and separately in his creation. The two self-expressions of the Father then would be unrelated.

As regards the person of the Holy Spirit, he has the task, both within the Trinity and in the hypostatic union, of uniting the man Jesus and the divine Logos, and then the human race with Jesus. Both Greek and Latin theology have termed him the "Gift." That is to say, without prejudice to his immanent role within the Trinity, he possesses from eternity a relatedness to creation. Augustine declares that the first gift of love is love. When Father and Son send the Spirit they send that love in which they themselves are "We" to unite the man Jesus with the Logos and mankind with Jesus. The incarnation of another person than the Logos then appears, at the least, unfitting, if not impossible and meaningless.

INCARNATION AND CREATION

These considerations put in a new and clearer light the Christo-centricity of creation that was discussed earlier. We have seen that matter has a directedness towards spirit, a directedness which is most fully realized in the human person. Further, the whole of creation has a directedness towards God. The evolution of the world has as its goal a union with God which does not yet exist. It has come to a preliminary climax in Jesus Christ. The process is not "purely natural," but takes place within a framework of grace; on the other hand, the emergence of Jesus is not an event beside or outside this process, but took place in and through it. God's intention in creating the world was that the world should come to himself. It is not as if God first of all created the world and then decided on a goal for it, but he first set the goal, and the form of creation was decided by the goal. The highest realization of this directedness of creation towards God took place in Jesus. In him creation is united with God most closely, so closely that any further union between God and the world would be pantheism. This unity then preserves the distinction, although the distinction does not imply distance, but closeness. It is of the greatest importance here that Jesus be not seen as an isolated figure. Even if this degree of union with God were to be achieved only once, in Jesus, still the function of Jesus here is to be the representative of mankind with God. To describe the intimacy of this representative function, the New Testament uses the word "brother" (Mt. 12:49; 25:40; 28:10; Mk. 3:33ff.; Lk. 8:21; Jn. 20:17; Rom. 8:29; Heb. 2:11f.). Jesus is to be the brother of all men. In him God has become our fellowman.

To say that all men are brothers because they bear the face of man or because they all come from the same God is not to give the deepest reason for their brotherhood nor to express its real strength. Brotherhood arises between men to the extent that they transcend themselves and that God gives himself to them; if men become brothers it is the effect of God's self-communication. But God's gift of himself to man reached its climax in Jesus, and he represents also the highest degree of human self-transcendence. It is in him then that we will find the most powerful source of human brotherhood. This is especially true of the risen Jesus, for the point of his resurrection was not to make him less human but more human. Also his resurrection makes it possible for him to be closer to men than he ever was during his earthly life, because we all know from experience that there is a sense in which the flesh divides while the spirit unites.

Because all men are united with Jesus as their representative and their brother, they share analogously in his divine sonship. God thus becomes the Father of all men, but his fatherhood is communicated through Jesus. John reports a beautiful statement of his expressing this: "There are many dwelling places in my Father's house; if it were not so I should have told you, for I am going there on purpose to prepare a place for you. And if I go and prepare a place for you, I shall come again and receive you to myself, so that where I am you may be also" (Jn. 14:2f.). The brothers of Jesus belong in the home of their heavenly Father. It must be emphasized again in this regard that the participation of men in the Sonship of Jesus means not a loss but a growth in their humanity. The knowledge that they are brothers in Jesus not only obliges but enables them to act towards one another as brothers. This behavior towards one another as brothers will take the most manifold forms and represents the culmination of what we call historical activity. Thus we come to the conclusion that, because of the incarnation, God himself has a history, not in the pantheistic sense of Hegel, but God has a history in the sense that his son Jesus has a history and by his life, death, and resurrection has inserted into human history a dynamism which cannot be exhausted. The fact that God has become man means that man has an obligation to act in history so that the brotherhood of all men is realized. The incarnation of God then assures both the secularity of the world and also its divinization (D. Sölle). The incarnation has both an existential and a futurist dimension: in Jesus we have a fellowman who is God.

To act in history means that we always search for new forms of economic, social, cultural, and political life. No form of social organization can ever be definitive. What may be the expression of genuine brotherhood today can become inhibiting and dehumanizing tomorrow. Especially the Christian can never dispense himself from taking part in the creation of any new social structures which a change in the times may demand. His norm, however, will always be the human community as a brotherhood and the individual as his brother, not a dogmatic ideology.

At this point the question forces itself upon us whether the Holy Spirit is drawn into the history of Jesus. After all, he is sent just as concretely as the Son (Gal. 4:6). According to Thomas Aquinas such a "mission" means that the person sent takes on a temporal form of existence (S. Th. I, 43–2). The divine Person enters into the temporality of creation, without himself becoming temporal. The Holy Spirit entered into salvation history with the "anointing" of Jesus and remains with him. The Spirit accompanies and informs the history of Jesus and so himself has a history. Since he continues to act in the Church, the community of Jesus, he has a history also in it and in the historical actions of the members of the Church. These relationships show that the incarnation itself already has salvific significance. We cannot distinguish between Christology and soteriology by saying that Jesus, because he was both divine and human, was capable of saving mankind. With the incarnation, redemption is already present, for in Jesus human nature has already been adopted unconditionally by God. This does not mean that the particular redemptive acts of Jesus, his death and resurrection, are superfluous, for the adoption of human nature by the Logos means that he took on himself a fully human life. All the acts of Jesus' life are self-realizations of the man-Jesus bound at the root of his existence to the divine Logos, and from this they have redemptive significance. We must say then that ontological and functional Christology (soteriology) form an intimate unity: the one implies the other.

## THE MYSTERY OF THE PERSONAL UNITY OF JESUS: ATTEMPTS AT AN EXPLANATION

Although the personal unity of Jesus in the duality of his natures presents us with a mystery which we know is not likely ever to be solved, still it is understandable that in the course of history theologians have made a number of attempts to increase, if only slightly, the light we have on this subject. We shall try to summarize briefly the most important theories.

The Thomist position rests on the doctrine of a real distinction between essence and existence, at least in its most consistent form (L. Billot, P. Parente, and B. Xiberta). A spiritual essence or nature is not yet a person; it becomes a person when to the nature is added subsistence or existence. Because essence and existence, nature and subsistence are really distinct, God can separate them, extending, as it were, the divine act of existence to take the place of the act of existence which would be proper to the creature. The force of the Thomistic conception is to emphasize that the human nature of Jesus has been adopted by the Logos but it is incapable of answering the question how a human nature could possess its own reality without possessing its own act of existence. It is questionable whether this "Thomistic" thesis really represents an extension of Thomas' thought.

H. Diepen gives another interpretation to Thomas' teaching. In his view Thomas does not maintain that the personal unity of Jesus is formally constituted by the fact that he has only one act of existence: being is an integral part of an entity and cannot be replaced by anything else, even by the divine act of existence. Every entity has being in accordance with its own nature. The immediate subject of existence is not the person but the nature, that is to say, it is not the person which exists so much as the nature, in Thomas' thought. The unity of Jesus is given precisely by the fact that he has one personality. His human act of existence, which is really distinct from his divine act of existence, is integrated with it to form one being. Jesus, therefore, is one integral being existing in two complete substances. Against Diepen, de la Taille has maintained that the human nature of Jesus is actualized by the divine act of existence, but in such a fashion that the Logos, that is, his act of existence, has a quasi-formal significance for the actuality of Jesus' human nature insofar as this actualization is the act by which the Logos makes himself a man.[4]

Duns Scotus and his followers make only a formal, not a real, distinction between nature and person. The two are defined differently, but in concrete reality they are identical. Personhood is not something added on to a spiritual nature but is its independence of another. The human nature of Jesus is therefore not a person because it is united with the Logos and so has lost its independence. This view seems to underestimate the significance of personal existence.

According to Suarez a spiritual nature becomes a person through the addition of what he calls a *modus substantialis*. In the case of the human nature of Jesus this is lacking and is replaced by another mode of existence, the *modus unionis*. Since existence and nature are not really distinct for Suarez, he considers that the human nature of Jesus possesses or is its own existence. It must be admitted that this view overcomes the difficulties of the Thomist position, but the idea of the *modus unionis* seems to leave us with just as great a problem.

In recent years lively discussion of this topic has begun again. The chief figures in this debate have been P. Galtier and P. Parente. Galtier posits a far-reaching autonomy of the human "I" in Jesus. He is concerned with this "I" from the point of view of psychology and he asks the question whether Jesus as man experienced in himself a human "I" distinct from his divine "I." This implies a distinction between the ontological realm and the realm of consciousness, that is, between the "I" of the person and the conscious "I." For a time Galtier posited in Jesus a substantial human "I" in addition to the psychological "I": the substantial human "I" being the individual human nature as the ontic principle of spiritual acts, and the psychological "I" being the inner center of consciousness to which all conscious acts are referred. Galtier can point to a number of passages in the New Testament which seem to support the idea of such a human, psychological "I" in Jesus. Further, he maintains that the divine "I" as such remains outside of Jesus' human sphere of consciousness so that he does not have human experience of it. Jesus' human consciousness functions entirely according to the laws of human nature and is not affected by the hypostatic union. Galtier does not deny that the human nature of Jesus is the instrument of the Logos, but he maintains that it would be crippled without its own center of consciousness. It seems, however, that a questionable philosophy is assumed here: there is a philosophical question whether the ontic and psychological levels can be so sharply separated as they are in this view.

Parente takes the opposite position as his point of departure. He assumes a real distinction between essence and existence and concludes that the divine person of the Logos, by conferring his own existence on the human nature of Jesus, has a direct influence on Jesus' human consciousness. By this he raises the human consciousness of Jesus to the level of the divine, and the divine person, who is ontically the only subject in Jesus, forms Jesus' one psychological "I" and so is the center of his human as well as of his divine life. The person of the Logos is the *principium quod,* the only acting subject is Jesus; the nature is the *principium quo,* the instrument. According to Galtier the human consciousness of Jesus has no direct experience of the divine "I" of the Logos: it is only through the Beatific Vision that Jesus learns what he truly is. According to Parente, by contrast, the human consciousness of Jesus does have a direct experience of its hypostatic union with the Logos, and of the "I" of the Logos as its own "I."

E. Gutwenger (*Bewusstsein und Wissen Christi,* Innsbruck, 1960) has attempted a partial synthesis of these two views. He considers that personhood cannot be separated from "I" consciousness, and he concludes that in Jesus there is no "I" consciousness without the awareness of being hypostatically united to the Logos. However Jesus possesses a human act-center, but its "I" is the "I" of the Logos. The Logos is not the efficient cause, but the formal cause of the human act-center. By this means Gutwenger introduces the human nature of Jesus into the life of the Trinity in a very intimate way. The difficulty with Gutwenger's theory is how such a human act-center, although possessing its own spontaneity, is not conscious of itself.

Perhaps a further clarification will come below when we consider the question of Jesus' knowledge and self-consciousness. In any event it should be emphasized here that the problem is whether personhood can be understood purely metaphysically, leaving out the psychological element. In point of fact, the psychological element is given little weight in Boethius' definition of personhood, which dominated medieval thought on this topic, while it is decisive for our contemporary notion of personhood. The medieval concept of person would not be destroyed if the psychological element were separated from it, and so the notion of a human psychological "I" would not necessarily imply the existence of a human person. Perhaps we can distinguish different levels in the notion of person, at least a metaphysical and a psychological level, in such a way that one could exist without the other.

Recent discussion of Christology has been greatly, and justifiably, concerned with the fact that Jesus lived in time and history. This is a necessary corrective for the influence of Greek metaphysics on the preaching of the Church, although it would be a mistake to think that Greek ontology was ever suitable for preaching. It was used to achieve some sort of clarity, rather than to reenforce the message of the Gospel.

The attempts that have been undertaken recently to make, as it were, a fresh start with Christology, such as those of A. Hulsbosch and P. Schoonenberg, must be seen in this light. Both authors interpret the figure of Jesus in a radically historical fashion. At the present time it is not clear how their theories are related to the doctrine of Chalcedon.

A number of Protestant theologians have carried this emphasis much further. W. Pannenberg (*Grundzüge der Christologie,* Gütersloh, 1954) considers that the Chalcedonian doctrine of the two natures must be abandoned, although the formulas "truly God" and "truly man" are essential statements of Christian theology. Jesus' union with God should not be viewed as the union of two substances: it is as this man that Christ is God. Jesus' resurrection was a divine confirmation of his unique claim to authority: and it is on this that his union with God and his divinity are based. Others have completely rejected the formula "truly God" for the sake of a purely anthropological and existential interpretation (R. Bultmann, E. Fuchs, G. Ebeling, H. Braun). Here, as H. Zahrnt has pointed out (*Die Sache mit Gott,* Munich, 1967), Jesus is viewed simply as a historical stimulus and Christ is merely a mythological symbol for a new understanding of human life (cf. H. Gollwitzer, *Die Existenz Gottes im Bekenntnis des Glaubens,* Munich, 1963).

The purely existential interpretation of Jesus has been defended very strongly by F. Gogarten ("Jesus Christus Wende der Welt," in *Grundfragen der Christologie,* Tübingen, 1966). We must be prepared to abandon the doctrine of the two natures in Jesus in order to preserve his true humanity. The decisive thing is the event that took place between God and Jesus and on which our salvation is dependent. God has revealed himself in the life and actions of Jesus as he has done nowhere else. The effect of Jesus' life is not to change the world, but to alter the relationship of man, and so of the world, to God. In this sense the Christ event has cosmic significance. The titles of dignity given to Jesus in the New Testament do not imply his preexistence, but state in effect that what happened in and through Jesus had its basis not in purely this-worldly relationships but in the salvific and creative power of God. These theories no longer take the statement of Chalcedon seriously or attempt to make sense of it for our time. Even to show that they are in harmony with the New Testament would seem to require at least a lifetime of labor.

## THE HUMAN MIND AND WILL OF JESUS

### The Problem of Jesus' Knowledge

Much has been written by theologians on the question whether and how Jesus knew that he was the metaphysical Son of God and how, with such knowledge, he could have lived a truly human life. However, if we take the New Testament as our point of departure, the problem of Jesus' knowledge comes to a focus in the question whether Jesus was not only ignorant but in error about the end of the world. The relevant passages of the New Testament do not allow a fully satisfactory solution because from the point of view of philology they appear to contradict one another. According to Matthew 10:23, it seems that Jesus expected to be transformed and to return as the "Son of Man" on the clouds of heaven while the disciples he was then sending out were still preaching. Mark 9:1 and 13:30 appear to support the same view. On the other hand, in Matthew 24:36 Jesus states that he has no knowledge about the time when the end will come, and there is evidence that he took some steps to form a community that would have some degree of permanence. It is no solution simply to eliminate from consideration one of these contradictory sets of passages. The followers of "consistent eschatology" tend to neglect the second group of passages. On the other hand, C. H. Dodd (*The Parables of the Kingdom,* London, 1964) tends to neglect the eschatological passages, that is, those referring to the future, and maintains that in Jesus' view the kingdom of God was not a matter of the future but of the present.

The demythologization school eliminates the entire problem. These writers hold that Jesus' message was not a matter of Jewish apocalypticism, but of prophetic eschatology, that is, that Jesus did not intend to describe the events that would accompany the end of the world, but to call the people to conversion of heart: men must decide for or against God. This message is termed eschatological in the sense that it has an ultimate and decisive character. The apocalyptic descriptions are simply a literary form to express this, just as Genesis' description of the creation of the world in six days is a statement that the world is dependent on God. Here the question whether Jesus expected the end soon or in the distant future is not a problem.

A. Vögtle suggests that Matthew 10:23 and Mark 9:1 are not original words of Jesus but go back to the first generation of the early Church and express its expectation of an imminent end. Likewise the linking of the destruction of the temple with the Parousia in Mark 13 derives from the early Christian community.

Rudolf Schnackenburg considers it is impossible to shed any useful light on the few words of Jesus that speak of the end of the world as coming soon. Even the early Church did not know what to do with these awkward fragments of tradition. He believes that Jesus' prophetic teaching was intended to nourish an eschatological hope, without inviting irrelevant calculations about the precise time of its realization.

Perhaps it can be said that these contradictory statements attributed to Jesus express the tension between the various stages of realization of the kingdom of God, between its beginning and its completion, between the present and the future. G. Bornkamm observes:

We must not separate the statements about future and present, as is already apparent from the fact that in Jesus' preaching they are related in the closest fashion. The present dawn of the kingdom of God is always spoken of so as to show that the present reveals the future as salvation and judgment, and therefore does not anticipate it. Again, the future is always spoken of as unlocking and lighting up the present, and therefore revealing today as the day of decision.[5]

With regard to the general problem of Jesus' knowledge we have no official doctrinal statements from the Church. The notion has long been common among theologians that from the first moment of his conception Jesus possessed complete knowledge of the world and the people he was to redeem. This theory presupposes that it is possible for the human soul to think and to know, even though the organs necessary for thought and knowledge, the brain and the central nervous system, are not yet developed. In such a view the genuine humanity of Jesus dwindles to the point of disappearing. In Mark 13:32 Jesus states that he does not know when the world will end. To explain this by saying that he did know it, but that it did not belong to his task as Messiah to reveal it, is to treat the New Testament with levity.

The most difficult question is: if Jesus possessed the beatific vision, how was it possible for him genuinely to suffer? In general, the traditional theological emphasis on Jesus' omniscience would seem to introduce the danger of monophysitism or even of a docetic idea of Jesus. It is simply impossible for a created human mind to keep before it the entire wealth of reality in the universe, and there is nothing to be gained theologically by ascribing such enormous knowledge to Jesus.

Karl Rahner has suggested that we must alter our notion of the beatific vision. He considers that such a direct vision of God does indeed necessarily go with the hypostatic union: as the ontologically highest actualization of created reality, the hypostatic union must be aware of itself, but the decisive element in this vision of God is God's ontological communication of himself, which in the case of Jesus becomes an existential element of his human subjectivity. The "vision of God" does not mean that Jesus continually "sees" the essence of God like an object in front of him; it is an alteration of the structure of Jesus' existence which can subsequently be objectified so that Jesus comes to understand himself ever more deeply.

An interesting and useful theory has been put forward by H. Riedlinger (*Geschichtlichkeit und Vollendung des Wissens Christi*, Freiburg, 1966). He rejects all the attempts made so far at a solution and distinguishes between the historical knowledge of Christ and his knowledge of the end or consummation. He bases his theory on an analysis of the New Testament, especially Philippians, the synoptics, Hebrews, and John, and on contemporary theory of history. By a thorough textual analysis he comes to the conclusion that the Christ-hymn in Philippians (2:6–11), which represents the oldest developed pre-Pauline, Christological statement of the New Testament, is an emphatic testimony that the Lord has delivered himself over to history, as well as that the emptying praised in the hymn is precisely the emptying of one who preexisted. It is Mark who gives the most concrete characteristics of Jesus' historicality, although already in Mark Jesus partakes of heavenly glory. In Mark Jesus is a man who lives fully in history subject to the course of everyday events. He experiences novelty in human encounters, is moved and led by unexpected events (e.g., Mk. 1:45; 3:5,21; 6:5f.; 7:24; 8:33; 10:14; 14:33ff.; 15:34–37). It seems that at the beginning he did not expect that his preaching would fail or that he would soon be faced with death. It was only when the leading circles stiffened in their resistance to him and the people more and more turned away from him disappointed that he began to speak openly of the necessity of suffering and death. Thus it was only in the clash with historical forces that Jesus came to see clearly the path he would have to take. Riedlinger considers it certain that Jesus was at least in ignorance concerning the time of the coming of the kingdom of God. Further, in his view it is possible that Jesus gave himself so completely to the idea of the presence of the kingdom of God here and now that to a later observer, looking at the matter from another perspective, the appearance of error would be unavoidable. However, a responsible Christology would not teach that Jesus was actually in error, so long as there is no solid historical evidence of that. Jesus' existence was historically concrete, that is, conditioned by whatever task lay before him, but this necessarily implies that his mental attitudes would be characterized as to a certain degree insufficient and provisional and so could be interpreted as failure and error. The historical character of Jesus' existence becomes especially clear in his confrontation with death (Mk. 14:34ff.). On the other hand Jesus' knowledge reaches into heavenly spheres (Mk. 1:10f.; 1:13ff.; 2:5; 9:2–8; 11:1–6; 13:1–37; 14:13ff.). In fact, in general the Gospel of Mark is not so concerned to point out the historical character of Jesus' knowledge, although it does this more clearly than the other Gospels, but to show that the knowledge of the Son of God went far beyond the world and history. In Matthew and Luke the historical characteristics of Jesus' existence are delineated less strongly, and there is more emphasis on the unearthly penetration of his knowledge. The Epistle to the Hebrews is concerned both with the preexistent and with the historical Jesus. By his simple statement that the "Word became flesh," John emphasizes the historicality of Jesus with a force that can scarcely be surpassed; yet he also ascribes to Jesus a knowledge

that goes far beyond anything human and stands in contradiction
to the ignorance that Mark describes. Riedlinger attempts to deal
with this state of affairs by rejecting the idea of the "beatific" or
"direct" vision of God traditionally attributed to Jesus, in favor
of a "historical" vision of God. By this he does not mean a special
type of knowledge, distinct from the rest of Jesus' mental life, but
the entirety of Jesus' knowledge, in which both historicality and
eschatological brilliance are conjoined in a manner which remains
ultimately mysterious. He continues:

We call the knowledge of Jesus "historical" because we see it embedded in the world and in time, in a particular epoch of the history
of Israel. The word historical is intended to preserve for us all that
Philippians says about *kenosis,* Mark about the concrete form of his
historicality, Luke about his progress in wisdom, Hebrews about the
humiliation of the preexistent One, and John about the Word becoming
flesh. It is intended as a reminder to us that the earthly life of Jesus
was lived out within horizons of thought and imagination that were
historically determined, that is, in ignorance, questioning, searching,
doubt and genuine progress in his understanding of himself and of
the world. By using the word historical it is also intended to say that
Jesus' earthly vision of God does not necessarily have to be thought
of as something continually present, either on a level below consciousness or at the "apex" of the soul. To acknowledge fully the
historical character of Jesus' knowledge is to leave room for the
possibility that he who was God, without ceasing to be truly man,
could deliver himself over so thoroughly to history that even in his
human vision of his own Godhead it was only with time that he came
fully to maturity, and that from time to time he experienced inter-
ruptions and also unique heights and depths in his vision of God. . . .
The phrase "vision of God" says that Jesus, not only in his knowledge
of God, but in his whole self-awareness and knowledge of the world,
was with God in a unique way above the world and time, that in fact
he was God himself. The phrase, "vision of God," should remind us
of all that Mark, and still more clearly, Matthew, Luke, John, and the
tradition of the Church have said about the heavenly glory of Jesus'
knowledge, about his unique I-thou relationship to his Father, about
his being filled with the spirit and with truth. But this in its turn
should not be understood in such a way that the fullness of glory
eliminates the earthly historicality and leaves room for only a docetic
understanding of Jesus' human inner life.

Although Riedlinger admits that it would be naive and mistaken to expect a definitive solution of this question, still it must be said that his view has provided a new basis for the further development of basic questions of Christology. From now on the inquiry must be concerned chiefly with the meaning of the historical, and of the historicity of man. Is man entirely embedded in history or are there elements in man that reach out beyond history? Is truth a purely historical phenomenon, or does it have any validity outside of history, and, if so, in what sense? Is it possible to maintain a radical historicality without submitting to total relativism?

With regard to the present question, the basic problem is likely to remain whether the hypostatic union, as taught by the Council of Chalcedon, could remain entirely hidden from the human consciousness of Jesus. If this is not possible, then the question is how Jesus, despite his awareness of God, could still act historically in any genuine sense of the word.

### Jesus' Will

It must be said of every creature: the more God acts on it, the freer it becomes. The assumption of the human nature of Jesus into a unity of life with the divine Logos did not only not endanger, but guaranteed, the human spontaneity of Jesus. We must say that precisely the presence of God in Jesus gave him a maximum of freedom. Freedom is not arbitrariness. It does not exist in a vacuum, but only in relationship to some object, that is, it is bound to a realization of the true, the good, and the human. Jesus' freedom was bound both to what was divine and to what was human, and not as two separate entities but each in the other. It was in his realization of what was truly human that Jesus accomplished the gift of himself to God, and through his dedication to God he achieved what was truly human.

Jesus Christ represents the highest realization of true human freedom. By his very presence among men then he represents the principal force active in human history for the realization of human freedom. Jesus' freedom in this sense is usually expressed by saying that Jesus' will, and Jesus himself, was "holy." This implies two things: that Jesus' will was defined in terms of God, from above, and that, from below, it was directed by his own decision towards God and towards his brothers.

As regards the influence of God on Jesus' will, this in its turn includes two elements, the self-communication of the Logos to the man Jesus, which is termed uncreated grace, and the effect of this on the man Jesus, which is termed created grace. The human nature of Jesus has been hallowed and sanctified through its union with the Son of God because and insofar as it participates in the uncreated holiness of God (*gratia unionis*). The union of Jesus' human nature with God is the highest form of grace, and is the basic form for all other grace. For this reason Jesus can be referred to as the original sacrament. Since Jesus is the center of human history, his union with God is the basis and the source of the union of all other men with God (*gratia capitis,* cf. Thomas Aquinas, S.Th. III, 6,1).

As regards the ethical or attitudinal holiness of Jesus, we mus first try to clarify an ontological question. In the discussions that followed the Council of Chalcedon, the question arose, how Jesus could possess human nature and yet be incapable of sin. One theory put forward was that, although Jesus possessed two natures, he had only one will, namely a divine one. This doctrine is termed monothelytism; as in many other theological debates, political factors played an important role in the argument. It was rejected first by the bishops of Italy and North Africa at a Council in the Lateran in 649, presided over by Pope Martin I, and definitively at the third Council of Constantinople, 680–681, the sixth general council. Accordingly it is an official doctrinal statement of the Christian Church that in Jesus there are two wills, a divine and a human, corresponding to his two natures.

In point of fact, the New Testament does distinguish the human will in Jesus from his divine will, in which he is one with the Father (Lk. 22:42; Mt. 26:39; Jn. 5:30; 6:38). As man Jesus had to learn obedience to the will of his Father (Heb. 5:8). Because of this twofold level of operation in Jesus, Pseudo-Dionysius speaks of his actions as "theandric," that is, both divine and human at once.

Although there are two powers of will in Jesus then, the close union between the human act-center in Jesus and the person of the divine Logos makes a contradiction between the two wills impossible. When it is reported in Mark 14:36 (cf. Lk. 22:42) that Jesus asked his Father to save him from death, this did not mean that his human will rejected the will of his Father: he added to the prayer immediately, "Yet not what I will, but what thou wilt." If Jesus had not reacted to the fate before him with pain and horror, he would scarcely have been human, but his complete acceptance of the will of God revealed itself in the fact that he was able to push through his own reaction of horror to a free act of obedience.

Freedom does not consist in the power to sin. It must be seen positively as the fact that a person decides freely and responsibly, without inner compulsion, to do what is good and right, that is, to do the will of God. By doing this he acts in accordance with his own nature. If we ask what was it that God willed, we must say that Jesus' life was dominated by one preoccupation, namely to set up the reign of God, his heavenly Father, and so to bring salvation to his brothers. To this task he gave himself without reserve. Jesus lets himself be led by the will of God at every step in his life (Jn. 10:16). To do the will of God is his meat and drink (Jn. 4:34). Even when the will of his Father leads him in the direction of death, he remains faithful to it. He must experience that whoever wishes to bring peace to a world dominated by human selfishness will be rejected as a disturbance and eliminated, precisely because he wants to bring peace. His path then is a path of suffering and of death (Lk. 22:37). For the sake of his Father's reign, Jesus gave himself over to the bitter fate of death (Mk. 8:31; 9:31; Mt. 16:21; Lk. 18:1–33; Jn. 11:8f.). The treatment of this in the New Testament is a particularly interesting example of the development of the early Church's conception of Christ. Mark represents Jesus as stricken to the very depths of his being; horror and dismay come over him; his heart is ready to break with grief. He throws himself on the ground and prays that the hour may pass him by, "Father, all things are possible to thee; take this cup away from me" (Mk. 14:33–36). In the hour of his death agony, he cries as if in despair, "My God, my God, why hast thou forsaken me?" (Mk. 15:34).

Matthew's account of the same events is considerably milder.

Here Jesus is in total submission to the will of the Father from
the beginning: "My Father, if it is not possible for this cup to pass
me by without my drinking it, thy will be done" (Mt. 26:42).
But in Matthew also Jesus cries out his abandonment by God
(27:46–50).

Luke portrays Jesus as essentially much more relaxed than in
Mark or Matthew. On the way towards crucifixion, he comforts
the women mourning over him (Lk. 23:27–31). After the crucifixion he prays for his adversaries, "Father, forgive them. They
do not know what they are doing" (Lk. 23:34). Luke does not
report his cry of abandonment by God. He promises paradise to
one of the thieves crucified with him, and he dies with a prayer,
"Father, into thy hands I commit my spirit" (Lk. 23:46).

Guardini illuminates the uniqueness of Jesus' attitude:

The fundamental character of Jesus distinguishes him from all the
other great figures of human history. Perhaps a brief comparison with
some of these may bring out more clearly the quality and breadth of
his attitude. For example, Socrates is driven to search for truth from
the inmost core of his being, and will not let anything turn him away
from this. Placed by calling before the final decision, he dies a death
which reveals his being and his work with the utmost clarity. Another
figure, Achilles, is also driven by the law of his own being, not this
time the law of truth, but the law of consuming action, and in carrying
this out he finds the fulfillment of his life. Both, Socrates and Achilles,
experienced their task as one familiar to them, and related to their
inmost being. With the Stoic the case is different. He experiences his
fate as foreign, and even hostile. He draws back into the core of his
being and closes himself off from the world outside. The basic events
in his life are not unfolding and development, but survival, holding
out, and withdrawal. A genuine character arises in this way too,
strong and alone, apparently cold but burning with hidden passion,
desperately brave, and manly to the point of unreasonableness.
Between these two extremes, of self-unfolding in a world of events
which lead one on, and simple survival in a hostile world, stands
the legendary figure of Aeneas. After the destruction of his home,
the city of Troy, he fulfills a divine commission, which leads him
to found a new city. He is kind, brave, sensitive to suffering, and
possesses an inflexible power to hold out in adversity, and to achieve
what he has to achieve.[6]

The figure of Christ differs from such prototypes of human life by the fact that he does not live out an attitude enclosed within the bounds of human history, but he is radically open to God as his heavenly father and so is open to the entirety of human history and of the world.

This openness includes both a negative and a positive element of ethical attitude. As regards the negative element, Jesus is free from all sin, that is, from all disobedience to God. He is in fact incapable of disobeying God (cf. the Decree for the Jacobites, DS 711; the Council of Ephesus, DS 122; and Chalcedon, DS 148). Scripture (cf., e.g., Is. 53:9f.; Lk. 1:35; Jn. 1:29; 8:46; 14:30; 2 Cor. 5:21; Heb. 4:15; 7:26; 1 Pet. 3:22; 1 Jn. 3:5) presents us with the following picture: with complete certainty and without a trace of anxiety or hesitation, Jesus could confront adversaries who hated him to the death and watched his every movement, and ask them the question: which of you can convict me of sin? He gives the impression of being completely sinless to disciples who are constantly with him and see him in all the situations of everyday life. From this calm and constant consciousness of sinlessness he preaches repentance and conversion; he forgives sins, is concerned for the salvation of others, warns of the dangers of riches. This means that he did not take sin lightly: he regarded it as the only real catastrophe. It is all the more significant that he considered himself free from it. He never gives evidence of having difficulties of conscience: even in the face of death he is not disquieted about his responsibility towards God or his fate in eternity. On the contrary, he gives comfort without asking to be comforted and apparently without needing it; he asks forgiveness for his enemies; he tells his disciples, "Set your troubled hearts at rest" (Jn. 14:1). He even tells them he has long desired to celebrate this hour with them (Lk. 22:15). Even in the final situation when there is no way out, he shows himself above all touch of despair.

Scripture describes the sinlessness of Jesus in a special way by its accounts of Jesus' struggles with Satan. Jesus had to undergo a struggle with the powerful and subtle adversary of God himself, whose aim was to maintain his own dominion over men by all the means available to him, by deceit and trickery, by lies and vio-

lence. Satan recognized immediately the threat which Jesus posed
to him, and summoned every possible effort for a counterattack.
He sees his dominion in danger and trembles (Mk. 1:24; 5:7–13).
The power that he summons up is made visible in the many cases
of possession which occur around Jesus. These are not accidents;
they derive from the fact that Satan sees his kingdom in danger.
However, his passionate resistance to Jesus shows itself even
more forcibly in the hostility that he arouses against Jesus' person.
The New Testament ascribes all the animosity shown to Jesus,
from Herod's persecution of him as an infant up to his betrayal
and death, to Satan. Satan's attack on Jesus is not only made
through other persons, but is also made directly against his will. In
three temptations he attempts to lead Jesus into unfaithfulness to
his task of establishing the reign of God. On three occasions he
urges him to choose the glory of this world in place of the glory
of God: at the beginning of his public life; on his way to Jerusalem; and finally on the Mount of Olives, where his natural
human fear before torture and death is exploited (Mk. 1:12f.;
8:31ff.; Mt. 4:1–11,16–23; Lk. 4:1–13; 23:31). But Jesus does
not give in; he is able to put resignation and despair aside, and the
attacks of his adversary break against the power of his love and
his obedience. Thus the decision as to the path that human history
will take in the future is made in the will of Jesus, ultimately in
his prayer in Gethsemane (E. Stauffer). Jesus has no part with
Satan (Mt. 7:21ff.; Jn. 14:3).

Jesus' victory over Satan is rendered definitive by the fact that
Jesus does not fight with the weapons which Satan uses. He does
not reply to hate with hate or to lie with counter-lie. This manner
of acting was apparently so new and unexpected to his contemporaries that it made him incredible in their eyes (Lk. 11:20).
The demonic forces are overcome solely with divine power, that
is, with the power of love and of truth (Jn. 14:30).

The positive side of Jesus' preoccupation with the reign of God
expresses itself in his consuming love for his Father in heaven
(Lk. 2:49; 23:46). Jesus has dedicated his life to his Father
(Mt. 26:39), and is prepared at any moment to give it up for him.
Everything that he does he does in union with the Father (Lk.
3:21f.; 6:12f.; Jn. 14:10; Mt. 11:27) and he lives in an un-

broken bond with him. His real life consists in the fact that he carries out the will of his Father.

This is revealed especially in his prayer, which is reported especially by Luke (3:21; 5:16; 6:12; 9:18,28f.; 11:1) and which consists in an intimate dialogue with his Father or in conversation with people about their Father. Because his heart is full of love for his Father, the words which come from him are all spoken either to the Father or about him. Because of his constant union with God, he never needs to ask pardon for his sins; it is only seldom that his prayers have the form of a request; for the most part they are expressions of praise and thanks (Mt. 11:25; Jn. 11:41). Jesus prays more for others than for himself, more for his Father's glory than for help in need (Lk. 22:32; Jn. 14:16; 17:1,24). He can only say what he has heard from his Father and can only do what he has seen with the Father (Jn. 5:19–47). He lives always as one who hears and receives. Jesus' life of prayer shows that the center of his existence is determined not by the historical circumstances in which he finds himself, but by his unique relationship to the Father (H. Riedlinger).

In such an interpretation, Jesus' prayer is not a mere appearance, a fitting in with the recognized customs of the community, a deceptive imitation for the sake of his onlookers. It is a matter of the greatest earnestness and importance for him. We will be able to comprehend this better if we remember that it can never be the purpose of human prayer to change God's mind so that as a result of the prayer he will give something that he would not have given without the prayer. The significance of prayer lies in the fact that it is a recognition of God by the one who prays and an expression of readiness on his part to receive from God. Prayer is thus a means by which man is changed, so that the God who is always ready to give can bestow salvation without doing violence to man's freedom. In his prayers of petition Jesus expresses the deepest characteristic of his being: his openness to God. In fulfilling his request, the Father reveals and confirms what Jesus had said of himself.

Love for his Father is the root of Jesus' lifelong struggle against faithlessness and smallness of heart, self-seeking and self-will, inauthenticity and untruthfulness, externality and legalism, narrowness and rigidity, and the blind service of tradition.

Jesus obeys the will of his Father freely and unreservedly throughout his life. Because of his dedication to his Father's will, Jesus is independent of all earthly bonds and yet has the warmest love for everything created and not only for his friends and apostles, but especially for sinners and those cast out by society. Love for his Father fills him with joy, peace, and sureness, with courage and trust. He constantly reminds his followers not to be anxious or afraid (Mt. 6:33; Jn. 14:1). All his actions, as reported by the evangelists, are the result and the revelation of his love for his Father. It is this which gives unity and simplicity to his life: it is the center in which he rests, from which he goes out, to which he returns.

It is of supreme importance that, in Jesus' teaching, love for God cannot be separated from love for men; in fact, it is only in this that love for God takes on concrete form. The relationship between the two is so close that there can be no love for God without love for men, and that a creative and helping love; love for God must be declared an illusion and self-deception if it does not show itself as love for men. More than this, Jesus declares that to love God it is not necessary to think of God: it is enough to love our fellowman (Mt. 25:31–46).

## Notes

[1] Translation: *Ante-Nicene Fathers,* vol. 3 (Grand Rapids, Michigan: Wm. B. Eerdmans Co., 1957).

[2] Translation: *The Church Teaches* (St. Louis: B. Herder Book Co., 1964), p. 172.

[3] "Current Problems in Christology," in *Theological Investigations* I, pp. 169–170.

[4] R. Haubst, "Probleme der jüngsten Theologie," in *Theol. Revue* 52 (1965), pp. 145–162.

[5] G. Bornkamm, *Jesus of Nazareth,* p. 92.

[6] Romano Guardini, *Die menschliche Wirklichkeit des Herrn* (Würzburg, 1958).

# Index